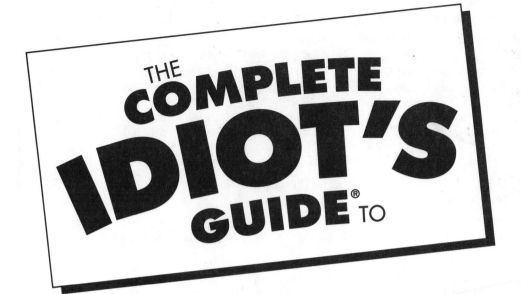

THE COMPLETE IDIOT'S GUIDE® TO

Publishing Magazine Articles

by Sheree Bykofsky, Jennifer Basye Sander,
and Lynne Rominger

alpha
books

Publisher
Marie Butler-Knight

Product Manager
Phil Kitchel

Managing Editor
Cari Luna

Senior Acquisitions Editor
Renee Wilmeth

Development Editor
Michael Thomas

Production Editor
Christy Wagner

Copy Editor
Krista Hansing

Illustrator
Jody Schaeffer

Cover Designers
Mike Freeland
Kevin Spear

Book Designers
Scott Cook and Amy Adams of DesignLab

Indexer
Tonya Heard

Layout/Proofreading
Svetlana Dominguez
Jeannette McKay

Contents at a Glance

Contents

Foreword

Freelance writers, you have three powerful allies on your side. Sheree, Jennifer, and Lynne have the insider knowledge you need to make a great start as a freelance writer—and succeed.

I've been in the publications business for over 25 years now, and I've seen the business change many, many times. Right now we are in one of the most dynamic periods of change, one in which the entire industry is being overhauled from top to bottom. Many of the old rules and ways of doing business are being pushed aside in favor of new techniques.

As the publisher of Bottom Line/Personal, I've seen publications multiplying—in numbers and in editorial pages to fill. It's very exciting. And you as a freelancer need to know how to best fit your talents into it.

Every publication has a slightly different set of guidelines, a slightly different set of needs. Learn these guidelines and needs before approaching anyone. While my own publications do not buy freelance material, every one of my staff writers was once a freelancer, and I know how important that career can be.

The Complete Idiot's Guide to Publishing Magazine Articles will equip you from day one to go out and be successful. Read their advice, and learn from it.

Martin Edelston
Publisher
Bottom Line/Personal

Introduction

Congratulations! By picking up *The Complete Idiot's Guide to Publishing Magazine Articles* you are one step closer to realizing your dream of being a published writer. The path to getting published in magazines, newspapers, and on the Web can be a bewildering one, but we are here to help you negotiate it.

We three authors—Sheree, Jennifer, and Lynne—have combined our knowledge and experience to help you get up and running as quickly and easily as possible. And what does it take to get started? The drive to learn, which, by purchasing *The Complete Idiot's Guide to Publishing Magazine Articles,* you have just displayed!

Between the three of us we have seen and done it all. Rejected? We've been there. Stuck for an idea? Happens to us all the time. Lost the contact at a top magazine you worked so hard to cultivate? Tell us about it. We'll tell you how to keep going, despite the slings and arrows of outrageous publishing fortune. So relax. You now have a friend in the business who can show you the ropes—actually, three friends!

What will you learn from the book we've written for you? All the steps, from start to finish. From the early stages and phases such as coming up with an idea, to querying an editor, to the real deal of interviewing, researching, and writing the piece. Hey, we'll even tell you how to turn it in on time!

And you've been hearing about what a hot market for writers the Web is. Well, we'll tell you which parts are hot and why. And even better, how you can get your own little piece of the Web world. It's such a big market that there are waggish writers who refer to the World Wide Web as Writers Working Weekly!

So settle in with this book and get ready to learn just how this freelance writing business works. It can be tough, but if you stick with it, there are few things more rewarding than seeing your name in print in a newspaper or magazine!

How to Use This Book

We've broken the process down into different phases. And we've kept in mind that, while some readers are primarily interested in writing for magazines, others might well be planning a Web writing career. But writing is writing, and the basics of getting your freelance writing published are the same in all genres and formats. We recommend not skipping a page.

In **Part 1, "Welcome to Writerland,"** we'll get your heart racing about life as a writer. You'll learn what the really great things about a career as a freelance writer are, from several people who lead those really great lives. You'll learn why the publications world needs freelancers, and why there is a growing need for freelance material. But we'll also give you an honest assessment of the downside of life as a writer—the rejection, the long waits between checks. You'll have all the information you need to decide if the life of a freelance writer is really for you.

With **Part 2, "Learning the Basics,"** you'll do just that. You'll learn basic professional writer's techniques for studying markets and generating ideas for articles. And then on to the big query question—writing an effective query letter to catch an editor's eye and get the go-ahead for your article. Once you land that first assignment, what then? Are you going to know what to do when the editor calls? You will if you read these chapters. You'll also learn who on the publication masthead does what and why. And to help you ace your first interview, we've given you lots of professional advice about researching and interviewing techniques.

Part 3, "Who's Gonna Buy Your Stuff?" moves on to more businesslike matters. You'll learn more about how newspapers and both consumer and trade magazines work these days and how you might be able to sell them your stuff. (Don't know what we mean by "trade"? Well, you'll have to read that chapter then, won't you?)

With **Part 4, "Online: The Newest Frontier,"** you'll get a glimpse at the glittering world of the Web. Glittering? Yes, there is money to be made for writers online. Despite the incredible advances in technology, the Web is still all about the written word. And you'll learn how you can be the one writing it! Learn about the major on-line magazines, who runs them, and what they buy. Find out how to market your services as a "content provider" to Web sites. Or—another way to strike Internet gold—just build your own dang site to get established as a writer!

Part 5, "A Short Course on Writing Effective Articles," gets you back to the basics to polishing your writing skills. Learn the difference between a feature article and a sidebar story. Find out how to hook your reader in the first few lines; how to write short, punchy pieces; and even how to decide if your idea is better suited to a full-length book instead of a magazine article!

The last part of the book, **Part 6, "The Business of Freelancing,"** gives you the knowledge you need to run your freelance writing business. Because it is, in fact, a business. You'll need to deal with invoicing, tracking various and sundry correspondence, and learning the basics of accounting. Taxes—did we mention taxes? Yes, they do follow you even into a life of writing. And contracts also rear their ugly heads. But never fear—we'll tell you what those lawyeresque paragraphs *really* mean.

Extras

Although we worked hard to present this info in as straightforward and easy-to-digest a manner as possible, there was some extra information we just couldn't resist telling you.

The Straight Scoop

"The Straight Scoop" sidebars contain bet-you-didn't-know information as well as anecdotes and helpful hints.

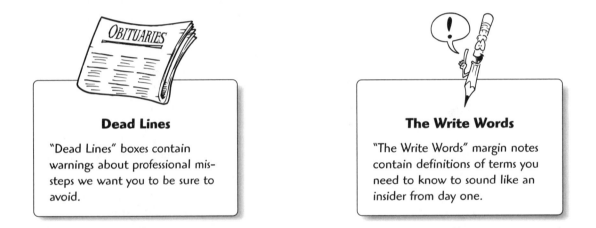

Dead Lines

"Dead Lines" boxes contain warnings about professional missteps we want you to be sure to avoid.

The Write Words

"The Write Words" margin notes contain definitions of terms you need to know to sound like an insider from day one.

Acknowledgements

Writing can be a lonely pursuit, but no one really writes a book alone. So we would like to pause and acknowledge some of the fabulous folks who helped us along the way.

Sheree would like to acknowledge, more than anyone else, Jennifer Basye Sander, for making all things possible.

Jennifer would have been lost without the constant advice and friendship of Sally Richards, freelance writer extraordinaire. And, of course, the love and patience of her husband, Peter, and two sweet little boys, Julian and Jonathan, takes the sting out of long lonely nights at the computer.

Lynne Rominger: I am indebted to so many people who helped me accomplish my goal of writing this, my first book, but must begin by thanking Jennifer Basye Sander. Jennifer, you have been and will always be my mentor; I've admired your tenacity and talent since our first meeting and used your career path as a model for my own. "Thank you," I fear, seems too small a sentiment to express my gratitude for believing in me as a co-author on this guide. Thanks also to Krista Minard, who gave me my first break into the glossy arena of writing, and Jack Hicks, my writing professor at UC Davis. More thanks goes out to my other co-author and awesome agent, Sheree Bykofsky, and to the multitude of wonderful writers and editors who agreed to interviews for the book—Kara Corridan, Sally Smith, Perry Bradley, Amy Hamaker, Joan Tapper, Mary Murray, Victoria Boughton, Brooks Clark, Kim Wright Wiley, Elena Macaluso, Ilene Beckerman, and Jim Thornton. Liz Allen Chmielewski and Jeff Maher also deserve my gratitude for their constant support, love, and friendship. And finally, I give thanks to God, my mother and father, and my brood of inspiration, Nickolaus, Sophia, Faith, and Hope.

Thanks to Our Tech Reviewer

The Complete Idiot's Guide to Publishing Magazine Articles was reviewed by an expert who double-checked the accuracy of what you'll learn here, to help us ensure that this book gives you everything you need to know about writing and publishing your work in magazines as well as newspapers and on the Internet. Special thanks are extended to Julie Polito. Julie is a freelance writer living in San Francisco and a former editor at *PC Computing Magazine*.

Trademarks

All terms mentioned in this book that are known to be or are suspected of being trademarks or service marks have been appropriately capitalized. Alpha Books and Penguin Group (USA) Inc. cannot attest to the accuracy of this information. Use of a term in this book should not be regarded as affecting the validity of any trademark or service mark.

Part 1
Welcome to Writerland

Let's start off by taking a look at just how great life can be as a freelance writer—the perks and the privileges enjoyed by those working as freelancers. You'll learn just what freelancers do, and why the magazine world relies on them. But, after all the positives are examined, we'll take a close look at a few of the negatives of freelance life.

Writers

Chapter 1

So, You Want to Be a Freelance Writer?

> ## In This Chapter
>
> ➤ The world of the freelance writer
>
> ➤ The markets for writing
>
> ➤ Why writing is such a great profession
>
> ➤ Books vs. magazines
>
> ➤ Professional writers share their finest moments

Welcome to the world of freelance writing, where every day is a challenge, and glamour and riches await you. Oh wait—does that sound like a slight exaggeration? Okay, you caught us. Freelance writing is not easy, but it is doable.

The life of a freelance writer can be a terrific one, with each assignment new and different. One day you might be researching a piece on travel to Afghanistan, and the next day you might be surfing the Web for a food piece about buying truffles online.

But freelancing also can be a frustrating life—a life of endlessly waiting for phone calls to be returned, for projects to be green-lighted, and for e-mails to be answered.

We three erstwhile professional writers—Sheree, Jennifer, and Lynne—will give you a solid overview of how to build a life as a freelance writer. Whether your dream is to become a full-time writer or to simply see your name in print a little more often, you'll find the information you need in the following pages. So, read on and learn.

The Write Words

A **freelance writer** is a nonstaff writer who sells work to a magazine, newspaper, or Web site. The freelancer is not employed by the publication and does not receive a salary or benefits; instead, the writer is paid an agreed-upon sum per article.

Words 'R Us

Who uses *freelance writers?* As a freelance writer, for whom would you write? The possibilities are endless. Here's just a short list of the types of markets that exist for freelance writers (we'll fill you in on all these different kinds of publications later in the book):

General interest magazines   Trade publications

Corporate newsletters   In-house magazines

Large newspapers   Free local newspapers

Web sites   Flight magazines

Publicity companies   Nonprofit organizations

It's clear that such dire predictions as Americans reading less and the printed word losing out to television and film were false alarms—the written word is stronger than ever. New magazines and newspapers are launched all the time—in fact, *The New York Times* recently reported three new magazine start-ups *every day.* Here are two examples of magazines that were launched in January 2000:

Kinko's Impress—A 300,000 circulation quarterly for small-business people, distributed in Kinko's copy shops.

Anti-Aging and Cosmetic Surgery—A 50,000 copy circulation quarterly that is both a general interest magazine about staying young and a professional magazine about running a successful cosmetic surgery practice.

The Straight Scoop

Magazines and newspapers frequently are described in terms of their circulation, which refers to how large a publication's readership is. Three types of circulation exist: paid circulation, free circulation, and controlled circulation. Paid circulation refers to the number of paid subscribers. Free circulation refers to the number of free copies that are printed and made available on give-away racks. A publication with a controlled circulation is a trade or industry publication that is sent only to qualified readers—those who are in the industry.

The Perfect Occupation

So what makes freelance writing such a great job, anyway? Let's look at some of the reasons that so many creative people dream of building a freelance career. Could it be that this is a great way to live?

The Ultimate Work-from-Home Career

Of all the different kinds of businesses or careers that you could do from home—everything from woodworking to sales repping to computer programming—nothing beats the business of being a freelance writer. After all, what do you really need? Your mind, your creativity, your curiosity, a computer, a phone, and maybe a fax machine.

Most writers find themselves a spare corner of the house or apartment and set up shop. There's no real need for a fancy neon sign, an engraved business card and matching stationery, or a company car. Not that those things wouldn't be kinda cool, mind you—particularly the neon sign. But the basic tools are, well, basic. They're also relatively inexpensive and mostly involve your talent and your persistence.

Dead Lines

Don't claim to have an assignment from a magazine or newspaper if you don't. Be honest with the people you interview. If you claim you're writing a piece for *Travel & Leisure* magazine when you aren't, one phone call to the editor will expose you as a sham. This can easily come back to haunt you, both with the magazines and your interviewees.

Perfect for the Terminally Curious

Full-time freelancer Sally Richards admits that a career as a writer suits her for this reason: "I am plagued with curiosity. As a reporter and author, you have license to be as nosey as you want, whenever and wherever you want."

Richards's point is a good one. Writers get to ask questions—really *deep* questions of all sorts of people. The President? Why not (if you can get past his press office)? A famous movie star? Think of a good angle for a *piece* you'd like to quote him in, and give it a try. Your next-door neighbor? Sure—you might get her to tell you all sorts of secret things if she thinks they will end up in an article.

The Write Words

A **piece** is professional shorthand for the article you're writing.

The Straight Scoop

How do you get to meet the people you admire most? Just call and introduce yourself as a writer working on a story for which you'd like their help—a quote, an anecdote, an interview, anything. Jennifer is a longtime fan of Mark Victor Hansen, of *Chicken Soup* fame. She knew that in addition to writing his inspirational stories, Mark was a longtime motivational speaker on the topic of goal-setting and self-improvement. She pitched an article to the editor of *Network Marketing Lifestyle* magazine about applying Mark's goal-setting ideas to the world of multilevel marketing. The magazine bought it, and she got to spend four solid hours with Hansen at his Newport Beach, California, office. Don't abuse this writer's perk, however. Call only if you are genuinely working on a story that you have sold or believe will sell.

As a writer, you can spend hours delving into a topic that fascinates you, write an article on what you've discovered, and not only get paid for the article, but perhaps also write off on your taxes what you spent doing it.

Imagine this scenario: You've recently developed an interest in the novelist F. Scott Fitzgerald. What really intrigues you is the time that he and Zelda spent living in Paris. This was an unproductive period in his life; if he wasn't writing, you wonder, what *was* he doing? So you decide to research that part of his life—in Paris. Fortune smiles on you, and you're able to sell an article on the topic to a literary magazine. Not only do you get to indulge your personal interests, you also get paid *and* can write off part of the cost of your trip to Paris! Does life get any better?

Along with the rest of America, Jennifer has recently begun spending time (and money) on eBay, the online auction service. Hoping to somehow subsidize her new shopping addiction, she put her creative thinking cap on to try to develop a good article angle. The world doesn't need another article about eBay itself, or about online auctions, so what sort of new and fresh angle could she approach it from? She looked more closely at the kinds of things she had been buying online—mostly used, high-end goods made by companies such as Hermes, Burberry, and Chanel. Here's the angle she came up with for her query letter:

> Much advertising ink has been spent by online luxury goods retailers, but their goods look so tacky and nouveau riche. Is it possible to use the Web to buy yourself an old money look? Disguise your newly minted e-commerce riches by dressing and decorating your home as though your granddaddy owned a large steel mill?

Now she gets to indulge her passion and feel as though she is spending time (and, of course, money) working.

Of course, you'll have to balance writing about your passions with writing about more mundane stuff sometimes to keep checks coming in. But freelance writing does give you the unique opportunity to explore your interests. Love French food? Become an expert freelance food writer. Did you major in English literature in college only to find that you don't get paid to read Jane Austen? Create a writing career in which you specialize in the English countryside and period as described in Austen's novels.

Must-Reads

Not only will developing a freelance writing career allow you to get paid to learn about interesting stuff, you also will get to spend hour after hour reading. Alas, no one will pay you for that part, but reading is a requirement. How else can you keep up with magazines and the kind of articles they're publishing? Browsing in the magazine aisles at Barnes & Noble isn't wasting time—it's helping you keep up with new magazines entering the marketplace. Reading small-town newspapers as you travel helps you discover interesting article angles that you can spin or revise in your own hometown. Burying your nose in the in-flight magazine isn't just a way to fend off a chatty seatmate—it's a necessary way for you to learn more about what kinds of articles in-flight magazines buy.

You also might be able to write off the cost of magazine and newspaper subscriptions as a business expense if you pursue freelance writing with any degree of seriousness. Check with your accountant to see what he thinks of your ability to write off your writing-related expenses. We'll talk more in the last part of the book about whether you need to sell your work to write off expenses.

Dead Lines

Don't dismiss small publications as not worthy of your valuable reading time. Any publication, no matter how small, might give you an idea for a story.

Travel Unlimited

Let's just get the bad news over with first—everyone wants to be a travel writer. Travel writing does seem to have the most cachet. The idea that you can spend your time flying first class to exotic resorts around the world, or lie by the pool with a drink in one hand and a pen in the other, jotting down your impressions of the poolside service and the hotel's architecture, sounds pretty glamorous. Is it a dream? Yep, it pretty much is. Let's take a look at the rocky landscape facing potential travel writers.

Travel editors at newspapers and magazines are completely overwhelmed with queries for story ideas. *The New York Times* Travel section gets so many queries that the publication prints the how-to-do-it information right there at the bottom of the page:

> Note to Readers
>
> The Travel section regrets that because of the volume of mail it receives, an unsolicited manuscript or article proposal cannot be acknowledged or returned unless accompanied by a self-addressed envelope. If a manuscript is accepted, the author will be notified before publication. Writers should not include photographs.

So, does that mean that you'll never be able to sell a travel article? No, but we do want you to know that the odds are pretty long to sell one to the major newspapers and travel magazines.

In later sections, we'll talk about how to craft articles that, instead of being actual travel articles, have a travel element to them. This will help you try to attain at least a dash of that sought-after travel writer status.

What About Writing Books?

Serious writers write books. They wouldn't lower themselves to writing for a glossy publication or a wrinkled fishwrap.

Oh, really?

The pages of magazines and newspapers are chock full with articles written by famous writers. Think those are personal essays about their fame and good fortune? Seldom. Many a successful book author is still hard at work meeting assignment deadlines for magazine editors. Why?

The Straight Scoop

Technological advances were supposed to have rendered words passé—the written word, anyway. But consider this observation from *The New Yorker's* "Talk of the Town" section: "The Internet is the first new medium to move decisively backward, for it is, essentially, written. When someone tells you that he has been online, what he has probably been doing is reading words that other people have written, and then writing some words of his own." The new media world still needs the old-fashioned writer.

Writing a book and then waiting for it to be published is akin to watching ice form. It is a slow, slow process. Researching and writing a magazine article, on the other hand, might well require only a week or two of effort, and then the piece appears in print just a few short months after you've turned it in.

Consider also the size of the potential reading audience. Even best-selling authors might have more people read their magazine articles than their books. For instance, Dominick Dunne writes many best-selling books, but he also writes regularly for *Vanity Fair*. His books sell in the many hundreds of thousands, but the circulation of *Vanity Fair* is in the millions; you can see that the magazine is helping to get his name out there to more potential book buyers.

Dead Lines

Don't be dazzled by the dream of someday living off royalties from a book. The last royalty check that F. Scott Fitzgerald received before his death was for $13.13.

The Straight Scoop

Even John Grisham is going back to magazines. Okay, so it's a magazine he owns—*The Oxford American*—and he isn't doing articles, he's serializing his latest novel. The book, *A Painted House*, will be published over the next year in serial form in the literary bimonthly. Grisham doesn't have any problem getting a book deal, though—why is he doing it this way? "It was so unlike his major books that we thought we should do something different," says Grisham's agent, David Gernert.

The income stream from writing books is also a slow, slow, slow one. Most publishers send out royalty checks twice a year, but newspapers and magazines pay within weeks. For writers who depend on writing as their sole means of income, magazine and newspaper work is critical to keeping the money flowing year-round.

Jennifer is the author of some 20-odd books (and many of them are indeed odd), so royalty checks arrive several times a year from publishers. Some books earn a bit of money, but some books don't. While the months between checks stretch by, though, she's all too happy to receive a biweekly check from *USA Today* for a freelance column she writes for its Web site. "It's the only regular income I've got!" she says.

Not only does writing for newspapers and magazines pay faster and reach a larger audience, but articles sometimes can take on a life of their own and turn into movies (or at least movie deals). The most famous example of an article that became a movie was one that appeared in a regional Texas magazine about the phenomenon of big-city guys dressing up like cowboys and hanging around Western bars on weekends. The piece was written by a magazine writer named Aaron Latham. Sound familiar? Ever heard of the 1980s' John Travolta movie *Urban Cowboy?* Latham actually sold several other articles to Hollywood as well.

The recently launched magazine *Talk* is in part based on the idea that there is synergy between well-written magazine pieces and the Hollywood movie business. Famous editor Tina Brown caused quite a stir when she first announced that her magazine (and Miramax Films) would retain the film rights on the magazine stories it published. Professional writers were not pleased by her attitude because traditionally those rights were owned outright by the author. (We'll give you a much greater understanding of the legal and contractual issues that writers face in a section toward the end of the book. First, the fun. Then, the dry stuff ....)

Writing and publishing articles in newspapers, magazines, and on the Web certainly won't stand in the way of your someday writing a book. In fact, they're the perfect stepping stone in that direction. They build your credibility. They give you exposure. And they might someday put you in the enviable position of having a book editor read your article and call you to ask you to expand it into a book! That happens all the time in the book publishing world.

The Cool Stuff Writers Do

So, are writers really cooler than other people? No, but sometimes it looks that way! Tell folks that you're a writer, and watch their eyebrows rise in admiration. Beats "gas station attendant" as a job title any day. The day-to-day life of writing isn't particularly cool or interesting, of course—one day in front of the computer is pretty much like any other day. But sometimes writers get to do incredibly cool stuff, like meet famous people or do daring things. Whatever makes a good story, writers will go out and give it a try.

We asked a number of freelance writers to share their finest moments with you. Here's what they had to say.

Dating for Dollars

Paula Munier not only got paid to write an interesting article about a video dating service in Santa Cruz, but she got a husband out of it as well: "I got an assignment from a business journal in Monterey, California," Munier explains. "A woman was running a local video dating service that was really successful. I interviewed her and felt that I had enough material to write the piece. But no, she insisted that I use her service, gratis, to get a better feel for what it was all about. So I did, and ended up meeting a man I later married!"

Hitting the Hague

Anne Basye, a Chicago-based editor and writer, has a number of corporate clients for whom she writes newsletter copy and in-house magazine articles. One client, the Evangelical Lutheran Church of America, called recently with an interesting proposition: Would Basye like to go to an international conference on nonviolence in The Hague? As you can imagine, it certainly didn't take her long to say "Yes!" She rubbed elbows with international leaders such as Bishop Desmond Tutu, and her entire trip to the Netherlands was paid for.

Getting to Know Gumby

Sally Richards says, "As a writer, I've been able to find and interview people who have been my icons. It has been an honor and a growing experience to meet them. What other job can you interview and do a photo shoot with Art Clokey (Gumby's creator) in the morning and Grace Slick in the afternoon? Grace Slick insisted on being photographed with a young raccoon. I found a dozen or so for her to pose with. And when her house in Marin County burned down some time afterward, she called me crying and said that the thing she missed losing the most in the fire was the photo from our interview. So I sent her another copy."

Shark Attack

What started as just an ordinary travel piece for co-author Lynne ended with a hug from a muscular and good-looking man. While researching a travel piece on NHL games for a city magazine, Lynne traveled to San Jose, California, home of the Sharks. The publicity staff for the Sharks gave her an all-access media pass that allowed her to wander at will around the stadium during the professional hockey game, getting a real behind-the-scenes look at what went on. (She showed remarkable restraint in not entering one of the places she had access to—the locker room.)

"As I was leaving that night after the game, the opposing team, the Los Angeles Kings, was also leaving the stadium," Lynn recalls. "Player Iann Laperriere emerged, and I chose that moment to ask the photographer accompanying me to take a quick shot. As the single mother of four, it was the closest thing to a date I'd had in many months."

Queen Elizabeth, Too

Like Lynne's all-access media pass, Jennifer still has her coolest media pass. In fact, it's framed and hangs in the guest bathroom in the hope that her friends might learn of her finest moment as a writer. The laminated media pass has the flags of the United States and Great Britain intertwined, with the words "The Visit of Her Majesty Queen Elizabeth, and His Royal Highness, the Duke of Edinburgh" across the top. "I never actually got near her," Jennifer admits, "but late in the day I did get to go to the airstrip and wave good-bye to her as she boarded her plane. Not only did I keep the media pass, but I also kept the white gloves I wore when I waved good-bye."

Idol Chit-Chat

San Francisco writer Lewis Buzbee met one of his literary idols, Raymond Carver, not long after Carver achieved prominence. "When I was just 23, I met him at a reading and went up afterward and introduced myself," says Buzbee. "I also worked up the nerve to hand him a copy of my first published short story. He wrote me a nice note."

One meeting and a nice note turned into three meetings—including Carver's over-night stay at Buzbee's house—and a three-year correspondence in which Buzbee conducted an interview with Carver through the mail. "The interview was published in the *Paris Review*," Buzbee says, "and is included in many Carver anthologies and scholarly papers. It has been translated into many languages around the world." A published novelist and writing teacher who also has sold freelance pieces to *GQ* and other magazines, Buzbee still credits this experience as the best thing that has ever happened to him as a writer.

Cookie's Fortune

Syndicated newspaper columnist Cookie Curci-Wright recalls fondly her long correspondence with one of her heroes—best-selling author Leo Buscaglia. She first wrote to just express her admiration and had the foresight to enclose some of her early newspaper columns. At the time, her columns were published only in her local San Jose–area newspaper. She and Leo wrote on similar topics—Italian families, generational stories, and fond memories of food and cooking. He liked what she sent and encouraged her to continue, even cheering her spirits when they flagged. "No one else carried a torch for my writing like Leo did," she says, "It really shored up my ego about my potential as a writer. It kept me going." They wrote back and forth for 10 years, until his death in 1998.

Fabulous You

In years past, writers were the unseen, unheard grunts churning out copy. But now writers sometimes can become celebrities. As with some of the famous magazine writers we mentioned before, including Dominick Dunne, the names of writers are recognized more and more. As you garner more *bylines,* you just might find yourself attaining a modest level of celebrity and renown.

One phenomenon that has helped raise the profile of writers is the increased use of first-person accounts. Magazines and newspapers no longer present only dry, third-person reportorial accounts of the facts. Instead, readers follow the tale of the erstwhile writer as he or she bumbles along on a bike trip through France, or tries to get a small business off the ground. The writer is a part of the story, not just the unseen hand behind it. So, when you're a character in your own story, you do achieve a bit of glamour.

My Calling Card

Being a published writer will separate you from the pack. It's also kind of a fun trump card to pull out once in a while. Sheree is a literary agent, one of many in New York City. But in a crowded cocktail party filled with other agents, she's the only one in America who can say, "I write the 'Ask an Agent' column on AOL."

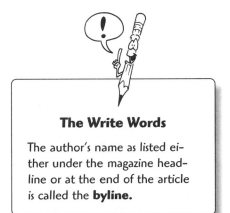

The Write Words

The author's name as listed either under the magazine headline or at the end of the article is called the **byline.**

Jennifer's neighbors nod their heads wearily when she announces that she has written yet another book. Then she casually mentioned that she'd wrapped up a deal to write a weekly column for the *USAToday* Web site. Hey, that got a bit of respect.

Lynne is a public school teacher by day and freelance writer by night. Do her family and friends ask her much about what happened at school today? Not really. What they want to hear about is whether she has finally succeeded in scheduling the interview with Eddie Murphy, or if she can get a backstage pass the next time their favorite rock band is in town.

So, are you ready to get going on your life as a hardworking freelancer? Ah, did we mention that it *is* hard work? Perhaps we haven't gotten to that just yet ....

In the pages of this book, we three—Sheree, Jennifer, and Lynne—plan to take you on an eye-opening trip through the world of freelance writing, showing you the ropes on everything from how to write a query letter that can catch an editor's eye, to how to craft an idea for an article that will get you repeated work.

In the meantime, read on to learn more about just why it is that magazines, newspapers, and Web sites need folks like you to keep on writing.

The Least You Need to Know

➤ Freelance writing requires little investment in equipment or office setup.

➤ Writers get the chance to indulge their own curiosity—and get paid for it.

➤ Publications pay much faster and more often than book publishers.

➤ Writers are often characters in their own first-person stories and develop a bit of their own renown as a result.

The Modern World of the Freelance Writer

Now that we've got your heart racing about the possibility of life as a freelance writer, you might have a question or two:

What are freelancers for?

Why would a publication or Web site hire one?

We'll answer those two looming questions in this chapter. But first, let's have a bit of a history lesson about the world of publications.

The Olden Days

Like so many traditional businesses, the world of magazines and newspapers was a fairly clubby one. What do we mean by "clubby"? Who you were and who you knew mattered more than a little in determining your success as a freelance writer. Editors reigned at a magazine or newspaper for years and years and repeatedly drew from the same stable of writers. Take the famous example of *The New Yorker* magazine, for instance, where the fiction editor who held that title for decades continued to publish the same handful of fiction authors—talented as they were—year in and year out.

Why look for new voices when the ones you already have are so good? That was a tough scene to break in to, and still is.

But in today's job-hopping environment, editors move from publication to publication. You can't always rely on the same freelance pals if you move from a fashion magazine to a financial magazine, or from a fishing magazine to a religious Web site. Editors need to continually develop new sources of writers they can rely on to write readable pieces in the style of whichever publication they're working for at the moment. That's where the talented freelancer—you—comes in. "It is no longer who you know, but what you write," writer Lewis Buzbee told us.

It's not just the mobility of editors that creates the need for more freelance material, but it's also partly due to the trends among reporters. Alison apRoberts, a staff writer with *The Sacramento Bee*, feels that there might be even more need in the future for freelance material at newspapers because so many journalism school grads are skipping the newsroom in favor of the Web. No longer will newsrooms around the country be filled with fresh-faced and enthusiastic J-school grads. Instead you might find frantic editors flipping through their phone files trying to decide which freelance writer to call.

Dead Lines

Knowing someone in the business might help you get started—after all, being well-connected never hurt. But personal connections will get you only so far. You still need to know how to write well to get work. Talent is the great leveler.

Ch-Ch-Ch-Ch-Changes ...

Competition is good—good for the industry and good for writers. In an effort to be heard and to reach more readers, magazines and newspapers are continually evolving. Interior design and type styles, cover looks and editorial voices—all are subject to change. And if a magazine undergoes a major change in the way it looks and sounds, there's a good chance that the editors will be looking for fresh, new writing voices. Again, that's a possible opportunity for you, the freelancer.

Another big change from the olden days (that is, the 1980s and mid-1990s) is the remarkable transformation in queries and submissions made possible by e-mail. Here's what life used to be like before e-mail:

➤ You identify a magazine you want to write for and send off a self-addressed, stamped envelope (SASE) requesting the author guidelines. Then you wait several weeks.

➤ You write a query letter to the editor and send it off in the mail. You wait several weeks.

➤ You finish your story and send it off to the editor.

The Straight Scoop

Magazines are in a constant state of flux, trying to find that one look and one voice that will help them leapfrog over their competitors to reign supreme. *Brill's Content* explains in a From the Editor letter why the magazine recently altered its design: "Some of our goals for the new design were intangible. We wanted a look that reflects the skepticism, but also the wonder and enthusiasm, that many of us feel about our media age. So we went for an approach you could describe as being sharp and bright, but not overly slick." As a writer, you need to stay on top of every change—including a change in design and a change in editors—at the magazines you want to write for.

But now life sometimes looks more like this:

➤ You visit the writersdigest.com site and download the author guidelines for the magazines you want to target.

➤ You send an e-mail query to the editor and attach clips to the message.

➤ You write the story and e-mail the file to the editor.

Dead Lines

Keep good records of your e-mail queries. When an editor responds, "Yes, I like the idea," you want to be able to remember just which idea it was!

Hyperspeed! No more trips to the post office for disk mailers, and no more mornings spent peering anxiously into a mailbox. Just fast answers to your questions. Well, editors still might not respond to your e-mail, just as they didn't respond to your query, but at least you'll find out much faster and be able to move on to the next person on your list.

Welcome to the New Media Landscape

You—and every other freelance writer—might harbor dreams of seeing your byline on an article in a big national magazine such as *Cosmopolitan, Esquire,* or *Newsweek.* Or, your dream might be to see your work published online with big sites such as *Salon* or *Nerve,* the literary erotica site. That could happen someday, but probably not right away.

The Straight Scoop

In newspapers, in magazines, and even on the Web, the number of editorial pages (pages available for the publication's writers) is directly proportional to the number of ad pages (pages sold to advertisers). If a magazine increases its number of ad pages, there is a corresponding increase in its number of editorial pages. This means that the publication will need more material from freelancers like you. Likewise, if ad sales fall, there is a cutback in size. In the late 1980s and the recession of the early 1990s, advertising fell off dramatically, and many large newspapers cut back on their nonnews sections such as food, business, and sports.

Most freelance writers start out with smaller publications. The really good news about this media-focused world we live in is that there are thousands of new opportunities in the form of smaller magazines, newspapers, and Web sites. What about the new inspirational magazine *Priorities: The Journal of Professional and Personal Success?* Never heard of it? It comes from the Franklin Covey folks, who sell datebooks and teach "Seven Habits of Highly Successful People" seminars. The author of seven books, Azriela Jaffe, let the folks at *Priorities* use an excerpt from one of her business books for free, and now she writes for them on a monthly (paid) basis.

Or how about *Home Business: The Home-Based Entrepreneur's Magazine?* No, it's not *Newsweek* or *Inc.*, or even *Fast Company*, but if you write about business, your time (in the beginning) is better spent querying the smaller publications that dot the new media landscape than banging your head against the mahogany doors at Time Warner.

How do you find new media opportunities? Think back to Chapter 1, "So, You Want to Be a Freelance Writer?"—there we granted you permission to browse through the magazine rack at the local bookstore and justify it as work. Well, that's how you find them. You find these magazines on the shelf, or in the seat pocket in front of you on an airplane, or mentioned in a newspaper article, or lying face up on your best friends' coffee table. New magazine launches happen every day, which means that every day new opportunities are opening up for you as a writer.

Hot Off the Presses

In this dotcom world we now live in, what kind of brave folks start up a paper-and-ink magazine? The folks at RENI Publishing, for one. Its new magazine for women entrepreneurs, *Venture Woman,* will send out its first issue in June 2000. "Magazines are something that women can carry around with them," editor Diane Sears Campbell explains. "Magazines aren't dead by any means."

The Straight Scoop

Writer Lewis Buzbee believes that it is not just the heated-up competitive world of media that has benefited writers, but also the idea of diversity. Newspaper and magazine stories and opinions are no longer written by a bunch of well-connected white guys, but by all manner of voices, young and old, black and white, gay and straight. "The opportunities to be heard have only increased," Buzbee says.

RENI Publishing specializes in niche publications, with newspapers targeted to commercial real estate developers and small business guides for the Small Business Administration. "It was someone at the SBA that first pointed out that women-owned businesses were a growing market," Campbell told us. "We see this as a business magazine, not a women's magazine—a magazine for established women business owners, the sorts of readers who would be picking up *Business Week, Inc.,* or *Entrepreneur.*"

Does this sound like a market you could write for? Send queries to:

Diane Sears Campbell
The RENI Building
150 Third Avenue SW
Winter Haven, Florida 33880-2907

Sticky Eyeballs

If two or three new magazines appear every day, 20 or 30 new commercial Web sites launch every day. And what's a Web site made of? Words and pictures, but mostly words. Even e-commerce sites such as Amazon.com incorporate editorial material into their Web sites—if not actual articles, then book reviews and other short pieces to keep their customers coming back.

Successful Web sites depend on repeat visitors. And how do you get visitors to come back to your site again and again? With interesting commentary, cutting-edge stories, and distinctive voices. And where does much of this material come from? Freelance writers.

A recent *USA Today* review of the newly launched Wal-Mart travel site had this to say: "Aside from a few packing and jet-lag tips, the travel site offers little *content*." What's that, you say? Content? Would that be words and articles?

Web marketing experts such as Ellen Reid Smith, author of *e-Loyalty* (HarperBusiness), believe that good content makes all the difference in launching a successful site. "The quality of your content is how you distinguish yourself from your competitors online," she suggests. "If visitors to your site don't see anything new or anything different, why would they ever come back?"

The Write Words

Written material found in a magazine or on a Web site is called **content.** Content is always distinguished from advertising.

Online Goldmine

In Part 4, "Online: The Newest Frontier," we'll dive deep into the new world of the Web to examine how freelance writers can find opportunities. But just to keep you reading that far, we'll tell you a secret now: Writing for the Web can pay well. It can also pay lousy, of course. But many freelance or contract writers are discovering that the prices they can command are many times what magazines and newspapers pay.

The Straight Scoop

When contacted by a financial Web site about developing content for them, Jennifer was more than a little reluctant at first. "I was under deadline for several books at once and just didn't see how I could add one more project. So to discourage them, I quoted the price that I usually charge my book publishing consulting clients—$125 an hour. 'Fine' was the response. 'How quickly can you start?'" Not only did they pay her $125 an hour for 60 hours worth of writing, but she also received stock options and a seat on their editorial board. "And they paid my invoice in two weeks!" she says. "If I had spent that amount of time working on a book project, I wouldn't have seen any money from it for months."

Why Editors Hire Freelancers

Newspaper and magazine jobs are highly sought after. Some publications have huge staffs, so why on earth would they want to buy a story from a freelancer? Why is it that freelancers are able to exist? There are two big reasons:

➤ Overhead

➤ Variety

Overhead

When a newspaper buys a story from you, the publication doesn't have to fund your 401(k). It doesn't have to pay medical benefits. Heck, it doesn't even have to give you a desk. All it needs to do is hand you a check when the work is over. The more material that a newspaper or magazine or Web site buys from freelance contributors, the lower its operating overhead. Employees are expensive—freelancers are cheap.

Laura Boswell is the managing editor for a division of an online version of a major U.S. newspaper. One of her first jobs was setting up a college football network of reporters to send back information after each game. "I hired college kids on campus," she says. "College kids were all too happy to earn an extra $75 a week for a few hours of reporting work. It would have been impossible to do all that with reporting staff—a logistical nightmare and a salary nightmare."

Variety

Although this is a book about getting your magazine and other articles published, we don't mean in *Variety* magazine. We mean "variety" as in a variety of voices, a variety of opinions, a variety of frames of reference, and a variety of freelancers!

Look in the first few pages of big glossy magazines such as *Vogue* or *Vanity Fair*. Is there an About the Contributors page? Read the profiles. Very few of the contributors featured actually work for the magazine. Here are two contributor profiles from a recent issue of *Working Woman*:

> We caught up with South African–born Vivienne Walt on assignment in Jakarta, Indonesia—the eighth country she's visited this year. The freelance journalist, whose work has appeared in *The New York Times,* the *Washington Post,* and *USA Today,* reports almost exclusively from abroad.

> "I've quit quite a few jobs myself," says Russell Wild, who wrote "50 Ways to Leave Your Employer." "But I've only been fired once. I was 17, delivering meat for a butcher shop, and I hit a gas pump with a station wagon." Happily self-employed now, Wild has written for *Maxim, Details, Success,* and *Cooking Light.*

Gee, their lives sound pretty swell—much more interesting than if a staff member had been assigned the story: "Staff member Jane Doe lives and works in New York City, were she shares a small apartment with four other young women, takes the subway to work in the morning, and sits at her desk all day." Wouldn't a magazine benefit from buying freelance material written by folks who are out in the world doing things instead of sitting at a desk writing all day long? Yes, and they do it all the time.

Sally Richards now works as a full-time freelancer, but she used to be a managing editor for a magazine. "When I was an editor, I liked having 50 or so reliable freelancers that I could call on. To use a cooking metaphor, it was like having a giant spice rack. And for each issue of the magazine I could mix up a new recipe. No two people write the same or approach a story from the same angle. By having a large number of writing voices at my disposal, I was creating a lively magazine for my readers that would not sound the same month in and month out."

Not only did Richards like the fact that she could add variety by using freelancers, but she also liked their proximity to their stories. "The closer the writer gets to the news source, the better," she says. "Having a freelancer go out and cover an event or conduct an interview in a far-flung place resulted in a much more vibrant story—much better than what I would have gotten if one of my newsroom people had called up and conducted an interview over the phone and written a story from that."

Finding the Best Sections for Freelancing

As a beginning freelancer, do you have a better chance of having your freelance material published in some parts of a magazine or newspaper rather than others? Yes.

"No editor is going to assign a long feature article to an untested freelancer," Krista Minard, editor of award-winning regional magazine *Sacramento Magazine* told us. "With a regional or city magazine, your best shot is to pitch ideas for the short sections in the *front of the book,* the 'what's new, what's happening' section. Our magazine calls it City Lights, but every magazine uses a different catchy title for it."

The Write Words

The **front of the book** is the first section of a magazine, before the major features begin. Magazine industry professionals often refer to their magazine as a *book.*

Bob Dreizler, the author of the financial planning book *Tending Your Money Garden* and some 80-plus published articles, believes that personal essays are a good way to start out. Most often found on the *op-ed page* (the opinions and editorials page) of a newspaper, these sections are in continual need of well-written personal views on a wide variety of topics. Bob even had a personal essay appear in the sports section of the *San Francisco Chronicle* about his young son catching a fly ball during a Giants game.

Take a close look at the papers in your town to see whether they use personal essays. Business magazines and newspapers frequently run personal essays about business-related topics.

Longtime writer Lila Anastas tried a few different times to crack one of the golden eggs of personal essays—the "My Turn" section in the back of *Newsweek*. "They get thousands of submissions a week for that section, so after my first rejection I decided to study what they did choose," she says. "I noticed that the essays they printed always started out with a personal anecdote before expanding to make a larger point. On my third attempt to get through to them, with an essay about a recent medical issue, I made it!"

Like other writers who make it into print on a regular basis, Anastas took the time to study what worked and made sure that what she submitted was in a similar vein.

The book review section of a magazine or newspaper is also sometimes receptive to freelance material. "I didn't know anyone there," Lewis Buzbee says of his early approach to the *San Francisco Examiner*. "I wrote up a sample review and sent it in. Sure enough, they called me to begin reviewing on a fairly regular basis."

The Write Words

The **op-ed page** is the opinions and editorials page of a newspaper.

Publications 101: Learning About Op-Eds, Q&As, and Other Types of Articles

We all tend to think of an article as a long, long piece that goes on for several pages in a magazine or that covers most of a big newspaper page. But there are all manner of different types of articles. Here's a quick primer:

➤ **Op-ed piece.** Usually a 600-word first-person opinionated essay on a topical subject you know firsthand

➤ **Personal essay.** A 500- to 1,000-word first-person essay on a personal subject

➤ **Review.** A 200- to 2,000-word critique of a book, movie, play, or restaurant

➤ **Service piece.** A 500- to 3,500-word third-person, informative, and educational piece that includes lists, phone numbers, and addresses

➤ **Q&A.** A 200- to 5,000-word third-person interview that includes your questions and the subject's answers

➤ **Profile.** A 200- to 5,000-word third-person interview without questions, using mostly narrative and quotes

➤ **News story.** A 1,200- to 2,000-word third-person informational piece that gives new, topical information in a serious format

➤ **Round-up.** A 500- to 3,500-word entertaining, informative piece, usually about where to find something specific

➤ **Cultural commentary.** A 600- to 6,000-word commentary or overview of a cultural phenomenon with an opinionated slant

➤ **Humor piece.** A 500- to 1,000-word humorous essay, often on a topical issue that could be personal, political, parody, or farce

There you have it, all the different types of articles that you might write. Memorize this lingo so that when you're talking to an editor on the phone, you don't need to ask, "Uh, you want me to write a service piece? Is that about waitresses?"

How Many Words?

You might have noticed that articles are defined in terms of their word count. What's word count got to do with it?

The publications business, whether it is magazine or a newspaper, is driven by page length. Well, actually, it is driven by advertising revenue, which in turn determines how many pages are available for the editors to fill up with words. The other pages are filled up by the advertising department.

It works like this: If the ad sales department doesn't sell enough ads to pay the bills for a 200-page magazine, it will quickly become a smaller magazine with less editorial content. On the other hand, if the ad sales department has a terrific month and sells twice as many ads as usual, bonanza! The editors can now afford a bigger magazine with more articles.

An editor always keeps in mind just how his finished product will look. Take the piece he assigned to a freelancer on sunbathing topless on the Riviera—how many pages should be allotted to that? Will he run pictures as well? Is that worth two full pages, or just one and a half? Or, perhaps instead he should use that long article he has on file about dog sledding during the Arctic summer. The sunbathing story will be only 1,500 words, which also will leave room to run a 250-word piece on skin cancer alongside it …. Get the picture?

Dead Lines

Don't turn in too much material. If you promised a 500-word story, turn in a 500-word story, not a 5,000-word story.

Putting together a publication of any kind is like decorating a house—you need to know which rooms the furniture will fit in. If you order a small mahogany side table for one room and instead an extra-long suede couch shows up, you've got a problem.

If an editor assigns you a story or gives you the green light on a story idea you've pitched, he also will let you know how many words he wants you to turn in. Why should your artistry and talent be crimped by such restrictions? Because your editor ordered a small side table to fit into a particular part of the magazine and doesn't want a big couch to show up instead.

So now you have a handle on why freelancers exist and what it is that they do. Let's move on to meet four top writers who make their full-time living from freelancing for a wide variety of magazines and newspapers.

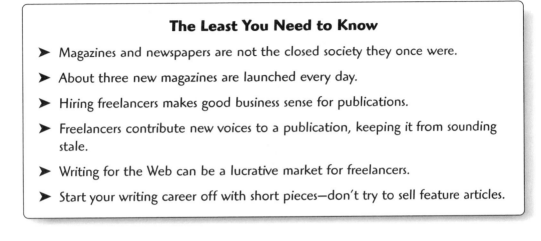

The Least You Need to Know

➤ Magazines and newspapers are not the closed society they once were.

➤ About three new magazines are launched every day.

➤ Hiring freelancers makes good business sense for publications.

➤ Freelancers contribute new voices to a publication, keeping it from sounding stale.

➤ Writing for the Web can be a lucrative market for freelancers.

➤ Start your writing career off with short pieces—don't try to sell feature articles.

Success Stories

The *successful* freelancer—you mean they're actually out there? Men and women whose career doesn't revolve around an alarm clock? Writers who actually make a decent living writing, working from assignment to assignment?

Stop the presses! Yes, they exist—quite well, in some cases. But the course they've chosen requires perseverance, an ability to overcome obstacles, and an inner confidence to ride out the dry spells without having a breakdown. Contrary to popular thought, the gig isn't all late mornings, bathrobe-clad until 3 P.M., feasting on M&Ms and coffee. In this chapter, you'll hear four successful writers express what works for them and what they've learned from living as a freelancer. They talk turkey about expenses, "ins" with editors, and even health.

Any freelancer will tell you this much: It takes more than a winning query or great clips to write for hire on a regular basis. Think of successful freelance writers as Olympic athletes, never resting on their laurels, but constantly honing and training their skills—mentally, physically, emotionally, and spiritually. Let the games begin!

Kim Wright Wiley

Although Kim Wright Wiley studied journalism in college, somehow she found herself managing investments for a living. But when her first child was born, Wiley decided to take a leap of faith and pursue her first love—writing—in the hopes of turning the typewriter into a full-time, stay-at-home career.

She didn't quit her day job initially, even when the query she sent to a now-defunct women's financial glossy, *Savvy,* resulted in her first assignment. "I cold-pitched the magazine on a short piece about investing for women," recalls Wiley. "I believe I immediately was at an advantage. At the time, the concept was fresh. I was a working woman in my early 20s giving stock advice." Wiley's one pitch blossomed into several articles with titles such as "The First Three Stocks Every Women Should Buy."

The Write Words

Shiny photographic prints are called **glossies** because of the finish required for sharp reproductions. High-quality publications use glossy paper. Hence, most national magazines that print all pages on shiny paper for a finished, professional look are referred to in the publishing biz as glossies. Think *Vogue*. Think *Glamour*. Think *Newsweek*. Think *Life*. Most freelancers strive for national, glossy assignments.

Mommy Washes the Clothes and Writes Award-Winning Articles

With a cushion of consistent assignments, Wiley finally decided to stay home with her daughter and write full-time. She'd found her niche. But Wiley's muse didn't focus solely on investment articles. She found that writing about ideas pertinent to her—specifically, the kids (she has two)—also earned the new freelancer assignments.

Now more than a decade later, Wiley writes full-time for national *glossies,* often commanding her own price for assignments. Her work has appeared in *Working Mother, Islands, Family Fun, Child,* and many other magazines. She is also the author of several travel books focusing on adventure seeking and globe-trotting with kids.

What follows is advice from Wiley in her own words. She recounts for us the path she took, what she's learned, and how to forge ahead on the road to a successful freelance writing career without a clip, a career in writing, or knowing anyone!

"Back to Me!"

Q: Where do you come up with the ideas for your stories?

A: My own life and the lives of my friends. At this stage of my career, editors call me with assignments about half the time, and the other half I come up with my own ideas. They're so autobiographical! I remember taking my kids shoe shopping when they were toddlers and wondering why kids' shoes were so expensive, and did it really matter if you got the $40 mall shoes over the $8 Wal-Mart version. So I did an article on "Why Do Kids' Shoes Cost So Much?" and sold it to *Parents*. I figure if I have a question or a problem or a desire to go somewhere, other people out there must feel the same way.

Q: From your experience, what works in a pitch letter?

A: A description of the idea in some detail, a summary of other markets you've written for, and an offer of clips upon request. I usually lead in with a question, then [explain] how my article will answer the question.

Q: What advice can you give aspiring writers about writing, the process and technique?

A: There's no substitute for having a good basic skill base. I wish I'd gotten out of journalism school knowing how to interview. It's an essential skill and one that's undertaught. If I had the chance to go back, I'd interview everyone in sight and practice pulling three or four quotes from a long interview. I had to learn that one the hard way.

> **Dead Lines**
>
> As Kim Wiley notes, interviewing remains an essential skill that all good writers must possess. You might not think that much preparation beyond the questions is needed, but think again. Everything from materials to research should be checked and double-checked before commencing an interview.

"It's Not Who You Know, Really!"

Q: Is breaking into the glossies really about who you know?

A: I broke in without knowing anybody. But it's undeniable that once you break in, it gets easier to sell your second piece, and your third when you know the editors. An editor who you've worked with before is more likely to say, "This isn't right for us, but call my buddy over at *X Magazine* ...." One thing novices don't understand is that publishing is a very small world. The fact that it's small works against you when you're trying to break in, but once you break in, it begins to work in your favor.

Q: With that said, then, how can someone on the "outside" break into the glossies?

A: I think you need to get clips at the less-than-glossies first—local magazines, airline magazines, in-house publications for businesses and hospitals. They don't pay well, but at the beginning you're just trying to collect clips. I wrote for anything during the first three years just to accumulate clips.

A Pocket Full of Expertise

Q: What's the best thing you ever did to advance your career? What moves did you make that you think brought you to the place you are now?

A: I developed pockets of expertise on certain subjects and wrote numerous articles out of those pockets. At last count, I've done over 20 articles somehow connected to fertility issues, for example, and over 40 about Walt Disney World. Strange things to be an expert in, I know!

Look for Wiley's works in national publications; you'll certainly notice a continuity in topics when reading her work. Moreover, take her advice and find your own pocket of expertise. The more you write on one or two specific subjects, the easier the research becomes—you already know the background information.

Brooks Clark

Brooks Clark credits an annual gathering of writers and editors on a lake in New Hampshire—called affectionately by all, "The Schmooze"—for cementing his freelancing career. "One summer, I told all my buddies, old and new, that sooner or later my company would fold and I'd be a freelancer," recalls Clark. When Clark's company did fold, he found himself on assignments for three publications within one week— *The Stanford Alumni Magazine, SI (Sports Illustrated) for Kids,* and the *Dartmouth Alumni Magazine.* The *SI for Kids* assignment earned Clark the cover and a trip to Puerto Rico. "Getting laid off was never such fun! he says.

And though Clark holds a "day job" as a speech writer, his freelance repertoire reads like a who's who of magazines and includes articles in *Sports Illustrated,* the *Washington Post Magazine, Attache, People, Kiplinger's Personal Finance, Lamaze Family, Life, Parenting, Working Mother, Success,* and *Outside for Kids.* Clark shares with us his writing dictums and perspectives on personal relationships and freelancing.

The Straight Scoop

Brooks Clark wrote—as an exercise for himself—a list of "Immutable Laws for Freelancers." On the list exists "Always Exercise." "Writing is a physical as well as a mental activity. If you get run down, your writing suffers," explains the veteran freelancer. "A freelancer is in charge of keeping his or her batteries charged. If you burn out, that's your problem, and you suffer horribly for it. When you get burnt out (for real), it can take weeks or months to really get your edge back."

Q: If you weren't writing, what would you be doing?

A: I might be an English teacher. I may yet end up running youth sports programs, since I do this right now anyway. (Clark co-directs a soccer league of 600 kids and is vice president of a competitive soccer club.) Truly, though, I've never once thought of doing anything other than writing in one way or another.

Q: What do you enjoy most about your job?

A: That moment when I have finished a story, turned it in, and know that it's basically okay. I get a rush of energy at that point that I truly love. I also love finding the good story that everybody else has overlooked.

Q: What do you enjoy least?

A: Being tired. Transcribing tapes.

Q: What makes you say, "I love this job!" What's been your favorite experience?

A: My favorite experience by far was getting 30 minutes with the University of Tennessee Lady Vols point guard Michelle Marciniak, then 30 minutes with coach Pat Summitt—who both answered all my questions in detail. There was not a wasted word in either interview, and the piece is still interesting today.

Life Stories

Q: Where do you come up with your ideas for stories?

A: I write sports parenting and parenting stories, so they come from my day-to-day experiences. I also specialize in the hidden history stories—especially reflections on the 1960s, which I experienced close-up in Washington, D.C., and through the eyes of five older siblings. Right now I'm planning a story on "my African brother," a Gambian student who lived with my family for five years—who led the student protests at American University—and an interview with the Rev. Kelly Miller Smith Jr., a churchman here in Knoxville whose father was one of the key people in the Nashville civil rights movement, which my father was also a small part of. So the interview would be two children of the civil rights movement reflecting on what it meant to us—who had no part in it at all.

You Gotta Have a Gimmick

Q: From your experience, what works in a pitch letter?

A: (a) Some wit and humor, (b) having a good story idea, (c) showing how you'd execute it, (d) demonstrating that you are a good writer who can pull it off, and (e) giving a nice way for the editor to call you or respond or say hello even if the answer is no. (Example: In the fourth or fifth paragraph, Brooks advises writing something like, "If you're interested, just give me a call. But what I'd really like to do sometime is a story on how sports can help kids with ADHD. I know it's touchy, but it's a big story out there.")

31

Q: What advice can you give aspiring writers about writing?

A: This is a lifetime study.

Q: The buzz about freelancing seems to be that "it's who you know." How true is this?

A: Totally.

In a previous discussion about this topic, Clark wrote in depth about "The Schmooze," saying, "The bottom line for the book: personal relationships are everything. Not just you and an editor, but the relationship of being able to say, 'This person is a good writer; she turns in good copy, no headaches, he's good at a + b.' That's how editors work—they ask other editors and writers." Though Clark can list many notable writers who spunkily set off on a sojourn at The Schmooze in New Hampshire and landed great assignments, the proverbial proof is always in the pudding. Good writing + Good ideas = Assignments. Perseverance and tenacity—getting you and your work out there can work wonders. In one word: networking.

The Straight Scoop

"Like any good freelancer, I use no-cost e-mail when it can avoid long-distance charges!" says Brooks Clark. And he's not the only freelancer to find that technology can have a cost advantage. Writers all over the globe frequently use e-mail as a means for preliminary interviews. Beyond the savings on long distance, e-mail interviews often prove more convenient for both interviewer and interviewee. Both parties can send and answer questions whenever time permits. Moreover, the writer needn't spend countless hours transcribing an interview. The interview arrives already transcribed in your in-box. Keep in mind, however, that some publications frown on all e-mail interviews. After all, it's harder to verify who's on the other end.

Q: Describe the best pitch letter you ever wrote.

A: It began, "Jim Morgan told me to drop you a letter ...." I got a call the next day. The best pitch letter I ever received began "Gary Smith said that you would be a good person to query ...." As I like to say to classes, [an opening with an introduction from a mutual acquaintance] says several things to the editor: (1) Gary Smith, one of the best magazine writers in America, remembers me, (2) Gary Smith knows where I am, (3) this person is a friend of Gary's, and (4) the query is good enough for Gary to have referred the writer. I called the writer immediately.

Q: Many freelancers say they "just know" when their pitch or essay submission wasn't even read and a canned rejection was sent without even looking at the proposed article. Even though editors adamantly deny that this ever happens, do you think it happens?

A: Yes, but it's part of the game. Just forget about it and send it somewhere else.

Brooks Clark's Immutable Laws of Freelancing

When Clark took a leap of faith and decided to devote himself to freelancing, he did something motivational and, at the same time, wise: He conceptualized and wrote down a list of rules to live by as freelancer. What follows is a list he still refers to when writing schedules and deadlines prove especially hectic. Follow these rules to remain focused on your choice to freelance:

➤ Never turn in the piece until it's done and you think it's perfect.

➤ Always turn in an outline or call to run over where you're going with the article with the editor.

➤ Always have a great attitude.

➤ The Inverse Law of Clips: Always send editors your fun clips or notes when you don't want or need anything from them.

➤ Always be realistic about your schedule.

➤ When in doubt or at risk of missing a deadline, call the editor.

➤ The story you're finishing right now is the most important story in the world. Worry about the next one next.

➤ Say no sometimes.

➤ Prioritize deadlines.

➤ Always exercise.

➤ Write it now, not tomorrow morning.

➤ Always know where the story is going before you begin writing.

Ilene Beckerman

Many people know of Ilene Beckerman from her best-selling book, *Love, Loss, and What I Wore,* the captivating story of her life told to us through the clothes she wore, and its sequel, *What We Do for Love.* But the native New Yorker has written about the Oscars for the *Los Angeles Times,* the good old days for *Victoria* magazine, the color gray for *The New York Times,* and different styles over the last millennium for *Weight Watchers* magazine. She also was a judge for *People* magazine's "Best and Worst Dressed" issue. Beckerman always presents her perspectives with humorous truth.

The Write Words

Samuel Johnson defined an essay as "a loose sally of the mind." Essays are, in fact, composition articles, infused with editorial, one's opinion—they're a think piece, per se. Generally speaking, reporters don't editorialize in their articles. **Essayists** do, however, and include more than observations in their exposition. An essayist's personal analysis of a subject usually reflects satire, strong sentiment, or humor.

Beckerman's writing career was launched at the age of 60 when her private collection of drawings and memoirs—photocopied at Kinkos as a present for her five children—somehow found its way into the hands of a book editor at Algonquin; *Love, Loss, and What I Wore* emerged on shelves nationwide soon after. "Gingy's" most recent title, *Mother of the Bride: The Dream, the Reality, the Search for a Perfect Dress,* looks lovingly and hilariously at one of life's happiest (and most stressful events)—the planning of a daughter's wedding—and is described by the author as "about $12^1/_2$ words" with a sneaky giggle.

Beckerman considers herself a "creator" and an *essayist,* who's still trying to figure out how to succeed in the freelance arena. She humbly discusses how lost she feels at having been thrust into the publishing world—wanting to write articles, but not knowing how to go about it at all. She wants to report, too, not just put her own ideas on paper. She yearns to write features. Get inside Gingy's head and learn about the writing beast within us all.

Exciting and Horrifying Endeavors

Q: What do you most enjoy about writing?

A: It's the most exciting thing I know. I enjoy the pleasure associated with creating something. When I was a child, I was shy. Writing was a quiet way for me to express myself. The words go across my brain like ticker tape. You pull them down and re-arrange them. Then you work and work and work on them until the final draft pleases you.

Q: What do you least enjoy about writing?

A: My first drafts. In my head, I have such an idea! I think I know what [the project] is going to be, but my first draft is never anywhere near where my mind thinks everything should be. It's kind of like when you go shopping and you see this gorgeous dress and you think, "I've got to have that gorgeous dress. It's incredible." But then you put it on, and you think, "Oh my god! This is horrible!" It doesn't look the same on as how you envisioned it.

Strumming to the Beat of a Different Drum

Q: Describe a typical day for you when you write.

A: I don't have a typical day. I've been with a lot of authors who say they go and write from 9 to 5 or they make deals with themselves about writing a certain number of hours a day. I just write when I have something to say. I am, however, very conscious of my deadlines. It's my good girl upbringing. Most of my ideas also come to me when I'm doing something else. Perhaps that's why I'm typecast as an essayist. I'm typecast. They always ask me to write about clothes. I remember how excited I was when I received a call from the op. ed. section of *The New York Times*. I thought, "Finally!" Do you know what they asked me to write about? Gray is the new black! I love to poke around the library and do what I call gentle research. I'd love to write a real reporter's feature. Do you know how to get one of those assignments?

Q: What advice can you give aspiring writers?

A: Number one—just write. Don't do your writing for money. Write because you have something to say, because you enjoy it. Just do it and get it down. Also, don't criticize yourself. Let it go.

Q: Considering that you, too, are trying to gain more glossy assignments and move away from essays, do you think "it's who you know"?

A: I do think that publishing is a small network. But it's no different than any other work environment. You've got people hustling, working, sucking up—access to wants is the same no matter what profession you choose.

Q: What writing are you most proud of?

A: I have some poems that I wrote when I was in high school. They were very "Dorothy Parker" and talked of broken-hearted love affairs. The fact that I had enough guts to write them then, type them, and keep them—I still have them—makes me enjoy them more than a photo. [The poems] have emotion and passion. There's no emotion in a photo.

Q: Do you read much, and what do you read?

A: I read *The New Yorker, Talk* magazine. *Harper's Bazaar. Jane*—I like to see what the young people are wearing. *In Style. W*—I love *W* because of the profiles. It's like what *Interview* was. I subscribed to the *New York Review of Books* and couldn't understand it. *Martha Stewart Living. Architectural Digest*. I love looking at beautiful things, and everything in *Architectural Digest* is so beautiful.

Beckerman's insights should serve as an inspiration to us all. She is proof positive that it's never too late to start writing.

Medicine Man Jim Thornton

In naming Jim Thornton as the winner of the 1998 National Magazine Award for his series of in-depth, first-person investigative health articles, the American Society of Magazine Editors (ASME) cemented his status as one of the premiere health and science journalists. But the awards don't stop here for Thornton, who prides himself on taking complex information and making it understandable and interesting for the masses.

This lauded writer currently contributes to *Men's Journal, Details, National Geographic Adventure,* and *Cooking Light*. He also has written for *Self, Glamour, Reader's Digest, Sports Illustrated,* and many other national glossies. Stop the presses! His work doesn't begin and end with popular magazines. The prolific writer boasts scientific papers published in journals, TV scripts, and even books.

For someone with such a huge repertoire of prestigious work, you might think he'd be a total snob. Not so. Thornton is refreshingly quirky, helpful, fascinating and, above all, candid. He talked at length about his arrival as a wildly successful freelance writer and offers up his own brand of advice for you:

Q: If you weren't writing, what would you be doing?

A: I don't know. I had a variety of jobs—shipping boy, whipping boy—I was pretty much a failure at all I'd done. The only other job I was marginally competent at was as a lifeguard at a resort for the rich—and then I was a school teacher. I got fired from that job.

Q: How then did you arrive at this career you have freelance writing for some of the most sought-after magazines?

A: [After getting fired] from teaching, I went to Iowa's Writer's Workshop. But I took fiction. Getting a second master's degree in journalism proved an excellent education for more literary magazine writing. Everyone's route is different. There are people who can slowly slip into freelancing just by sheer force of talent. Journalism classes (taught me) concrete skills, the nuts and bolts. The impulse for a lot of writers is introspection. But for journalism, you have to go out into the world and ask people questions. I was in the arm chair category until I took journalism. I always wrote from imagination.

While a graduate student at Iowa, I went into the *Iowa City Press Citizen* with some ideas and met the editor, and (he) hired me. In the early to mid-1980s, my wife and I moved to St. Paul, and I wrote for *Minnesota Monthly*. They didn't pay very well; I used to have to crank out a lot—everything from real estate to articles on duck artists. Slowly I accumulated some decent clips. Then, I think, I started to send out essay-type things to New York publications and got some nice rejection notes.

Then in 1987, my identical twin was getting married. I called up editors and said that I was going to be in New York and asked if they would mind if I stopped by. All agreed. I went in. They let me stay. I schmoozed and joked around. By the time I got back to Minnesota, I had an assignment with *Sports Illustrated,* my first national.

Pretty Fishy, Eh?

Thornton's first national story covered transgenic walleyes cross breeding into a super fish. Says the writer, "*SI* liked the idea because is was quirky." Soon after, Thornton saw in the paper a story on some guy racing poodles in a dog sled contest. What did the entrepreneurial writer do? He called up the fishing editor at *SI*, who said, "Go ahead and do that, too!"

Q: What do you enjoy most about freelancing?

A: Since those initial publications, I've pyramided my way up the pay scale. I enjoy that instead of 10 articles, I can now do one or two longer articles (for the same pay). I also enjoy the adventure stories. (For instance, he covered a story for *National Geographic Adventure* where he jet-skied in Siberia.)

Q: What do you enjoy the least?

A: The stress of not knowing if I'm going to get enough work. I'm the sole support for the family. It's not as bad now, but back when I first began, normally I'd have enough work and then it would evaporate and it was terrifying.

Q: From your experience, what works in a pitch letter?

A: I don't really do that ... I never did a whole lot of it. You know how they always say come up with one finely crafted idea? I don't do that. I give the editors 25 ideas, each in 2 single-space inches of copy, with little details. [The editor] can go through the list and make proactive selections. Tune the slant.

Q: What advice can you give aspiring writers?

A: Be persistent. In all elements, be persistent. Be persistent in attracting the best interviews. Be persistent in getting editors to like you. I remember thinking, "There are just born great writers, and I'm not one of them."

Look for Thornton's work at a magazine near you!

The Straight Scoop

If you are lucky enough to have an editor of a magazine offer to look over your work, send it to him, for goodness sake. If you don't or you procrastinate, the door just may close on the opportunity. You'll spend the rest of your career kicking yourself for not making it all happen that much sooner.

Cheap Advice: One-Sentence Tips from the Pros

➤ Do the freebies, like radio shows, as they often turn into paid writing assignments.

➤ Never cop an attitude when asked to rewrite a piece.

➤ Always return an editor's phone calls.

➤ When you've written for a publication three or four times successfully, don't be afraid to ask for more money on your next assignment.

➤ Give yourself time off from writing—at least one day a week.

➤ Always refer frequently to your assignment sheet to ensure that you write the right story—the editor's vision of the piece.

➤ Meet your deadlines.

➤ Meet your deadlines.

➤ Meet your deadlines.

The Least You Need to Know

➤ According to the writers in the trenches, the possession of great clips and a fabulous query remain good ways to garner an assignment—but not the only way. Networking ranks as high as strong writing, in some cases.

➤ Even previously published writers worry about the next assignment and work on perfecting their craft.

➤ Write about that which you know, and develop "pockets of expertise."

➤ Don't give up if you aren't able to earn an assignment in a national publication. Start with smaller publications, gather strong clips, and work toward achieving a byline in a national glossy.

➤ Develop a system, a schedule, and stick to it.

➤ Finally, write because you enjoy writing and because it is something you must do for yourself; write because it is a part of who you are. Don't do it for the bucks!

Chapter 4

The Editors Talk

In This Chapter

➤ Learning which editor to send queries to

➤ What makes a good query letter

➤ How to break in to national magazines

➤ What editors look for in new writers

If you want to write for magazines, there's no avoiding them: editors. Editors are the almighty gods and goddesses who sit on Magazine Mount Olympus, deciding what gets inked and what gets tossed. Editors stand between the freelance writer and his or her entry into the glamorous life of the glossy printed page.

What do editors want? What the heck do they do? What's the difference between a features editor, a managing editor, and any editor? Most important, which one receives and reviews queries?

In this chapter, we introduce you to five honest-to-goodness editors—the supernatural powers of print. Just as Odysseus navigated the whims of Poseidon, Circe, and myriad other immortals to find his way back to Penelope, we'll play Athena to your Grecian king and give you an inside look at the editors. In their own words, you'll learn what freelance offerings please these gods and what makes them want to shower the freelance writer with thunderbolts.

The Hierarchy of the Gods: Learning Which Editor Does What

What's in a name? Mucho—especially when you consider that a query letter addressed vaguely to "Editorial Department" will get you nowhere fast. Finding your way around Magazine Mount Olympus, therefore, remains a must in your pursuit of a freelance writing career.

The Write Words

The **masthead** is a list of all the editors, artists, designers, editorial staffers, and sometimes advertising executives for a publication. You'll typically find it printed within the first few pages of a publication.

The Write Words

The **editor-in-chief** supervises the editorial staff and oversees every story, department, and column, shaping the content, tone, and personality of the magazine. Depending upon the size of the publication, the editor-in-chief may wear many hats, including editing the piece before turning it over to the designer for layout.

The easiest way to get the lowdown on who's who in Editor Land is through the *masthead* of the magazine or newspaper you're interested in. You'll typically find the masthead printed within the first few pages of the publication; it's a listing of all the editors, artists, designers, editorial staffers, and sometimes advertising executives at the publication. The masthead is your lifeline to real people with names who, I might add, open and read mail—*your* letter pitching that incredible feature idea.

You might notice that several editors—all with different editorial titles—exist within one publication. In one magazine, you may find an editor-in-chief, a managing editor, a features editor, an associate editor, a health editor, and a beauty editor. Another magazine might list only an editor-in-chief and a managing editor. The number of editors and their respective topic specialty is determined, in most cases, by the size of the publication. For example, even though a city and regional magazine might feature a health story each month, the publication's *editor-in-chief* or managing editor probably assigns and edits the stories, whereas a national woman's glossy magazine might possess a single editor devoted to procuring and editing health features, a health editor.

The best way to find your way to the right editor is to call the publication. Tell an editorial assistant in one sentence the basis of your idea and ask her to whom you should send the pitch. Another good tactic? Categorize your story. Is it health-oriented? Then pitch the health editor. You get the idea.

The Ladies Come and Go, Talking of Michelangelo

Okay. Easy enough, you think. Just send the query to the editor-in-chief, the top name on the masthead, right? Baaaat! Wrong. Pitching the editor-in-chief often works with regional publications, such as city-oriented magazines, but national publications require a tad of logic and a little research.

By the way, always call and confirm that the editor listed on the masthead to whom you plan to send your pitch still holds the position listed. Editors are notorious for moving within and to and from different publications. Just because *Working Mother* lists Catherine Cartwright one month doesn't mean that by the time your pitch letter arrives, she hasn't moved on to another magazine.

Regional Athena, *Sacramento Magazine's* Krista Minard

Sacramento Magazine, where Krista Minard runs the shop, is a monthly publication devoted to covering the four-county region of California's capital and has hit racks for more than 25 years now. Minard's duties, however, extend beyond the area's popular glossy. The magazine group Sacramento Magazine Corporation also publishes numerous "contract" publications, such as chamber guides and convention and visitor magazines, including the *Northern California Golf Guide* and the *Sacramento Medical Guide.* All in all, Minard might oversee, orchestrate, and edit more than 25 publications a year! That's pretty good, considering that her first job with the magazine was as a receptionist; she got her foot in the door and answered the phones until an opening occurred where her true talents could be showcased between the pages of the publication.

Q: What's your typical day like?

A: There is no typical day after the initial walk in, which involves checking voice mail, checking e-mail, checking regular mail—never fewer than 80 pieces a day—then it all depends on what's happening. For example, right now I'm working on six publications: The February issue of *Sacramento Magazine* is shipping out, so I'll be doing some last-minute proofreading. Copy for the March issue is due from writers, so I'm receiving files, converting them, and fielding phone calls from writers who are going to be late. The *Northern California Golf Guide* is inserted into the March issue of *Sacramento Magazine,* so I'm getting copy for that, too. The publisher is actually editor-in-chief on the golf guide, so there have been plenty of meetings with him this week to discuss the content and what needs to be done with the copy. It's time to assign the editorial for *Sacramento Magazine's* April issue, so I've got to review the lineup with the publisher and call some writers. Also, in contract publishing, I'm working on a couple of projects. *Roseville Magazine* needs to be proofread one last time; I'm waiting for a call from the head of the Elk Grove Chamber of Commerce so I can concept the editorial for the magazine; perhaps most pressing in the contract pubs is the

Community Guide, which we publish for the Sacramento Metro Chamber. That copy is in from the writer but needs to be processed and organized and given to our designers within the week. This morning there was a department head meeting to attend, and we discussed the strengths and weaknesses within the company. Not surprisingly, one of the weaknesses we've tagged for the editorial department is this: We need more staff!

Q: What qualities do you seek in new writers?

A: Enthusiasm, ability to write well, accuracy, tight writing, and willingness and ability to come up with ideas that are right for the magazine.

Q: How much about freelancing is "who you know"?

A: My favorite freelancers are people I've worked with for many years. Some of them were writers for previous editors here; others are people I've met in other situations and have expressed interest. For example, one of the best freelancers is a woman who lives down the street from me. When I moved to the neighborhood, she heard through the grapevine that I was the editor of *Sacramento Magazine*. I heard she taught journalism at the local high school. There was always a mutual respect, but we rarely spoke. I ran into her in a coffee place one day, and we had a conversation about her students and my internship program.

A year or two later, while I was pregnant with my first daughter, I saw her sitting on her porch holding an infant. I stopped, admired the baby girl, we talked—again very rushed—about daughters, motherhood, and pregnancy and the fact that she had left her teaching job to stay home with her baby. She was doing some columns for our local newspaper. I liked her; she liked me, and while I was on maternity leave we visited a lot, and sometime in that time, she asked me about writing opportunities. I assessed her work, and when I got back to the office, tried her out on a short story. She did a great job, so I assigned her something else—and from there, she has become one of my biggest contributors.

Magazine Stalkers

(Even though Minard acknowledges a willingness to try out new writers, she adds this:)

But before I'll take a chance, I have to have some sense of the person's ability and the person's nature. We get a lot of what we call "magazine stalkers." These are the people who bombard us with queries and ideas, and there's always an undertone of desperation. They really want to work for *Sacramento Magazine* and seem to view it as a glamorous deal, but when we try them out on a story, their writing turns out to be very weak, loose, and devoid of depth. Or, they turn out to be public relations writers .... Often it's hard to tell the difference between a stalker and someone who will turn out to be a great contributor, and this is one reason why I will not try out even the most promising-looking writer on anything longer than a [300- to 500-word] piece.

Q: What's the best way to break in?

A: Send a query letter detailing an idea for a story that is fitting for *Sacramento Magazine*. Don't call. Don't e-mail. Don't fax. Send the letter, complete with a *SASE*. Don't tell us why we should publish your story. Just tell us what the idea is and give enough detail so that we can figure out where it might fit. And do some research. If the subject was just covered in the magazine, we're not going to do it again *in any way* for several years. Focus your thinking on the short stories in the magazine—City Lights, particularly ....

The (pitch) letter should break from the traditional four paragraphs that ends with "Would *Sacramento Magazine* be interested in ...?" Those are dead giveaways that the person is a student in a Writing for Publication class. While I don't immediately discard them, particularly if the idea is good, I do go into it knowing that the writer is inexperienced.

In finalizing her interview, Minard listed "no-nos" for both writers wanting to break into the magazine as a contributor and writers who frequently contribute. Among her "no-nos" are ...

1. Faxed or e-mailed queries.
2. No *SASE* included.
3. Letters addressed to "Dear Editor."
4. Regularly missed deadlines.
5. Submitting incomplete information.
6. Complaining about editing.
7. Misspelling names in a story.
8. Writing too long and expecting the editor to either run it all or cut it for you.

To take a peek at *Sacramento Magazine*, navigate online to www.sacmag.com.

The Write Words

All editors ask for a **SASE**—a self-addressed, stamped envelope—to accompany any article submission or query.

Islands Girl: Editor-in-Chief Joan Tapper, *Islands*

Scuba diving, sun bathing, and boogie boarding. Ever dream of a writing assignment where you whisk off to Ambergris Caye or Fiji, frolic in the sand and surf, dine on exquisite resort fare, and basically—let's face it—vacation for your pay?

Aahhh, the life of a travel writer (sigh). Writers lucky enough to land travel assignments get paid for reporting on tropical treks, sun kisses, and Mai Tai madness. But getting such a gig requires providing the proof in the poi, according to *Islands* Editor-in-Chief Joan Tapper, who shares advice on how freelancers can break into travel writing.

The Straight Scoop

Jane magazine likes to invite everyone to the party that is their publication—readers, writers, everyone. When you open the magazine's cover, you're entering *Jane*. In keeping with the publication's friendly tone, *Jane*'s Web site shows off baby pictures and offers up brief notes and quirks about its staff. Editor Suzan Colon gets our vote for "Most Inspirational," as the staffer's bio insists that Colon "was dragged away from a bucolic life as a freelance writer for publications as diverse as *Details* and *DC Comics* to work at *Jane*." Colon was recently crowned senior writer/editor at *Jane*.

The Write Words

An **in-room publication** is something that a resort provides to its guests. The magazine is placed in the room, much like an in-flight publication.

Who's That Girl?

Perhaps her childhood in the Windy City propelled Joan Tapper toward warmer, more temperate shores. Or maybe it was trudging to masters classes in comparative literature on bone-chilling mornings at Harvard University. Whatever the reason, Tapper has made a career in vacationing, first as an editor at *National Geographic Traveler* and since 1988 as editor-in-chief of *Islands*, an international travel magazine focusing on (what else?) the islands of the world. In 1996, Tapper earned directorship of Islands Publishing Company, which includes *Resorts* and *Great Hotels*; *Sojourner,* an *in-room publication* in Aspen, Colorado; and multimedia and custom publishing divisions. Under Tapper's leadership, *Islands* magazine has won numerous top prizes from the Society of American Travel Writers.

Tapper's Truths and Answers

So you want to jet off to faraway lands and write about your adventures for a living? Hold the tote and the carry-on bag, and read what the person who "shapes the overall focus and tone" of a 220,000-plus circulation travel magazine advises the prospective freelancer. We played Q&A with the 30-year veteran of exotic locales and found out what characteristics Joan Tapper looks for in new writers.

The Straight Scoop

The Society of American Travel Writers (SATW) is a professional association that promotes responsible journalism, provides professional support and development for members, and encourages the conservation and preservation of travel resources worldwide. Membership into the society requires sponsorship and a track record of travel writing with integrity. For complete guidelines, navigate the SATW Web site at www.satw.org. In addition, SATW offers an annual directory with listings of more than 1,000 of the top travel communicators in the United States and Canada. You'll find everyone from prominent travel writers to top travel editors, to communications executives representing tourist attractions. Either print out the order form on the Web site, or call 919-787-5181 for more information.

Q: What do you look for in new writers—besides his or her ability to write?

A: Ability to write is foremost. I also look for his or her sense of this particular magazine and what we're after. I'm interested in reliability and imagination, of course. I'll try a new writer on something that's low-risk, but when it comes to spending a lot of money on an assignment—this is a travel magazine, after all—I'd rather go with a writer (or a photographer) who has performed well for us in the past.

Q: How can someone on the "outside" break into your publication?

A: An outsider should study the magazine and write a pertinent, imaginative query aimed at a low-risk—front or back of the book—department. Or be willing to try a feature *on spec*.

Q: Describe the best pitch letter you ever received.

A: Bob Morris, who later became one of our contributing editors (and later the editor of our short-lived

The Write Words

On spec stands for "on speculation" and means writing a piece on the *chance* that the publication might purchase the rights for it. In other words, the editor shows an interest in the idea but might not want to risk advancing the expenses—especially in a travel story—and paying the fee for rights on the chance that the writing turns out weak or the feature flops. You, the writer, have no contractual guarantee that your hard work is going to pay off. Nevertheless, you can prove yourself on a spec assignment, which then may result in contract assignments.

Dead Lines

Harper's Bazaar Features Director Mary Murray doesn't mince words when giving advice to writers wishing to break into the pages of America's hallowed fashion glossy. Authoritatively Murray resounds, "Read the magazine. Don't insult me by sending me a generic pitch letter that's obviously been sent to 50 other magazines out there. I can tell when a writer doesn't read or know the tone of *Harper's Bazaar*. And don't tell me that a topic is important to women. So what? It doesn't matter if the topic is important to women. What matters is if the topic is important to our readers."

dive magazine, *Aqua*), broke in with a query on Boca Grand, Florida. It was a place that he knew and that was near his home, so travel expenses weren't exorbitant. His query was lively and interesting and used the techniques we prize in the magazine: anecdote, dialogue, theme. And his clips were good.

Q: Give your top list of things freelancers shouldn't do. What turns you off to a new writer immediately?

A: Don't query me without ever looking at the magazine. Don't try to convince me that you know what I want better than I do. Don't send a laundry list of ideas. Don't call the night before you're leaving on a trip. Don't miss a deadline without alerting me. Don't try to palm off a sloppy, casual story.

Q: Many freelancers say they "just know" when their pitch or essay submission wasn't even read, that a canned rejection was sent without anyone's even looking at the materials. How do you respond to these writers' perceptions?

A: I don't believe it. Most editors are honest and overworked, and they look at the queries that come to them. But they won't spend a lot of time with something that does not grab or hold their interest. If I can't make it past the first paragraph, I won't go further.

Where in the World Is Joan Tapper?

Have a pitch that'll put wind in Joan Tapper's sail? Send it to *Islands* magazine, P.O. Box 4728, Santa Barbara, CA 93140-4728.

The Whole Kid and Kaboodle: Health Editor Kara Corridan, *Child*

Kara Corridan made what many writers jokingly call "a move to the dark side." Corridan, you see, spent many fruitful years freelancing—most recently as a *Working Mother* regular—only to take a full-time position as an editor at *Child*. Corridan oversees all the health-related stories for the parenting publication that offer valuable advice on caring for and raising children from infancy to preteen years. Interestingly, Corridan lives the single life and has no kids, yet has her finger on the pulse of children's health issues.

Insight from the Dark Side

Corridan assures us that Darth Vader doesn't lurk behind the desk at *Child*. Rather, hers is the sage wisdom of Obi Wan Kenobi as she offers fresh-from-freelancing advice on the inner sanctum of an editorial office and on getting your foot in the door of freelance magazine writing.

Q: If you weren't an editor, what would you be doing?

A: I'd still be involved with magazines as a free-lance writer.

Q: What do you enjoy most about your job?

A: I most enjoy helping shape an article that's already in great condition from the writer!

Q: What do you enjoy least?

A: I least enjoy haggling with the art department over space for stories, *heds, deks, captions,* and so on.

A Peek at an Editor's Day

Q: Describe your "typical" day, as best you can with the crazy pace of a publication.

A: [On] a typical day, [I read] e-mails; listen to voice mails; start editing or working on lineups for upcoming columns (I edit four health/safety columns, one of which I also write, as well as the health and safety features); have lunch, usually at my desk; read the paper; go back to editing/writing. In the midst of all this, of course, I'm fielding calls from writers and PR people, attending various staff meetings and press events, and having the occasional "desk side briefing" with PR people.

Q: What do you look for in new writers?

A: I look for recent clips from national magazines. I appreciate the writer sending along a great story idea as well, but if [he has] great clips and [is] just writing to introduce [himself], that's fine, too.

The Write Words

A **hed** is short for a headline, the title of the story, while a **dek** is short for a decked head, the brief opening or short introduction that gives the reader an idea of what the feature will cover; the decked head is usually one to two sentences.

The Write Words

Captions are explanatory copy that may identify the who, what, where, when, why, and how of a picture, but they also may tell something extra to amplify a message or illuminate a point. The caption may tell the reader what happened before or after the picture, for example. The caption strives to give the reader information about the activity in the photo that is not obvious from looking at the picture.

Dead Lines

Don't ever cold-call an editor you haven't worked with and pitch a story idea over the phone. *Child* magazine's Kara Corridan explains why she dislikes phone pitches from writers: "First, it puts me on the spot, and second, even if I love the idea, I'll still need something on paper. It's just a waste of time for everyone."

Q: The buzz about freelancing seems to be that "it's who you know." How true is this? Do you work mainly with writers you personally know?

A: No, I wouldn't really say it's who you know when it comes to getting work from an editor. Of course, it certainly helps catch my eye if a writer can mention the name of a colleague right off the bat, but it's just as nice to hear from a good writer I've never worked with or heard of.

Q: How can someone on the "outside" break into your publication?

A: Again, someone can "break in" here by sending impressive clips and possibly a fresh idea or two. It's that easy and that hard.

Q: Describe what makes a good pitch letter?

A: Any pitch that's brief, two grafs or less, includes ideas for a smart sidebar, and tells me something I didn't know is [a query] I'll want to follow up on. A writer I didn't know recently queried me with an intriguing pitch—she described a new behavioral technique I'd never heard of, gave the credentials of the person who came up with it, told why it's working in her family, and detailed a few possible sidebars. I was interested but had lots of questions. I passed it on to my articles editor and editor-in-chief. I asked the writer to flesh out the query, which she did, and it led to an assignment.

Q: What's the best thing you ever did to advance your career? What moves did you make that you think brought you to the place you are now?

A: I'd say the most helpful move in my career was starting as an editorial assistant. I learned incredible amounts about what makes a story idea work, how to write coverlines, how to write tight items, and what it takes to have a successful relationship with an editor. Another helpful job was being a freelancer because it enabled me to write about all sorts of topics—and work on a hundred things at once.

Q: What is the story of which you are most proud? Why?

A: The story I'm most proud of isn't one that appeared in *Child* or even one I edited, but one that I wrote for *Shape* (March 2000). I completed the Avon breast cancer three-day, 60-mile walk, and wrote a diary-style piece about it. My mother had breast cancer, and I trained during the whole time she was in treatment, so both the walk and the story meant a great deal to me.

Rock-a-Find-Baby

Got the goods on soundly sleeping babies or another article idea for *Child* magazine? Write impressive ideas and send outstanding clips to Kara Corridan (or the appropriate editor), *Child* Magazine, 375 Lexington Avenue, 10th Floor, New York, NY 10017.

Trade Tactics from Above: Editor-in-Chief Perry Bradley, *Business and Commercial Aviation*

Perry Bradley hangs his hat each day as editor-in-chief of *Business and Commercial Aviation,* a 40-plus-year-old trade magazine that covers operations of turbine business aircraft and regional airliners. "We're known as the leading how-to operations and management magazine in the field, and we have circulation of about 50,000," says Bradley. Bradley's career in aviation journalism took root when he found the perfect mix of his love of flying—he's piloted since the age of 15—and writing while working on an aviation newsletter. He has been with B/CA for five years now and oversees a staff of about 15, including production and administration. "We have four writers, plus me, on staff, and we use a cadre of about six freelancers with high regularity," attests the editor. Here's the advice he gives you for entering the trade writing zone.

Into the Wild, Blue Yonder

Q: What do you enjoy most about your job?

A: I like the access it affords me (and others on the staff). We regularly talk to the very top people in our industry—people with thousands of employees and billions in revenue. That's an experience I wouldn't have elsewhere. We also get to spend a lot of time with top officials in the government. For instance, one of our reporters was with the FAA administrator on a flight on New Year's Eve, which she took to demonstrate her confidence in FAA's Y2K fix. We also do a significant amount of traveling—both domestically and abroad. Finally, I love airplanes and aviation—that's what got me into this line of work, and that's what keeps me in it.

Q: What do you enjoy least?

A: Being editor carries with it an administrative burden. You have to sort out people's problems, ride them about deadlines, keep track of the corporation, monitor budgets, come up with—and implement—new business ideas (or at least the editorial component of new ventures). The administrative stuff is the least interesting part of my job. However, I also realize it has to be done—and I take the view that by doing it, I shelter the reporters and other staffers from having to worry about it. In that respect, it's somewhat rewarding.

Q: What do you look for in new writers, besides his/her ability to write?

A: Ability to write is a starting point, but even more important is subject-matter knowledge, an ability to report, knowledge of the conventions of journalism, and *enthusiasm*. You'd be amazed at the number of freelancers who don't show any enthusiasm. Writers—especially freelancers—who approach their work as if they are in a service business will put a smile on the face of many an editor. I also look for writers who do their homework and take the time to understand the audience our magazine serves and the type of stories we run.

What's That Noise?

Q: The buzz about freelancing seems to be that "it's who you know." How true is this? Do you work mainly with writers you personally know?

A: Who you know is important in trade publishing. Our industry is small, and the core writers covering it are all pretty well known to the industry and to each other. However, like all professions, we always need fresh blood. Since who you know is important, writers who want to crack in should take the time to get to know people in the business.

Q: Give your top list of things freelancers shouldn't do. What turns you off to a new writer immediately?

A: Two things: Don't look to an editor for ideas. I'm not an ATM. I need people who are interested and motivated enough to come up with proposals on their own. Secondly, don't feign knowledge or understanding. Ask questions. It's what good writers and reporters do for a living. Finally, take a minute to find out something about the magazine before approaching me. You'd be surprised at the number of shotgun approaches we get that display an obvious lack of knowledge about who we are and what we do.

Q: What's the best thing you ever did to advance your career? What moves did you make that you think brought you to the place you are now?

A: I was enthusiastic and curious, and I built relationships with people in the business. I had a simple strategy that paid off—I always sit in the front in press conferences, and I always ask at least one question. People in the industry get to know you that way—and they appreciate the interest and enthusiasm.

Q: Many freelancers I've spoken with say they "just know" when their pitch or essay submission wasn't even read, that a canned rejection was sent without even looking at the materials. How do you respond to these writers' perceptions?

A: Often they are probably right on. When I was first trying to get a job at a newspaper, a friend who was a reporter told me to be patient. Her logic was that most editors got where they are because they were good writers and reporters, not because they are great managers. Also, the volume of mail most editors receive is phenomenal. Writers who make it easy for me to say yes do well—that is, people who have done homework, have demonstrated ability, and are going to be responsive. Probably the best approach to a pitch is to find out everything you can about the magazine, come up with a couple ideas you think would work, and call the editor (or e-mail) and let him or her know you're a service-oriented writer who can help by giving great copy that will work for the magazine.

Once you hook them, provide details. And for god's sakes, pay attention to meeting deadlines.

Back to Basics—Writing!

Q: What is the story that you are most proud of? Why?

A: I did some reporting on how the government intends to use the Global Positioning System in the future to give aircraft more freedom in where they fly and a better margin of safety. I like the story because I took some very complex technical and political issues and distilled them down to a point that the reader could get through it and really understand why they should care. I also like the piece because it was one of the most thoroughly reported stories I ever wrote. In general, the ones I'm most proud of are the ones that involved the most reporting. At a trade magazine, you have to make yourself an expert in lots of areas. You know that somewhere in your audience there are readers who know a hell of a lot more about a given topic than you do. When you do so much reporting that you feel good about talking even to those folks, you've done your job well.

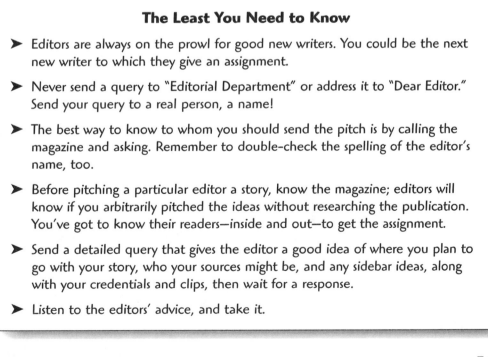

The Least You Need to Know

➤ Editors are always on the prowl for good new writers. You could be the next new writer to which they give an assignment.

➤ Never send a query to "Editorial Department" or address it to "Dear Editor." Send your query to a real person, a name!

➤ The best way to know to whom you should send the pitch is by calling the magazine and asking. Remember to double-check the spelling of the editor's name, too.

➤ Before pitching a particular editor a story, know the magazine; editors will know if you arbitrarily pitched the ideas without researching the publication. You've got to know their readers—inside and out—to get the assignment.

➤ Send a detailed query that gives the editor a good idea of where you plan to go with your story, who your sources might be, and any sidebar ideas, along with your credentials and clips, then wait for a response.

➤ Listen to the editors' advice, and take it.

Chapter 5

So, Is This *Really* for You?

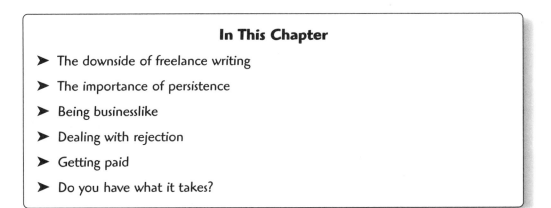

In This Chapter

➤ The downside of freelance writing

➤ The importance of persistence

➤ Being businesslike

➤ Dealing with rejection

➤ Getting paid

➤ Do you have what it takes?

Four chapters of the glory of the freelance life. So far we've pretty much given you the triumphs and none of the defeats. Hey, we're not cruel. You bought this book to learn how to sell your writing to magazines, newspapers, and Web sites. Why would we crush you in the first few pages by telling you about the slings and arrows of outrageous publishing fortune? No, we knew you'd need to get pumped up about how really great this life can be. But now it's time to lower the boom. Here's the clear-eyed chapter where we urge you to consider whether a life of rejection, disappointment, isolation, and endless waiting is for you.

If you can make it through this chapter and still want to write for pay, then you have our permission to go ahead and give this freelance life a serious shot. Don't say we didn't warn you, though ....

Enough of the Glitz and Glamour—Here's the Dirt

Your heart is pumping with the possibilities. Like Anne Basye of Chicago, you want to go out and cover a world peace conference. Like Lynne and Jennifer, you'd like to have a cool framed press pass or two hanging on the wall in a blatant attempt to impress your friends. Or, like a lot of writers, you want a life that sounds like it's straight off the About the Contributors page in *Vanity Fair*.

Would you be surprised or disappointed, though, to learn that most writers see their work more often in the *No Name News* than in the glossies? Or that the folks whose lives we portrayed so tantalizingly had to bust their behinds for *years* to get to where they are now? And would you be surprised to also learn that most writers think it's fine and dandy to see their work in the *No Name News* on a regular basis—as long as the check clears?

The Straight Scoop

"I was so thrilled when one of my corporate newsletter clients called about sending me to Europe to attend a big conference for them," business writer Anne Basye of Chicago told us. "And I was also a little ashamed. Because I had begun thinking that I really needed to raise my rates with them, that I just wasn't charging them enough. But hey, they can go on paying me a hundred bucks a month for ever if they send me to The Hague every so often!" So, do these kinds of cool things happen all the time to folks who write newsletters? Sorry, only once in a blue moon.

Help Wanted

Suppose you came across this job listing in the *Really Great Jobs Times*:

> Freelance writer—Must be able to meet short deadlines under enormous pressure, go for long periods of time without hope of a check, be pleased by the small sums of money that do show up irregularly, be regularly ignored or treated shoddily, and still smile about it. Must also be endlessly crafty and creative, never dull or repetitious, always cheerful and optimistic, and able to spend long periods of time alone in front of a damn computer.

Hey, get your resumé out now! Who do you call for this job?

Who Really Makes It as a Freelancer

Who makes it as a freelance writer? Only the very talented? Only the ones who go to the right schools? Only the ones who look good in the late morning sipping espresso in the corner of a café with a laptop on the table in front of them?

None of the above. Well, maybe *some* of the above. But here are the people who *really* make it as writers:

Persistent people make it as writers.

Are you surprised? You thought it was the espresso sippers with the laptops, right? Well, if they're persistent, chances are that the espresso sippers *will* make it. And if *you* are persistent, you will make it, too.

Why is persistence so critical? What about talent? Ideas? Skill? All those things you need, yes. But here's why persistence is so darn critical: There will be many times as a freelance writer when you:

➤ Won't have any work at all. No assignments, no green-lighted projects, no nothing. You will need to be persistent enough to keep going.

➤ Won't get your phone calls returned. The key source you need to complete your piece just won't deign to call you back, and you will need to be persistent enough to keep trying anyway.

➤ Won't have any money in the bank. And the next check won't be coming until the end of the summer. You will need to be persistent enough to survive the dry spell.

➤ Won't be sure if you have made the right decision in pursuing this as a career or hobby. And you will need to be persistent enough to keep trying until some sort of sign arrives—a good one or a bad one—and helps you make that big decision.

Will success come quickly? You need to be prepared if it doesn't. Many writers do try again and again and again before they get their first break. Once the losing streak is broken, however, the second break should come pretty quickly.

The Organization

You're persistent, are you? Persistent enough to keep reading through that last section, anyway. Is persistence the only non-talent-related trait you need? Sorry. Another critical element in making it as a freelance writer is this:

Organization

The Straight Scoop

"I don't believe that you have to go through a long period of suffering when you first de-cide to begin writing," Dena Amoruso told us. "It is possible to begin a writing career and be making a decent living in just a few months." How? "By finding a niche that needs you. I write for the home building market—newspaper columns, Q&As, builder profiles, and even some publicity material that goes out without my byline. It will take you a long time to break in if you are going after the same part of the market that everyone else is trying, but take the time to study what kind of information is needed—and then write it."

Most successful freelancers are extremely organized people. That kinda contradicts our mental image of the writer—those creative yet sloppy folks whose apartments are lit-tered ankle-deep in scraps of paper with Really Important Thoughts written on them, who are brilliant but scatterbrained, and who look good with that dainty cup of espresso in the café but are apt to walk off and leave the laptop sitting there.

Here is the real picture of how successful freelance writers run their lives. They've developed systems for keeping track of any number of things, including these:

➤ **Query letters.** How many are out, who they went to, and what they were about

➤ **Article ideas.** Files bulging with scraps of paper torn from newspapers, maga-zines, and random thoughts jotted down on napkins

➤ **Contacts.** Carefully tended Rolodexes with editors and their publications noted carefully, business cards from potential information sources, or interview possi-bilities

➤ **Deadlines.** A large erasable whiteboard filled with upcoming deadlines, or e-mail reminders

➤ **Tickle files.** Reminders to call and re-pitch editors who have asked to be re-minded about something. "Call me again in May, I might use that for a summer travel round-up …"

➤ **New outlets.** Copies of new magazines or newspapers to approach, information from media columns about who is starting what and moving where

Ya Gotta Be, Like, Businesslike, Ya Know?

So, you want to become a writer so that you can spend time on the phone schmoozing with editors about what's happening in the world. Perhaps you have visions of making witty insider comments about Jerry Seinfeld, Tom Cruise, or Will Smith, or posing your theories on how the Middle East can finally achieve lasting peace. Well, you might get the chance to do that, after you've worked with someone for a while. But editors are busy people, and what they need in their lives is a writer with a good idea who can be counted on to turn in a publishable piece in the time required. They don't need someone who wants to chat them up on the phone for hours on end with no particular purpose.

If you want to be a writer, you need to be businesslike. (Sounds so unwriterly, doesn't it? If we talented writers were businesslike, we would become something other than writers—something like bankers, or venture capitalists ....) You need to be able to place a call to an editor, get right to the point, and let that person get the heck off the phone and back to the hundred other tasks he was trying to complete this morning.

Not only will a businesslike, no-nonsense demeanor serve you well with editors, but it also will help you take a more mature approach to your career as a writer. Remember, writing is a business, and it's a critical part of the publishing business. Understand that you're setting yourself up for failure if you think for one minute that it is about *you and your talent.*

Dead Lines

Yes, deadlines are a big, big deal. You can't just call up an editor and tell her that the dog ate your disk. No matter what has happened in your life, it really doesn't matter to the editor. Her schedule is predetermined by the publication's needs, not yours. "I forgot" is not acceptable. Post your deadlines in a very visible location and *meet them.*

Biz School

In addition to having a businesslike attitude, it will also serve you well to have a businesslike understanding of the financial side of publishing. The more you understand about how it all works (big hint: it all has to do with money), the easier it will be for you to see how you can better fit in and prosper.

How do you learn more about the business of publications? Here are a couple ways to do it:

➤ *The New York Times, The Wall Street Journal,* and *The New York Observer* all devote a great many column inches to covering the media business. They frequently write about magazines and newspapers, both the businesses and the people. The tabloid *New York Post* also has a media column by Keith Kelly that has a big following among media people themselves.

➤ *Editor and Publisher* is the trade magazine for the newspaper business. The publication has a Web site at www.editorandpublisher.com.

➤ MediaWeek runs a cool Web site at www.mediaweek.com that is jammed with hot information about the business.

And when you do develop more of a relationship with an editor, ask about the business. Make sure that as your career as a freelance writer grows, you come to a point where you can read a paragraph like the following snippet from MediaWeek and understand not only what it says, but why it could be important to you:

1999 was a record-breaking year for McGraw-Hill's Business Week, which ended the year up 22.6 percent in ad pages, to 5,118.1. In terms of revenue, the title is expected to tally $442 million, a 22 percent increase over 1998, says publisher William Kupper.

The Straight Scoop

Neophyte writers won't have much luck cold-calling editors to ask them out to lunch to discuss the writer's career. Why would an editor want to spend a lunch hour helping someone who may never actually write a blessed word? All editors know about wannabes—folks who want to be writers and spend a great deal of time daydreaming and planning for a career that never really happens. That's a waste of time. But you might be able to get an editor out to a restaurant by expressing a desire to learn more about how the business of publishing works. If you direct your questions toward the business of publishing—and better yet, ask enough questions about the editor's career—by the end of the lunch, the editor may well ask you, "So, what is it that *you* write?"

Why does it matter to a writer how many ad pages were sold? That's what determines how much space is available for editorial. What's a *title?* That's industry speak for *magazine,* also sometimes referred to as a *book.* And where did the .1 come from in 5,118.1 pages? Advertising pages are divided into a variety of sizes, everything from a full page to $1/3$ to $1/8$, to the tiny little ads for restaurants and hand-knit sweaters for dogs that decorate the sides of *The New Yorker*'s back pages.

If none of this makes sense to you now, don't give up. It takes a little time to learn the jargon for any industry. Don't be afraid to ask if someone uses a term you don't know.

Growing a Thicker Skin

Hmmm … this life of a writer is growing ever less appealing, isn't it? But wait! It gets worse. One very real thing that writers must grow accustomed to is rejection.

It's like perpetually living in the seventh grade, hoping that the right guy or girl will look your way at the school dance, and then sagging with dejection when you spot him or her walking off toward the dark part of the gym with someone else.

Or, it's like working hard on a project you're certain will please your boss, turning the report in so proudly—knowing that your career is about to jet toward the stratosphere once she reads it and recognizes your brilliance—only to see it sit day after day unread in her in-box.

Are you crying yet? Sure, we're making up silly scenarios here, but the crushed emotions behind them are all too real. There will be many, many times in your life as a freelance writer when your feelings will be hurt. Not only will your work be rejected, but there also will be many times when you are flat-out ignored or forgotten.

Do writers send out query letters that are never acknowledged? You bet. As the author of 20 books and countless articles, Jennifer sometimes found her letters ignored. "It is kind of a weird feeling, to have worked so hard on what you thought was the perfect query letter, enclosed the perfect clips, and even a SASE," she says. "You drop it into the mail with such great hope and expectations, and then … nothing. It's kind of creepy, like it didn't really happen at all."

Lynne has certainly had the same experience, as has Sheree, and all of our friends who are writers. And, we are sorry to say, it will happen to you.

"I Can't Go On This Way!"

How can writers possibly suffer all that rejection and still go on? And not just go on writing, but continually endure such treatment day in and day out? Some writers keep plugging away because rejection just doesn't bother them. Some writers keep plugging away because they are determined to make it. And some writers keep plugging away because, when you finally do sell something, the money ain't too bad.

Hello, Is Anyone Out There?

Ready to hear even more bad news about the real life of a writer? It's pretty lonely sometimes. There's no collegial crowd of coworkers clustered around the coffee pot. There's no one to swap weekend warrior stories with. There's no one but you, your computer, your phone, and maybe a cat or dog to keep you company.

It can be quiet, awfully quiet—just the sound of your own fingers clacking away on a keyboard and not many ringing phones. And depending on your workload, maybe the phone won't ring for days on end … except for those pesky telemarketers, of course. The UPS driver might stop by. The meter reader comes around once a month. But other than that, you're on your own, pal.

The Straight Scoop

How fast will you be rejected? In this day of high technology and fast freight, it can happen pretty darn quickly. Jennifer's fastest-ever rejection came from the op-ed page at *The Wall Street Journal:* "I wrote what I thought was an extremely witty and insightful personal essay during the beginning of the turmoil in Indonesia a few years ago. Addressing it with great confidence, I overnighted it to Max Boot, the editor of that page. Early the next morning, my fax machine rang. Who could be faxing me that early? It was *The Wall Street Journal* passing on my piece. From the time I dropped it in the FedEx box to the time the paper spat out of my fax machine was maybe 16 hours." Oooo, that one stung. And with so much being done with e-mail nowadays, rejection could actually happen in seconds.

Dead Lines

Many a time writers have been portrayed as drunkards. Alcohol, according to the stereotype, was a necessary part of the creative process. That's not true, of course. Be wary of gravitating toward the liquor cabinet in your times of loneliness or rejection. There are far too many examples of writers whose talents and lives have been destroyed by alcohol abuse.

Lonely writers sometimes get together with other lonely writers. (Most communities have writers groups—ask at your bookstore, check with the library, and keep an eye on the events calendar in your newspaper.) But however you deal with it, loneliness is the freelance writer's one faithful companion.

Who Pays What (and When)

Enough of this other stuff, let's talk about something really important: money. Can you really make any money as a freelance writer? More important, can you make *serious* money as a freelance writer? We have two answers—yes and yes. Okay, so it pales in comparison to the kind of dough that e-commerce IPO guys are making. It's still big money, though, and (as you'll discover in the section on writing for the Web) it can even include stock options!

A dollar a word is the basic formula that most large publications follow for the articles they choose. That doesn't sound too bad now, does it?

Alas, some pay less than a buck a word, and some don't pay at all. Some pay on acceptance; some *pay on pub*; some pay *in copies*. Here's a sampling from the writer's guidelines of a few different kinds of publications:

➤ *New Mexico Business Journal.* "Payment, as you might suspect, depends on the nature and length of the article. Generally, writers of 'major' pieces can expect to receive between $200 and $400, more on rare occasions (hey, we're a small company trying hard). That top end describes the scale: other pieces might fetch $50 to $200, depending."

➤ *Hemispheres.* "Payment for articles is upon acceptance and the return of your signed contract. Amount varies by length, location in the magazine, and other factors and is negotiated with the writer."

➤ *Cosmopolitan.* "Payment is commensurate with quality of work."

➤ *American Baby.* "Between $800 and $1,000 for feature articles, depending on article length and whether the author has written for *American Baby* before, is paid upon acceptance. First-person experiences pay $500 upon acceptance. Crib Notes pay $100 upon acceptance."

So, not everyone—particularly the bigger players on this list, such as *Cosmo* or United Airline's in-flight magazine *Hemispheres*—is willing to say how much they pay to writers.

Check out the valuable information at the *Writer's Digest* Web site. You can access the writer's guidelines for a vast quantity of different types of publications and save yourself many a phone call and SASE. Point your mouse to www.writersdigest.com and click on Writer's Guidelines.

Dead Lines

Don't overlook the amount of time that you put in *before* you begin writing a piece, or the time you'll put in *after* you've written it. Fact-checking, rewriting, hashing things out with the editor—it all adds up. So while the idea of a dollar a word might dazzle you now, it might not look like such a terrific payoff by the time the check actually arrives.

The Write Words

Publications that "**pay on pub**" send payment for an article when the magazine in which it appears has been published. If you turn in a story in June that is scheduled for the September issue, don't check your mailbox anytime soon.

The Write Words

Some smaller literary magazines don't pay money but pay **in copies.** They send their contributors copies of the magazine as a payment of sorts.

Is the Check in the Mail?

The writer's guidelines for *The New Mexico Business Journal* note that the journal pays "on the 15th of the month of publication." Some other publications pay on acceptance. Alas, no one sits down and writes you a check the minute you're finished working. More often, it will be many months between the time you write the piece and the time you endorse the check. In the final chapters of this book, we devote some time to the business of freelancing. You'll learn more practical advice on how writers manage to live with this kind of spotty cash flow.

Deciding Whether This Is the Life for You

Well, what do you think about becoming a writer now? Have we frightened you into putting this book back on the shelf? We hope not. But it wouldn't be fair to paint only a rosy picture of what the freelance life is like.

When you establish yourself as a writer, all this bad stuff is pretty much behind you, right? Nope. Even writers who have been supporting themselves handsomely for years with the money they earn from their words sometimes send out unanswered queries, get the brush-off from an editor on the phone, or peer anxiously out the window for the mail carrier, hoping like heck there's a check in the bag.

Still with us? Good! Now that we've got all the gloom and doom behind us, let's move on and learn more about how to write articles that sell!

The Least You Need to Know

➤ The freelance life can be one of rejection, disappointment, isolation, and endless waiting.

➤ It might take months or even years of trying before you make your first money as a writer.

➤ Although a talent for writing is critical, so too is persistence, organizational skills, and a businesslike attitude.

➤ Successful writers develop a thorough understanding of the business and money side of publishing.

➤ Payment varies, depending on the size of the publication. Time of payment varies as well.

Part 2

Learning the Basics

Now that you know what freelance writers do, how do you learn how to do it your-self? Right here, right now! Here is a basic course in writing the all-important query letter, structuring articles, researching, and conducting interviews. From your first as-signment to your first fact-checking request, here is everything you need to know in order to operate as a professional in the publications world.

Chapter 6

Studying the Market

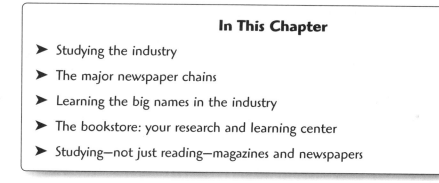

In This Chapter

➤ Studying the industry

➤ The major newspaper chains

➤ Learning the big names in the industry

➤ The bookstore: your research and learning center

➤ Studying—not just reading—magazines and newspapers

"How to succeed in business without really trying"—great name for a musical, lousy idea for a career plan. Writers hoping to build a successful career in freelancing will need to try and try and try and try yet again. Other than working on your writing and querying skills, how else can you consciously try to improve your chances of success?

The best way to succeed in any business is to *study the business*. Make no mistake—magazine and newspaper publishing is big, big business; online publications are also moving into the big money realm. We touched on this topic in Chapter 5, "So, Is This *Really* for You?" but let's delve into it a bit more here.

Becoming a Student of Print

Writers often think there's something not quite right about knowing the business side of publishing, that it might somehow taint their talent, or that writers ought not to have to clutter their minds with the dirty side of the business where the money is made.

Sorry, but the fact is that you *do* need to know this stuff. Would you open a shoe shop without first learning about the shoe business? Or start a café without first learning who your suppliers might be? If you're going to be in this business, you need to *be* in this business.

Reading Is Fundamental

As a freelance writer, it behooves you to present yourself as a knowledgeable insider. The more you can think, talk, and act like other successful freelance writers, the savvier that editors assume you are and the easier your chosen path will become. But unless you actually live in New York City or some other publishing capitol, and unless you really do work in the newspaper business or magazine business, how are you ever going to achieve that knowledgeable air? The same way you learn anything else in life: read.

Dead Lines

You'll hear this advice over and over again—do not query a magazine unless you have read several copies to get a feel for what it is all about. Querying blindly means certain rejection.

You've already learned about some of the online sites for the media business, places such as MediaWeek (www.mediaweek.com). Try to spend more time cruising online through the major newspaper and magazine sites. And for those of you who still like to curl up in bed with a good book, we'll give you a few to start with.

In Cold Type

Want to know more about the history of the newspaper business in the United States? There are many dry histories about the press on the library shelves, so why not read about the more colorful *people* behind the press? You can get a fascinating behind-the-scenes glimpse at *The New York Times* by reading these books:

➤ *The Times of My Life: And My Life with the Times,* by Max Frankel (Random House). In this memoir, Max Frankel, the now-retired executive editor of the *New York Times*, recounts his 45 years with that paper.

➤ *The Trust: The Private and Powerful Family Behind* The New York Times, by Susan E. Tifft and Alex S. Jones (Little Brown & Company). This book follows four generations of the Ochs and Sulzberger families as they build the NYT into a powerful and influential voice.

Tired of the *Times*? Then read about the *Post* instead—the *Washington Post*, that is. Here are two books that will lift the curtain in the Capitol:

➤ *Personal History*, **by Katharine Graham (Vintage Books).** This Pulitzer Prize–winning book is the memoir of the most powerful woman in the newspaper business.

➤ *A Good Life: Newspapers and Other Adventures*, **by Ben Bradlee (Touchstone Books).** This book gives a lively account of the business by the longtime editor of the *Post*.

Chains of Gold

Another important piece of the puzzle for freelance writers is to familiarize themselves with the major newspaper chains. Decades ago, there were strong independent newspapers in towns across the country, but as in other industries, newspaper ownership now rests in the hands of increasingly fewer companies that own increasingly more newspapers. Here are the big players:

➤ **Gannett.** In addition to owning *USA Today,* Gannett owns more than 75 regional papers, ranging from big-city papers such as the *Detroit News & Free Press* to small-town organs such as the *Visalia Times-Delta*.

➤ **The E.W. Scripps Company.** This company owns 30 papers, including the *Cincinnati Post*, the *Knoxville News-Sentinel*, and the *Denver Rocky Mountain News*.

➤ **McClatchy News.** Based in California's state capital of Sacramento, the publisher of *The Sacramento Bee* also owns 22 other papers.

➤ **Knight-Ridder.** The second largest newspaper group in terms of circulation, Knight-Ridder owns 53 daily and suburban papers.

➤ **The Hearst Corporation.** This company owns and operates 20 papers around the country. See the following sections for more information about the Hearst media empire.

This is only the tip of the newspaper-chain iceberg. Take a close look to see who owns what in your area. And be warned—newspapers are bought and sold every day.

Dead Lines

Try to read and learn as much about the business as possible, but don't try to fake your end of a conversation with an old newspaper hand. If an editor drops a name you don't recognize, go ahead and say, "Who?" rather than pretend that you know.

The Straight Scoop

The *Columbia Journalism Review* has long been hailed as the arbiter of good writing and professional reporting—not to mention some inside scoop about the newspaper business. Now you can get it all online by checking out the publication's Web site, at www.crj.org. The site also has a great "who owns what" section so that you can check to see who owns the paper you're querying.

Magazine History

The life of a newspaper is a colorful one ("Stop the presses!"), but magazines are equally intriguing. Not many magazine *writers* have been compelled to write about their experiences (with the notable exception of folks who worked at *The New Yorker*—they've *all* written books). Magazine *editors*, on the other hand, have written some good behind-the-scenes books.

Probably the best of the lot is *In and Out of Vogue* by Grace Mirabella. No longer available from the publisher, this book is worth searching for. Try one of the online booksellers that offers an out-of-print service. Grace Mirabella gives good dish about the world of fashion publications. She was the editor at *Vogue,* until she found out one day (in the midst of a massage) that she'd been fired. Not one to slink off in defeat, she instead founded *Mirabella* magazine. Good woman, good book.

The Straight Scoop

So you'd like to read a book about *The New Yorker* magazine, but the selection makes your head swim. How is it that one magazine has inspired so many books? The latest entry is *Gone: The Last Days of* The New Yorker, by Renata Adler. Here is her explanation of why she joined the staff at the magazine: "I started writing so I would have something to say when people at parties asked me what I did."

Fashion magazine folks seem to write more often than news magazine folks. Diana Vreeland wrote *DV,* and John Fairchild of *Women's Wear Daily* and Fairchild Publications wrote *Savage Chic.* Both would be of interest to freelancers who plan to write for women's magazines. If your dream is to see your work featured in *Travel & Leisure,* go ahead and skip 'em.

The Godfathers

Think you know a fair amount about the American media? Good for you. But for those of you who are just dipping your toes into the publications world, here are two names you should know. Chances are that you'll never meet either one of them, but what they own and what they do will affect you as a freelance writer:

➤ **Rupert Murdoch.** The Australian-born owner of News Corp. A big player in television (Fox) and book publishing (HarperCollins, William Morrow, and Zondervan), Murdoch owns the *New York Post* and the magazine *The Weekly Standard.* The list of overseas papers he controls is quite extensive.

➤ **Si Newhouse.** The owner of the privately held media giant Advance Publications/ Condé Nast. Among the magazines owned by Si Newhouse are ...

Vanity Fair	*Details*
The New Yorker	*Wired*
Glamour	*Jane*
Architectural Digest	*GQ*
Bride's	*House & Garden*
W	*Gourmet*

In addition to these magazines, Newhouse owns 24 local newspapers and the Sunday magazine supplement *Parade.* At one time he also owned the book publisher Random House, but he has since sold it to Bertelsmann, a German publishing conglomerate.

Dead Lines

Be careful whom you complain about or make fun of. In conversation with an editor (or worse yet, in a letter or e-mail), be very careful not to malign other magazines that might be in the family fold. "Those jerks over at *House & Garden* have owed me for a story for six months," you might say to the editor of *Bride's* magazine—which is owned by the same parent company. And, hey, how were you to know that *The New York Times* owns the *Boston Globe?* The best approach, of course, is never to badmouth anybody.

Here's another name you should know: William Randolph Hearst. He was a very interesting guy, the one who built Hearst Castle, and the one who inspired the movie *Citizen Cane*. He's dead, of course, but the media company that bears his name owns some 20-odd newspapers and the following magazines:

Cosmopolitan	*Good Housekeeping*
Esquire	*Floor Covering Weekly*
Harper's Bazaar	*House Beautiful*
Colonial Homes	*Popular Mechanics*

As far as media companies go, a few you'll want to know about are Meredith, which owns the *Better Homes and Gardens* franchise of books and magazines; the Washington Post Company, which owns *Newsweek* and more than three dozen local newspapers; and Primedia, which owns *New York, Seventeen,* and *Modern Bride* magazines. How do you find out who owns a magazine? Open it up and look at the bottom of the masthead page.

We could write an entire book about who owns what, only to find that—because of takeovers and acquisitions—it would be outdated the minute it was published!

Synergy

So what's up with all these companies? Don't magazine publishers publish magazines and newspaper publishers publish newspapers? That certainly was the tradition, and they are two distinctly different types of businesses with different types of problems. But nowadays, the big buzzword is *synergy,* and traditional companies are morphing into "media companies" that own all manner of media.

How does this work? If a media company owns both a magazine and a newspaper, the newspaper could build interest in forthcoming issues of the magazine. For example, you might see "This month's *Vanity Fair* reports …" in a newspaper article. That works even better when the same company owns a book publisher and a movie company, too.

How You Fit In

Rather than obsessing about who owns what, is there a way to keep up with what's going on in the media? Jennifer keeps track by subscribing to *Brill's Content*. Now in its second year, *Brill's Content* bills itself as "The Independent Voice of the Information Age" and focuses the harsh light of scrutiny on members of all facets of the media, from newspapers and magazines to television and film. Of course, it's also a fun read. You'll learn a great deal about the publishing business from this magazine.

Now that you have a handle on what's happening in the media world, is there a way to make sense of how you as a freelancer fit into it? You do fit in, perhaps more now than ever before. A very real byproduct of all this conglomeratization is a concern over the role of the press. Can reporters and staff writers really speak freely and report accurately if they're worried about stepping on the toes of someone else in their media family?

On the other hand, freelancers can say whatever they darn well please. It might not actually get printed, but they can say it. Of course, using freelancers also helps large conglomerates keep their overhead down, thereby keeping their board of directors and their shareholders happy.

Hanging Out for Fun and Profit

Are your eyes glazed over yet from the tangled web of who owns what and why? Other than trying to memorize the corporate family trees on the off chance that someone quizzes you someday, is there some other way you could be spending your research time? Yep. You can sit down with a cup of coffee in a quiet corner and actually read a magazine.

No doubt there are quiet corners in your house, the coffee is free, and you have a few magazines lying around. But we prefer to go where the action is. Surround yourself with rack after rack of shiny new magazines and carefully folded newspapers from around the country, each one filled with the promise of hope for your fledgling career. Sit with an overpriced espresso in hand. Hang out in a bookstore hour after hour, and know that the time you are spending is *important*.

Learn to Read a Magazine

Oh, come *on!* Learn to read a magazine? *The Complete Idiot's Guide* series is geared for beginners, yes, but surely this is stooping to a new low!

You know how to read a magazine—of course you do. But we want you to be able to *read* a magazine. Read it like a map that will lead you to your goal of seeing your own work appear on the same pages as established writers. Here are a few things we want you to pay close attention to in your reading: the Letter from the Editor and the About the Contributors pages.

The Letter from the Editor

You can learn a lot from an editor's letter. For one thing, you'll learn a bit about the editor's personality, and sometimes you'll find out quite a bit more about his or her personal life. Does the editor have children? Is he married? Does he live in the country? Editors breezily reveal all kinds of personal stuff that might help you zero in on the perfect article idea for the magazine.

Here's a snippet from what Bernadette Grey, editor-in-chief of *Working Woman,* had to say in her letter in the front of the January 2000 issue: "Just a few years back—when both of my children were still in diapers ...." She then describes how she took up running early in the morning as a way to both exercise and unwind. That's good information to know about an editor—that she's a committed runner and that her children are no longer tiny babies. File this away in your memory bank. Who knows when it will come in handy?

Can you always assume that the editor is the perfect example of the magazine's ideal reader? Heavens, no! Don't forget that Helen Gurley Brown edited the youth-oriented *Cosmopolitan* until she was in her 70s, long past when she had to worry about "How to Tell If He Really Likes You."

The Straight Scoop

Careful readers of the January 2000 issue of *Success* magazine might have noticed something odd about it—and it might have saved them the trouble of querying the magazine with article ideas. The articles had a certain staleness about them, an odd way of referring to things that would take place in the fall and winter of 1999 in the future tense. What happened? The magazine ran out of money before the fall and winter issues were ready to go to the printer. When an investor finally appeared, the *Success* staff picked up right where they had left off by printing the issue that was ready to go to the printers, even though it was material that had been written many months before. Is *Success* out of the woods yet? Be sure to call before querying—it's a good magazine, and we wish them well.

What else can you learn by reading the editor's letter? You'll learn whether the magazine has recently changed focus, whether it just launched a Web site, and whether it just won a major industry award. That's all stuff you should pay attention to if this is a magazine you hope to write for someday.

About the Contributors

In Chapter 2, "The Modern World of the Freelance Writer," we dazzled you with the descriptions of contributors to a recent issue of *Working Woman* (the freelancers that Bernadette Grey hires). Do we want you to read this section of a magazine just so you'll burn with envy for their glamorous lives? Not really. We want you to remember that it really is possible to write for magazines, that all kinds of people are freelancers, and that someday your name might well show up there, too.

Other Things to Look For

Here are some important questions to ask and answer as you read a magazine:

➤ What are the major sections of the magazine? You want to sound knowledge-able in your pitch letter to the editor, so look carefully to see what they call their front-of-the-book sections. *The New Yorker* calls theirs "Talk of the Town."

➤ Is this a brand new magazine? Check the volume number to learn how many years it has been in existence. Volume 3, number 1 means that this is the first issue in the third year. Newer publications might have a greater need for new freelancers.

➤ What is the magazine's tone and style? Hip and irreverent? Ponderous and scholarly? What kind of approach will you need to make?

➤ Who is the audience? Is the tone geared toward teenage girls, middle-aged women, or private pilots? Make sure that you have a thorough understanding of the magazine's audience.

Does this seem like a colossal waste of time? Some freelancers do consider the time that they spend researching the market a financial drain. No one is paying them to do it, so why should they bother at all? Better to spend the time in front of the keyboard, right? We disagree.

The Straight Scoop

Build a network of other freelancers with whom you can swap current information by joining your local writers' group. By joining a writers' group, you not only can enjoy the company of other writers, but you also can benefit from what they know, such as which magazines pay the most and which ones don't pay at all.

The more time you spend reading magazines, particularly the very magazines in which you hope to see your work featured, the greater your feel for what kinds of articles have the best chance of getting the green light. Editors repeatedly say that the single greatest mistake freelancers make is pitching a story that's inappropriate for the maga-zine. "It's clear from the first line that they've never even bothered to pick up one issue," is the refrain. Make sure that you are never guilty of this sin.

Reading the Papers, Too

Can you scrutinize newspapers for information, too? Sure you can. Familiarize yourself with the op-ed pages and who the editor of that section is (it should be listed near the top of the page). Study the sections that might carry freelance work, including the food section, the travel section, and the business section. Study the bylines to see if most of what the newspaper carries seems to be written by staff members or freelancers. Make sure that the idea you have for a terrific article wasn't just covered in a recent issue.

Get the Kit

Lynne likes to take her research one step further than just reading the magazine. She likes to study the *media kit*. A media kit is the packet of information that the magazine sends out to prospective advertisers. You'll find all manner of information about the magazine's circulation and, more important, its readership. Average age, income, interests, and other helpful demographic information about the magazine's readers are prime pieces of information contained in a media kit. You also might be able to get another critical piece of information—the editorial calendar.

The Write Words

A **media kit** is the packet of information that the magazine sends out to prospective advertisers. How do you get the media kit? You have to call the advertising department. If they ask, be honest and say you're a writer. Don't pretend to be a prospective advertiser.

An editorial calendar is the internal document in which the editors lay out their ideas for the focus of the coming year's issues. For example, the January issue might focus on health, diet, and careers to take advantage of the heightened interest in self-improvement at that time of year. March might center on travel, and perhaps the June issue will be the weddings issue. If you have this information in advance, you can pitch article ideas directly to the editor based on what you know the magazine is looking for. (You'll want to pitch them well in advance, of course, say three or four months. In January, most magazines are thinking about spring fashion. In September they're looking at Christmas.)

Here's a snippet from the editorial calendar of a major women's magazine (naturally, we can't tell you which one):

March: Hollywood fashion

April: The dotcom issue

June: The American family

July: Preview of fall runway news

If you had this information in hand right now, you could start pitching the editor a story about planning a large-scale family reunion for its June issue, or an interesting piece about a wacky e-commerce company for the April issue.

Sometimes it seems that all the magazines are covering the same few topics. The food magazines are all writing about truffles. The *shelter magazines* are all writing about chintz. The fashion magazines are all writing about pashmina. What's a writer to do? In the next chapter, you'll learn how to put all your hours of publication study to work in generating new and interesting ideas.

The Write Words

Shelter magazines are decorating and interior design publications such as *House & Garden*, *Architectural Digest*, and *Elle Design*.

The Least You Need to Know

➤ Become a knowledgeable insider by studying the publications you'd like to write for.

➤ Try to acquire a working knowledge of who owns what in the media world.

➤ Read newspapers and magazines with an eye toward learning what kind of material they might be interested in buying from you.

➤ A publication's media kit can be an invaluable source of information about a publication's audience and about its upcoming editorial plans.

➤ Spending time learning about the market will pay off in your ability to target the right editors.

Hmmm...

Hmmm...

Chapter 7

Generating Ideas for Articles

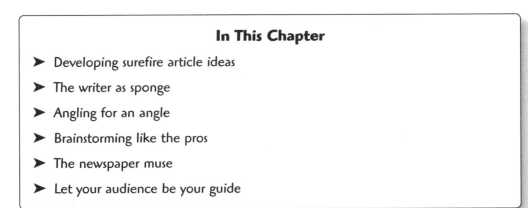

In This Chapter

➤ Developing surefire article ideas

➤ The writer as sponge

➤ Angling for an angle

➤ Brainstorming like the pros

➤ The newspaper muse

➤ Let your audience be your guide

So now that you've spent hours sipping coffee and reading magazines and newspapers, you're raring to generate some article ideas. If the real estate mantra is "Location, location, location," the article-writing mantra is "Ideas, ideas, ideas."

What separates a successful freelance writer from a writer who struggles endlessly to get even one piece accepted is quite simple: the quality of their ideas. Writers with great ideas for articles get work. Coming up with ideas is not that difficult. Coming up with *great* ideas takes a bit more effort. Let's learn how to do it.

What *Do* People Want to Know?

The most successful magazine and newspaper articles are readable, informative, and thought-provoking, and they introduce the reader to something or someone new. You're confident that you can produce a written piece that is readable. You believe in your ability to transmit information. You can take a stand, if necessary. But new? With so many words flowing unceasingly from so many writers, what the heck can you find to write about that hasn't already been covered a thousand times? Seems impossible, doesn't it?

Well, it's not. Coming up with a great idea for an article is what is going to get you work. Coming up with great ideas all the time is what is going to get you *consistent* work. Coming up with great ideas is simply a matter of tapping into what it is that people want to know.

So what is it that people want to know? Here are a few basic things that *everybody* wants to know:

➤ How to save time

➤ How to save money

➤ How to be loved

➤ How to make money

These four basic *angles* are the basis of many a successful article. Don't believe us? Let's analyze a few from some current publications:

➤ **"Debt-Defying Acts," by Patricia Kitchen, *Working Woman*, January 2000.** This article gives details the author's struggles with paying her bills on time. It's a combo of the save time/save money/make money ideas.

➤ **"Let's Get Ready to Rummage!" by Brett Martin, *Joe*, Fall 1999.** This article in coffee powerhouse Starbucks's new magazine looks behind the scenes at the popular PBS show *Antiques Roadshow*. Why is everyone so curious about how much their Uncle Sam's old uniform is worth? They want to make money. That is the basic desire behind the popularity of the show, hence this article.

➤ **"Off-Season Caribbean," by Laura Landro, *The Wall Street Journal*, Weekend Journal section, March 17, 2000.** This is a high-end twist on the save money theme. Instead of paying thousands of dollars a night for a swank hotel room on hip St. Barth's, this article helps readers spend only $710 for a night at the Hotel Carl Gustaf by traveling to the island after Easter.

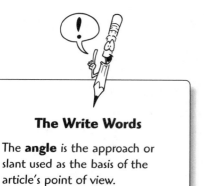

The Write Words

The **angle** is the approach or slant used as the basis of the article's point of view.

Use these four basic themes in combination with just about anything, and you can come up with a great article idea. Watch this:

Topic	Angle
Investing	Save time/save money/make money
Food	Save time/save money/be loved
Travel	Save time/save money
Children	Save money/save time
Pets	Be loved/make money
Houses	Save money/make money
Furniture	Save money/make money
Gardening	Save money/save time/make money

Take gardening, for example, a hobby that interests vast numbers of people across the country. Much has been written on the topic already, but if you apply these different angles, you can come up with article ideas such as this one:

"Lawn Care in Half the Time"

"Twenty Plants for Under Twenty Dollars"

"Grow Money in Your Garden by Raising and Selling Scented Geraniums"

Try it with the topic of children, and you could get these:

"Bargain Theme Parks: Four with Free Admission"

"Bargains Online: How to Buy Used Children's Clothing Online"

"Streamline Your Mornings with These Make-Ahead Sack Lunches"

We could go on, but you get the idea. Whenever you stumble across an interesting topic, apply one of these angles to see if you can't come up with a saleable idea.

Five Hot Markets!

A recent *Writer's Digest* article titled "5 Hot Markets for the 21st Century" claimed that freelance writers could pretty much keep themselves in assignments by writing variations on the themes that most interest the millions of aging baby boomers: health, money and retirement advice, entertainment and travel, family matters, and essays and humor.

The Write Words

The **target audience** is the group of people (the larger the better) that will be interested in reading about the subject of your article. Always match your target audience to the publication.

Remember, what interests you probably interests other people as well. Sit down and start a list of the things that *you* most want to know about. Chances are good that there's a good magazine article topic somewhere on the list and a *target audience* to write it for.

Play the Percentages

Writer's Digest cited scads of statistics about Boomers in their article on the five hot topics. As a freelance writer on the lookout for article ideas, you need to start paying attention to statistics, too.

American Demographics magazine (and Web site at www.americandemographics.com) is filled with fascinating articles and sidebars about unusual demographic trends. You might come up with an article about the travails of left-handed life after reading about how many Americans are left-handed. Or, perhaps you're inspired to write an article about city folk adjusting to life in the country after reading about how prevalent this movement is. Start to keep an ideas file in which you can toss clippings with odd facts or statistics. Who knows when they might come in handy?

The Straight Scoop

"This generation is in no rush to trade the Rolling Stones for kidney stones," says the editor of *New Choices,* a magazine targeted to the over-50 set. Baby boomers are indeed a huge potential reading audience for any publication, and many magazines are targeting them directly. So get started now to build a freelance career writing articles of interest to this influential crowd.

Keeping Your Eyes and Ears Open

As a writer on the lookout for inspiration, you must become a sponge of sorts, continually absorbing fresh ideas, fresh information, and unusual facts or tidbits. If you have a tendency to stay home all day long with the shades drawn and the television and radio turned off, you might have chosen the wrong profession.

Writers need to absorb the world around them, to continually talk to new and interesting people, and to read newspapers, magazines, Web sites, even billboards. And they always need to always ask, "Is there more to be said about this? Is there a different way of looking at this problem? Are other people interested in this topic, too?" Leave your writing and researching antennae up all the time.

Dena Amoruso writes for the New Home News section of realtytimes.com and for newspapers on purchasing and owning new homes. Every week she comes up with not one, but two ideas for articles. How? "I write on the same topic all the time—real estate for consumers," she says. "In order to keep inspired and abreast of everything going on in the industry, I subscribe to all the trade journals and spend a lot of time cruising the industry Web sites."

One of Jennifer's favorite methods for coming up with new ideas for books and articles is kind of a sneaky one—she eavesdrops. "I just want to know what people are thinking about, talking about, wondering about," she admits. "I try not to be too obvious about it, of course, and I don't think I've ever been caught. And it has helped me tap into new areas of interest to write about."

The Straight Scoop

Say you read an article in your hometown paper that has given you an idea. But if you write something similar, aren't you stealing the idea? No, not if you take the article as inspiration and develop it into something else. "I read a newspaper account in the *Sacramento Bee* about how popular four-car garages have become in this area," says writer Dena Amoruso. "And then I wrote a column about how four-car garages are ruining the suburban streetscape."

What to Avoid Like the Plague

It's hard enough to sell an article when you're first starting out. Why make it even tougher on yourself by trying to sell an article on a topic that has been done to death? Here are three overpublished areas that you would be well-advised to avoid:

Travel with children to Disney World

Trouble with air travel (luggage, lines, and so forth)

Trendy exercise methods such as Tae-Bo, Pilates, and yoga

Surefire Brainstorming Techniques

Some days you will stare out the window, unable to come up with even one more word, let alone an actual usable (and saleable!) idea for an article or essay.

Are there secrets the pros use to keep their synapses firing even when fatigue has set in? Uh-huh. We've asked a few successful freelancers about their creative methods and how you can use their techniques to craft your own success.

Judy Zimmerman, a successful travel writer who sees her pieces published in newspapers around the country, is a big believer in forecasting. Any time there's an article or a round-up issue of a magazine that includes a forecasting piece about what might happen in the future, Judy studies it for clues. "I sold a piece on space travel [for ordinary people] simply because it was a new thing and hadn't been covered much before," she explains. "Those year 2000 magazines, the ones that had predictions and lists of what will be happening in the future, are great idea generators!"

Health writer Jim Brown has this to say: "I've been writing about the health industry in California for many, many years, now, first as a staff writer, then an in-house editor, and now a freelancer. Although you'd think the ideas for fresh angles and articles would dry up after a while, they never do. As a matter of fact, they just keep growing." By specializing in one area, Jim has established himself as a true expert in the field and at the same time has built up an impressive body of contacts. "The more I know, the more I can think of to write about," He says Not only does he know the people in the field, but he also knows the editors at the publications who buy stores on this ever-changing topic.

Dead Lines

Never send a query to a magazine without first researching some of its more recent issues. The worst thing you can do is send off a query for an article to an editor who has run something on the same topic—it makes you look foolish and unprofessional.

In addition to subscribing to trade industry journals and cruising Web sites to spark ideas for articles on the home-building industry, Dena Amoruso sometimes falls back on another technique: "There are many days when I am two hours from my deadline and the screen on my computer is absolutely blank. At times like this, I just close my eyes and say a prayer." And sometimes, she tells us, it works!

You've already heard about her eavesdropping method, but Jennifer also generates idea after idea not only for articles, but also for nonfiction books by using a fairly simple method—she reads the newspaper. Okay, so she reads *many* newspapers, sometimes three or more a day—primarily *The New York Times, The Wall Street Journal,* and *USA Today.* Read on to learn her method.

News Clips

What's in the paper today? News stories are often a good jumping-off point for a magazine article. The article could expand on the idea or look at it from a different angle or in the context of a different community.

Here are some headlines from today's *New York Times* that hold potential for magazine articles:

➤ **"Trouble for Women in the Mess Hall."** This short article in the science section reports a much higher percentage of eating disorders among women in the military than in the general population. It speculates that it has to do with military weight requirements and the pressure of being a woman in a man's world.

This would be great as a lengthy magazine article that focuses on two or three real women in the military and how they handle their body image from day to day.

➤ **"Schmoozing with Dolls in Chicago."** This feature story discusses the extraordinary success of American Girl Place, a retail store opened by the manufacturers of the American Girl dolls. The store has a restaurant, a theater, and a "dress-like-your-doll" clothing division. In its first year of business, the store has produced $25 million in revenue and attracted customers from all over the country.

This could be the basis for a wonderful first-person account of taking a young girl to this doll Mecca, possibly a travel piece.

➤ **"Handing Out Modern Art by the Bushel."** Private collectors Peter and Eileen Norton have just donated 1,000 works of modern art to 29 different museums.

The collectors themselves and the artwork could be the focus of an interesting personal profile.

See how it works? You can do this very same thing every morning as a creative exercise. Just sit down with the newspaper and a sharp pencil, and start circling headlines that intrigue you. Brainstorm articles that could grow from what you have found. Much of what you think up will be useless, but if you do this often enough, you'll begin to consistently develop strong ideas for articles. Give it a try.

Dead Lines

Does the word plagiarism mean anything to you? It should. We've been encouraging you to read the papers looking for ideas. However, we do not suggest that you plagiarize articles someone else has written. Always do your own work, re-reporting a story and digging up fresh new information. Always fact-check names and numbers as well. Make a story your own before trying to sell it.

The Straight Scoop

So *The New York Times* has already written about American Girl Place. Doesn't that pretty much wreck your chances of writing about it, too? No. Why not pitch an idea about the store to a doll magazine? There are plenty of smaller publications and smaller markets to whom you can sell a story like this.

Custom-Fitting Your Ideas to Your Audience

Once you have an idea for an article, how to you know which way to focus it? What kind of an angle should you take? You decide in advance who you want your audience to be.

Let's take the example we used earlier about *The New York Times* article on military women and eating disorders. If you were going to write a major article on it, how might you shift the focus to reflect your reading audience?

➤ For a magazine with a young readership, such as *Cosmopolitan* or *Jane,* you could focus on young women just entering the military.

➤ For a health magazine, you could focus on the military's fitness and weight standards for women and contrast them to the population in general.

There you go—one idea, two angles for two different audiences.

Let's try it again with an article that Jennifer is working on now, the idea about acquiring an old-money look online. Here's how she is focusing it for two different magazines:

➤ For a money and investment magazine, she's focusing on the amusing idea that you can use your newly made Internet riches to acquire an old-money look.

➤ For a women's magazine, she's gearing the piece more toward her reactions to what she actually bought—how wonderful it all seemed to be until the box with someone's used ball gown actually arrived ....

Some writers can consistently create new ideas for articles and just as consistently think of new ways to angle the same articles to sell and re-sell them to different types of magazines.

The Straight Scoop

Jennifer made a fast buck not long ago: She picked up her local paper, read a story, and sold a story to a Web site 20 minutes later. How? She had read a long article about a local business in which a young boy gave his mother business advice that paid off in lucrative contracts. "Pokémon, Mom," the boy said, urging his mother's translation service company to seek out Pokemon work. Sensing a hot story, Jennifer called her editor at Fortune.com and told her the high points. "Go for it!" the editor said. By the end of the day, Jennifer had reached the boy at home, interviewed him about what he thought the next hot business trend would be, and wrote a 300-word piece for the Web. See why you should always read the paper in the morning?

Now that you have a handle on researching potential magazines you'd like to write for and developing the ideas to pitch to them, let's work on the hard stuff—actually writing an article. The next few chapters take you by the hand and guide you through the critical steps of querying an editor, getting the assignment, and doing your first live interview. It might be terrifying stuff, but once you do it, you'll be a pro!

The Least You Need to Know

➤ Successful freelancers come up with ideas that sell.

➤ Freelancers can use newspaper articles as inspiration for a piece with a different angle.

➤ Common themes that can be applied to almost any topic are how to save time, how to save money, how to be loved, and how to make money from the topic at hand.

➤ Articles that target baby boomers have almost endless appeal to magazines nowadays.

➤ Statistics and odd facts can spark an idea for an article.

➤ Brainstorm ideas daily. Most will not be useable, but you will learn how to create ideas consistently.

Chapter 8

Writing a Winning Query

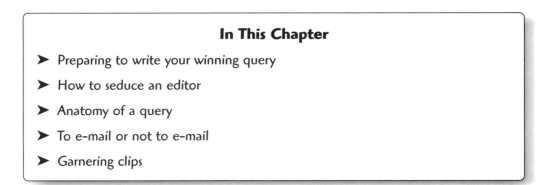

In This Chapter

➤ Preparing to write your winning query

➤ How to seduce an editor

➤ Anatomy of a query

➤ To e-mail or not to e-mail

➤ Garnering clips

Conceptualizing the article was the easy part, right? After all, you're a creative person. The sheer abundance of ideas, however, may be swimming around in your head like a school of fish or smacking into each other like bumper cars. Maybe you're overwhelmed by the number of publications out there. Or maybe you're unsure about how to approach the publication.

Not to worry. Here's where we make sense and put sensibility to your pitch by providing an understanding of the query and the *query* process.

Walk in My Shoes

Let's step inside the editor's shoes for a moment. The editor serves the publisher as style-maker of the magazine and is responsible for fulfilling the publisher's vision—its positioning, who will buy it, what type of stories will be covered, and so on. Ask yourself this: Would you trust your boss's vision—his or her creative child, per se—to a complete stranger? And, oh, incidentally, thousands of dollars ride on your decision.

Dead Lines

Why do publications always ask for a SASE? Returning submissions and answering queries can prove costly and time-consuming. When you don't include a SASE, you say several things about yourself to the editors: You don't care about their guidelines, the success of their magazine, or their time. Exhibit politeness and place an importance on the rules of the publication by including a SASE with all queries and submissions.

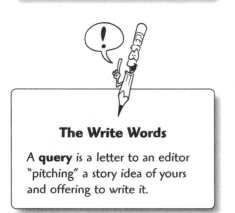

The Write Words

A **query** is a letter to an editor "pitching" a story idea of yours and offering to write it.

You get the point. Taking a chance on an unknown, unproven freelancer is risky business for an editor. Many an editor can recount horrifying tales of new writers who either floundered or sunk, leaving blank space for the editor to fill *after* deadlines.

Sacramento Magazine Editor-in-Chief Krista Minard tells of a new freelancer she entrusted with a huge real estate feature. "He called me two weeks before the deadline and said he couldn't do it, and then wanted me to make him feel okay about it!" recalls Minard. This writer's pull-out from the story left Minard scrambling for a competent, proven freelancer who could write a formidable and comprehensive feature in one week.

The Seduction: Approaching the Editor

Yet editors, as visionaries, constantly seek fresh blood to enliven the pages of their publication. They are in search of creative forces like you to contribute to the vision. Even if working with an unknown writer remains risky, all the editors we spoke with acknowledged the continual search for an innovative voice and a bold, new writer to add to the ranks.

In a nutshell, most editors are on the prowl for new writers, and that's good for you. Most editors, however, choose to work with only a few new writers who prove in their initial pitch and then their first assignment that they write well and can translate the tone of the magazine to the story. Look at the task at hand: earning an assignment from a magazine—like a date—requires a little strategy combined with a little flirting before getting to first base. Let's begin the *query* seduction.

Be Prepared

Let's say that your article will profile several celebrities of the 1980s with a "Where are they now?" angle. In what publications will your idea best fit? Go grab the latest edition of *Writer's Market* and find out. You'll probably come across *Cafe Eighties,* a quarterly magazine featuring articles for the 25 to 35 set with a focus on 1980s' nostalgia in the Contemporary Culture section. You'll most likely also spot several other magazines where your article may find a niche. Moreover, in several paragraphs under each entry, you'll learn the who-to, what-to, where-to, and how-to of submitting your query.

The Straight Scoop

With listings for more than 1,300 consumer magazines, 450 trade publications, and 8,000 editors, *Writer's Market* remains the definitive work source for the freelancer.

Great! You've scanned the pages of *Writer's Market*. Now what? Get your hands on several copies of each of the magazines you intend to query. Read them. Read them again. Read them again, again. You may find that your idea doesn't fit the editorial content after all. You've just saved yourself the trouble of writing a query destined for an editor's wastebasket. If the overall content does fit with your idea, however, commit the voice of the magazine to your innermost being, and call the publication.

Don't Come on Too Strong

Now you do a cold call. Stop the presses! Don't use this call to pitch your idea. Never pitch an idea over the phone, unless you have a strong working relationship with an editor. This is a different type of call, a call that gains you one more step in the seduction. During this call, ask someone in the edi-

Dead Lines

Sending a query to the subscription address of a magazine marks you as inexperienced. Though the subscription service typically will forward your query to the editorial office, the editors will question your competence as a journalist if you can't even send a query to the right place.

torial department to whom you should send a query regarding an article idea about (fill in the blank with your cool idea). Editorial assistants are a good place to start, as they are accustomed to fielding these types of calls. Double-check the spelling of the editor's name you're given, and verify the editor's title (Managing Editor, Health Editor, Big Kahuna, whatever). Now you're ready to flirt!

Let the Flirting Begin

Now the flirting begins in the form of a query letter. Though creativity and originality remain pluses, every editor with whom we spoke listed the same distinguishing characteristics of an outstanding query. Here they are ….

The Write Words

When an editor for a magazine refers to a story **proposal,** he or she is talking about a "pitch" or a query letter. It's the same thing. When you make a pitch, you are sending your proposed idea.

Hook, Line, and Sinker

Hook your editor with a strong opening. If the editors snooze before the end of the first paragraph of your *proposal,* you lose. Writer Kim Wright-Wiley likes to lead with a question. She then answers the question within her proposal. Other writers use hard statistics as openers. Let's say you want to write an article for *Child* about a neurological disorder sweeping across populations of elementary school children. Begin your letter to Health Editor Kara Corridan with a statistic like this: "One in eight elementary school children has been diagnosed with a severe neurological disorder in the United States this year." Immediately you've shown Corridan the audience for the piece (all those parents of elementary school-age children), and you've probably hooked her with a pretty startling statement.

The Straight Scoop

Even though it's not about "who you know," it doesn't hurt if you know someone. If you possess an introduction from either an editor or a writer, let the first sentence of your query express the connection. Successful freelancer Brooks Clark says the best pitch letter he ever wrote began, "Jim Morgan told me to drop you a letter." Clark received a call the next day. Remember to return the favor some day for another aspiring and talented neo-phyte freelancer.

Be Specific, Darn It!

Specificity rules in the assignment-garnering query world. In two to three paragraphs, you've got to tell the editor what you will be writing about and the approach you will be taking. Clearly describe your idea, the approximate length of the final product (will it be 200 words or 2,000?), possible expert interviews and anecdotes, and the date by which you can produce the finished product.

Harper's Bazaar Features Editor Catherine Hong says the quickest way for a writer to earn a rejection on a query is "lack of specificity." She credits a "well-detailed proposal, citing specific sources, anecdotes, everything pertinent to the article," as the best way to break into the prestigious glossy.

I Only Have Eyes for You

Quite simply, express why *you*, not someone else, should write the piece. Come on, this is seduction, baby! Show the editors your writing mojo. If you have clips from here to kingdom come by way of *Vanity Fair* and *People,* you wouldn't need to flirt so much, but you've purchased this book to find out how you can achieve clips from *Vanity Fair* and *People.* So why are you the mother-of-all-writers for the article?

Let's examine some ways you can shine here. First, how might you be close to the story? Are you an expert in the field you'll be writing about? For instance, if you're pitching a parenting piece on behavior problems, are you a child psychologist? Or do you work with children? Is there a first-person connection? Are you the parent of a child suffering with behavior problems? Could your insight or anecdote lead the article?

Tell the editor what you've discovered so far. Give the editor a taste of your research and your writing. And if you do have clips, mention them here.

Signed, Sealed, Delivered, I'm Yours

Include a SASE. To quote Forrest Gump, "That's all I have to say about that."

The Waiting Game

You licked the stamp and sent the query. Now what? The waiting game, of course. Patience is a virtue, in this case. Many editors receive hundreds of queries and submissions a day. Along with their duties of running a glossy publication—editing copy, assigning stories, shipping out proofs, and meeting production deadlines—they behold stacks of mail each day with their name emblazoned on the envelope, waiting to be read and answered.

Dead Lines

Want to kill your chances immediately at receiving an assignment off your pitch? Then follow these tips:

➤ Misspell the editor's name, the publication's name, or any words at all in the query. They hate it at every magazine from *Cosmipolitan* to *Marta Stewirt Living* to *Aviaton and Space Tecknology.*

➤ Include grammar error. Don't never do that one.

➤ Quote Granny's thoughts about what a hot-dog writer you are! (Relatives aren't editors.)

Big Beautiful Woman Editor-in-Chief Sally Smith honestly acknowledges that she "may not read a query for up to two months." Your *Writer's Market* typically provides in each entry the length of time a publication may take to answer a query. Wait at least that long, and then call. Make one rehearsed, nonpestering call. Depending upon the outcome, either let go and move on to another magazine or idea, or rejoice in the assignment.

Sound Effects

Every editor interviewed for this book—from regional publications such as *Sacramento Magazine* to national glossies such as *Working Mother*—adamantly agreed that the difference between a good query and a fantastic query is the ability of the writer to convey the tone of the magazine in the pitch.

When Lynne Rominger recently interviewed a sound technician for a theater company, the engineer stressed the importance of designing the sound for each production: "You wouldn't want to hear *The Sound of Music* the same way as *Jesus Christ Superstar. The Sound of Music* is very natural, while *Superstar* is 'in your face.'" Likewise, a writer wouldn't write a pitch letter about a serial rapist with the same voice or tone to both *Mademoiselle* and *Law and Order*. "Know the magazine" rings often and loudly from the lips of editors.

A Query to Aspire Toward

The following query to *The Washington Post Magazine* earned Brooks Clark an assignment. Why? Because Clark employed several elements of a great query. In fact, the letter is a perfect example of a great query from start to finish. Here are just a few of the strong elements he included: First, he immediately apprised the recipient of a mutual contact, thereby establishing credibility. Next, he provided the editor with the placement of the piece, the "why" the publication should print his idea ("I imagine you guys will be running a variety of looking-back-on-1968 stories"). His understanding of the type of features the magazine may choose to print also provides the editor with the knowledge that the writer knows the magazine and knows the type of content and stories it prints.

Clark also details in an engaging way (the narration of a story involving a prominent politician) the premise and direction of the unique and widely appealing piece. The writer even expresses the tone he hopes to deliver in the piece ("... he gave us that feeling [which I would want the piece to communicate] of Kennedy's passion).

Finally, Clark showcases—even flaunts—his superior writing skills with a "tad" of his style and personality thrown in for good measure. The editor who read this query knew that Clark not only had a great idea that fit the magazine's feature lineup, but that he also could deliver the goods at the caliber of writing the magazine demanded. One final note: Clark introduced—quickly and to the point—another possible story, just to pique the editor's interest yet again. Check the pitch out now to see a query done right.

January 14, 1993

Linton Weeks
Managing Editor
The Washington Post Magazine
1150 15th Street, NW
Washington, D.C. 20071

Dear Linton,

Jim Morgan suggested that I drop this query off to you. I imagine you guys will be running a variety of looking-back-on-1968 stories, especially around April, and the idea that follows (for which I am the midwife, not the writer) might fit in the mix somehow.

Last summer I was reminiscing with a childhood friend about 1968 (we were in sixth grade at St. Albans at the time), and I brought up a remarkable moment in our lives: a Saturday afternoon in that momentous April—less than a week, I think, after the assassination of Martin Luther King—when a few kids in my neighborhood were gathered in our school library and were filmed asking questions of Bobby Kennedy for a campaign commercial.

I have some very clear memories of the day. Kennedy arrived in a red Chrysler convertible immediately after touring the riot areas downtown. (His face was bright red, I assumed from the heat of the flames and his emotional response.) My friend Paul Lee (precocious, politically savvy, and ready to change the world) had positioned himself at the library table directly across from Kennedy and *grilled* him—with questions about nuclear disarmament, hunger, the inner cities, Vietnam, everything. And Kennedy had been magical in his responses. He didn't patronize. He listened. He answered honestly, and he gave us that *feeling* (which I would want to communicate in the piece) of Kennedy's passion, charisma, caring, understanding. (I'm not hot-dogging you, either—it was palpable; and remember, we were only 11 or 12 at the time.)

Paul, now an architect in Oakland, California, got my attention when he told me he remembered every word that Kennedy had said to him that day. I told him to write it all down, and he has. For a taste, here is a paragraph:

> *Kennedy started by greeting us, letting us know he was pleased to spend this time with us. Then he surprised us. Instead of diving into politics, he asked if we had any favorite poems we could share with him. We were required to memorize a poem every week in school, and most everyone raised his hand. He was playing to the whole room and wanted to draw everyone in. He pointed over those of us near the front to an older boy in the very back. I was relieved. Next, Kennedy shared some verse by Alfred, Lord Tennyson. One phrase still sticks with me: "... my purpose holds to sail beyond the sunset, and the baths of all the Western*

stars, until I die." Kennedy talked about how beautiful the images were to him. They expressed a feeling about our lives being on a quest, reaching out in uncharted directions, with confidence in a better tomorrow ....

Later, Paul recounts Bobby's answers to several of his questions, and notes at one point that, while Kennedy was waiting for his car, "I had a remarkable, tangible feeling that he somehow had an awareness that went beyond himself, that in his mind he was in touch with the hearts and aspirations of the American people."

Paul became a devoted admirer and campaign worker for Kennedy and—like everybody else—was devastated by his assassination in June. Paul was numbed, he realized now, in a way that he has only recently come to understand, which in my mind is true of many of us, and an important point of the story. After 25 years, we are all beginning to feel the passion again. (Start Fleetwood Mac music here.)

There are a couple sidelights to this story. One is that, after all this time, I (or I should say, my intern here at *Special Report*) tracked down the three one-minute ads that were made from that session to a political film library in Oklahoma. They sent us a copy and, sure enough, there was Paul (with Buddy Holly glasses) looming on the screen for long stretches. The camera also lingers on two old buddies, Randy and Nick Smith. (Randy, now a lawyer in New Orleans, said he was putting his memories on paper, too.) Kennedy was just as we remembered him. So the story has an illustration.

The other sidelight is that Paul gave a copy of his manuscript to Ted Kennedy and got back a passionate, hand-typed response. In it, the Senator says that Paul's descriptions of Bobby moved him, and he offered some of his own. It's really something.

So, if this grabs you, let me know (phone number). I told Paul I'd be happy to rework the raw material taking whatever angle you think might work. If it isn't right for you, I'd love any suggestions you might have about what to do with it.

Things are going well down here in Knoxville. I've enclosed our most recent issue of *Special Report,* for which I recently became the managing editor. Sometime I want to query you about tracking down my Gambian brother—that is, an American University student who lived with my family for many years, spent many years in prison in Gambia for some political reason, and whose wife (a Sierra Leonese) and four daughters live in D.C. It's about two families, white and black, who've shared a lot over these 30 years. Hard to get a handle on, but some day ....

Best Regards,
Brooks Clark

Serial Dating: The Multiple Approach

Some new freelancers wonder whether they should send the same query proposal to more than one magazine at the same time, a strategy called multiple submission. Why put all your eggs in one basket? Well, because the magazine might tell you to. Some publications couldn't care less about whether you submitted your idea or complete manuscript to another magazine along with submitting to them. On the other hand, some magazines want the exclusivity associated with the idea, concept, everything!

Determining whether you can send the query to only one potential editor or many requires, again, a little research. You possess two options: (1) At the risk of sounding redundant, look it up in *Writer's Market* or (2) call the editorial department and ask. Whatever you do, don't wing it and send multiple submissions without checking. Murphy's Law dictates that's when two magazines will want to snap up your idea, and then nix you and the article because you broke rules and submitted to several outlets. We know. It bites to tie up an idea for months, hoping that you land the assignment. But if you want to play in this league, you've got to follow the rules.

E-Mail Etiquette

In our technologically advanced age, we move at the speed of light. E-mail has replaced the post office in the work office—except when it comes to periodicals. Though many magazines do accept e-mail submissions and queries, many more don't and prefer snail mail over the George Jetson approach—which, by the way, allows hard-copy clips to accompany the pitch. Once again, it's easy to find out if a magazine will accept your e-mail query: Call. Look in *Writer's Market*. Send for guidelines. Whatever you do, don't assume anything and send an electronic submission without checking.

Getting Clipped

Most glossy magazines require *clips* of your previously published writing. Here's the Catch-22, right? How do you get the clips if you need the clips to get the clips? You probably don't possess a clip from *Cosmopolitan*—yet. Instead, you may have an extraordinary essay or feature written for the neighborhood newspaper. Hey, it's still a clip.

How about your alumni magazine? Lynne Rominger achieved her first glossy clip by writing a personal essay about attending UC Davis with her mother for the "Aggies Remember" column of her alumni magazine. She sent that clip with another essay submission to *The San Jose Mercury News*. *The San Jose Mercury News* printed the new essay and, voilà! She had another clip—this one from a top five media market.

The Write Words

Samples of your published work are called **clips,** and usually, an editor will want to see them before assigning you an article. Clips help the editor determine whether your writing meets the standards of the magazine.

So, don't panic if you lack clips. Start small and work up to glossy features. Here are the basics, however, concerning clips:

➤ Don't mention clips if you don't have them.

➤ Include clips only if they showcase a professional caliber of writing.

➤ Include no more than three clips.

➤ Make sure that whatever you send remains representative of your strongest, most journalistically sound and expressive work.

➤ Never lie and say that you possess clips when you don't.

The Least You Need to Know

➤ Always address your query to the editor by name—never to the "Editorial Department."

➤ Check *Writer's Market* for guidelines before querying, or call the magazine directly for query specifications. Be sure to ask whether the magazine accepts multiple queries and submissions.

➤ A good query includes a strong lead, concise but specific details about your proposed article, and the reason you should write it. And don't forget the SASE.

➤ Show the editors you query that you know the audience, the style, and the voice of the magazine.

➤ As quickly as we all move in the technological age, most magazines still seem to prefer snail mail over e-mail. Check with a phone call before querying electronically.

Chapter 9

Your First Assignment

In This Chapter

➤ Meeting the editor's vision—not yours

➤ Conducting your research and staying organized

➤ The importance of meeting your deadlines

➤ Be your own fact-checker

Now that you've written a winning query, an assignment will soon follow. Fantastic, eh? But what do you do from there? In this chapter, we'll show you what happens next, the inner workings of the editorial process from assignment to production and everything in between. You'll learn about an assignment sheet, a lineup, and your role as a writer with a feature within the lineup. We'll also give you some tips on researching your topic and meeting your deadlines.

The Envelope, Please: Your Idea Has Been Accepted!

Congratulations! The editor called to tell you she loved your pitch and wants you to write the piece. Getting from idea to query to *assignment* probably felt like scaling Mt. Everest. We know you want to grab all your friends and celebrate, but you can't. Not yet. As a freelance professional, you need to get the facts about pay, rights, and deadline. Then you need to start researching and writing.

What? You didn't hear us? Writing. That's right, no procrastination. The byline remains just over the horizon, so as Maria told the children in *The Sound of Music*, "Let's start at the very beginning."

The Write Words

The **lineup** is a listing of all the elements of the particular issue, with the number of pages each element will be. The lineup lists all the departments, features, sections, and page numbers. It's the plan, or outline, of the issue. Every lineup is pretty general, perhaps giving the title, a brief synopsis, and the number of pages devoted to the story.

The Write Words

When the editor asks a writer to produce a specific article for a fee, the writer is then on assignment with the magazine. The article is the **assignment.**

I See a Vision—the Editor's!

Once you get an assignment, the editor will send you an assignment sheet and possibly the issue *lineup*. The assignment sheet details everything that your article should include and offers the editor's vision of the article—complete with sidebars, boxed information, and content. Sometimes the editor will include the art director's vision, too. Additionally, the assignment sheet will state your deadline and pay.

Wait a cotton-picking minute, you say. Didn't you send your own assignment sheet of sorts with the query? We can hear you now: "I haven't written a word yet, and the editor is already changing the article!" Well, yes and no. She may have tweaked the concept to better suit the magazine, but isn't the point that you have the assignment? Your idea spawned the article that you now have been given the opportunity to write. Be happy. Shut up. Study the assignment sheet.

You Want What?

Believe it or not, sometimes writers make the grave mistake of assuming that the article they've been assigned is the article that they pitched. Not so. Free-lancers Brooks Clark and co-author Lynne both express the necessity of poring over the assignment sheet. Clark lists ignoring the assignment letter and writing the wrong piece as one of the top things a writer can do to turn an editor off—meaning, of course, no more assignments. "It happens more than you think," says Clark. "And more than once I've done all the reporting, sat down, taken another look at the assignment letter, and realized that I was about to write the wrong story."

The Straight Scoop

As the creator of an idea, you own several unalienable rights—until you sign them away. The right you'll most likely sell away with your articles is first serial rights. This means that the writer agrees to let the magazine or newspaper publish the article for the first time in any periodical. The right to subsequent publishing of the article remains with the author. Other rights that affect writers include one-time rights, second serial (reprint) rights, all rights, electronic rights, subsidiary rights, and dramatic, television, and motion picture rights. For a more complete description of these rights, go to Chapter 25, "Contracts and What They Really Mean."

Co-author Lynne neglected to scrutinize an assignment sheet once on a pets' feature and entirely missed an important component—a celebrity focus! "When I initially spoke with the editor, the story idea concentrated on pets as healers, comforters, and friends, with several boxed paragraphs devoted to pet services such as sitters, rescue agencies, and tips for picking the right pet," she recalls. The assignment sheet, however, denoted a huge pictorial with celebrities and their pets. Lynne scrambled in the last week before deadline to line up and interview almost 30 notables and their pooches, parrots, kittens, and fish.

Remember: Scrutinize the assignment sheet, and ask for clarification on anything you might not understand. Then attack the piece with the editor's vision, not yours.

An Assignment Sheet Sample

Assignment letters come in all shapes an sizes. While one editor might send you a concise assignment sheet that says you've got the gig and to go for it, another assignment sheet might detail the sources you should use, the *slant* of the piece, what information should be covered, and what should be included in sidebar boxes. The assignment sheet's content depends entirely on the editor. Here is an example of a more typical assignment letter:

Dead Lines

Big Beautiful Woman Editor-in-Chief Sally Smith recalls a writer who was assigned a 2,000-word article and submitted 17,000. Instead of writing one article, this writer wrote the equivalent of eight. Bad move. *Sacramento Magazine* Editor-in-Chief Krista Minard says, "Perhaps the worst offense is writing long and assuming the editor will run it anyway—or worse, expecting the editor to cut it!"

Sample Assignment Sheet

March 15, 2000

Kim Wright Wiley
Address

Dear Kim,

It was good to talk with you this morning. I'm delighted that you can work on the Central America/Mexico special section for our September/October 2000 issue. This one seems very straightforward (for a change), and I know you can give it a lot of flair.

As I said on the phone, the advertorial text will stretch for 6 to 8 pages. I've attached the information sheet that advertising gave me, but basically, there's a 500-word intro on how to plan a winter vacation to the area, followed by sections on each of the featured places. These should be 350 to 400 words each (2,500 total) and should highlight the three not-to-miss things to do in each place. We should have the information in stages beginning at the end of March. The very last of it should be in by mid-May. Final deadline for the text is June 5.

You'll be working with Jim Buckley, a freelance editor. His phone number is 805-555-5555; fax is 805-555-5555.

For the text, we'll pay $3,000, on acceptance of the manuscript. In addition, we'll pay for miscellaneous phone and fax expenses, with receipts.

This is a freelance assignment, on a work-for-hire basis. You will not retain any rights to the work.

Please sign a copy of this letter and return it to me. We look forward to working with you, and please don't hesitate to call if you have any questions.

All the best,

Joan Tapper
Editorial Director

The Write Words

A **slant** is a device used by magazines in the articles to appeal to their readership. For instance, one magazine may insist on inspirational endings, while other magazines may begin all articles in first person. This common approach to the articles within a magazine is termed the slant.

All Work and No Play: Research

Everyone who hated the research paper in high school, raise your hand. That's about the whole population. Unfortunately, if you don't love research or can't at least tolerate research as a means to an end, get out of the freelance business now. Freelancers spend as much time (if not more) researching an article as they do writing the article. And just like in high school, your sources and documentation count. Sure, the editor won't hold you to MLA format, but he may request more information about a source, so you'd better be prepared. To that end, keep your research organized and credible.

Give Good Research

Develop a system—files, notebooks, whatever—where you keep every source, note, Web site printout, and scrap of paper. The keen eyes of editors, proofreaders, and fact-checkers alike may ask you to go back and verify a name, rank, or serial number. If your research is comprehensive, detailed, and organized (at least in one place, for goodness sake!), you'll be ready to shoot the answer back in seconds flat. On the other hand, if you need time to seek out the sources again—in other words, if you've given bad research—the powers that be will think twice before assigning you another piece.

Jennifer keeps her information all stacked on her desk. What may appear messy to the untrained eye works for Jennifer, who knows just which stack contains the information that she needs. The writer also keeps individual folders with clips, notes, and scraps of paper for future ideas. Though the assignment might only glimmer in the recesses of her mind, when it arrives, she's ready with a folder full of research. "I also use a lot of gray plastic file storage boxes, without files in them," she says. Jennifer keeps information important to the story or book she's working on in the storage boxes.

Likewise, Lynne developed a surefire system after a few scuds missed the target. "I can't tell you how horrible it feels when an editor says, 'You've got the last name on so-and-so different in two places. Which way is correct?' or 'Who gave you the information for the chart?' and you can't immediately offer the answers because the research or notes were sloppy," she admits.

Today, Lynne keeps copious notes on legal pads for each assignment and always asks how to spell every name as the first interview question. She keeps all notes, pamphlets, Internet sources, and everything else in distinct "research genre" folders, which are then stored within one hanging folder and identified by the article theme on tabs. "Now when an editor asks about something, I pull the file and rattle off the answers while she's still on the phone," Lynne says.

Often, the magazine will receive a call or letter from an irate reader who questions the content of an article. If it's your story, you'll score points with the editor if he can go back to the reader armed with watertight, rock-solid sources and information. Both literally and figuratively, cross your T's and dot your I's.

Variety Is the Spice of Life

Your research as a freelancer may take several forms. Not all research involves late nights spent at the library looking up ancient articles as background information. Part of the mystique of writing remains the thrill of active research—reporting on destinations, people, and events. You'll want to access and use any or all of the following research vehicles for your article, depending upon the need.

The Internet

Of all the research vehicles available to you, the one that can cause the most trouble for a neophyte journalist remains the Information Superhighway. Many writers rely on the Internet to provide them with background information, studies, and source leads. But with the easy access for anyone to post anything online, writers need to be especially wary of what they choose to accept as credible information.

Think logically. Government sites, professional association sites, university sites—these all offer credible information. You can be comfortable citing a report off the Census Bureau site or from an article at *USAToday* Online. But a Web page with "Joe Schmoe's Hella Cool Ways to Count People" as a headline should raise a red flag.

Good places to begin your online research are search engine sites such as these:

➤ www.askjeeves.com

➤ www.altavista.com

➤ www.yahoo.com

➤ www.netscape.com

Dead Lines

Newspaper search engines—where you can find past articles from the paper—often charge for pieces past a week old. Watch out! These fees can rack up quickly, especially if you are on deadline and desperate for the information to complete your article.

These sites can also lead you to periodicals online, such as specific newspapers. If you type "Los Angeles Times," for instance, in the search field of one of these search engines, you will likely find the newspaper's site. Even better, the link will send you directly to the online edition, which might also provide a search prompt to look up articles the publication printed. Hence, you've found another great place to research. In addition, search engines can lead you to government and university sites, great places to gather credible data. Again, just use one of the search engines listed previously, and enter the agency name or university name that you seek. The engine will rev up and find the sites for you.

You get the idea. And remember: The information out there is only as good as the person offering it.

Books

Up-to-date books are a great way to glean information on a topic. Moreover, the authors can turn expert for your article.

For example, while researching an article on women who chose not to have children, Lynne came across a book entitled *Pride and Joy: The Lives and Passions of Women Without Children,* by Terri Casey. Not only did the introduction provide Lynne with some statistical information for the piece, but the author provided an interview. Casey, herself child-free, gave Lynne wonderful and insightful quotes to use in the body of her article. Casey the author became Casey the expert for the feature. Book authors, in general, are more than happy to be interviewed and talk about the contents of their books because the feature then provides the book author with publicity and can increase sales. You both win: You win with great information and sound research, and the book author wins with the publicity hit.

Periodicals

You don't want to quote the competition's recent article on the same subject. What you want to do is locate news stories or information that gives credence to your article. For instance, if you're writing an article about daycare and *The New York Times* just happens to print a front-page story on a 20-year study concerning child care in the United States, cite it! Moreover, look at the key players in the article. Perhaps you'll gain a couple experts for *your* article.

Studies/Reports

You'll find these either online or in the ivory towers of university libraries. Depending on your article, studies may prove an integral facet. For an article on child-free women, for instance, Lynne found a recent study that cited the exact percentages of women within the U.S. population who actually chose not to have children. The information was significant because the study differentiated between women who couldn't have children and women who chose not to have children, whereas Census Bureau reports indicated only households without kids. In this case, the study enriched the piece for the reader.

On-Site Observations

This research typically proves the most fun for writers. You're out and about, hanging with dignitaries at a nonprofit event, watching a professional sporting event and interviewing a player, or eating at a five-star establishment. You observe and take notes on everything you see, hear, smell, touch, and taste. Hey, you pitched the pregnant women skydiver story. Now jump out of the airplane!

Interviews

A complete discussion about interviewing appears in Chapter 10, "The True Gen: Interviewing." Without giving away the whole enchilada, you find the experts or those to profile and sit them down for a little Q&A with tape recorder and notebook in hand.

Movies/Documentaries/Literature

Perhaps you want to quote a poignant line from a movie or liken a political figure to a tragic character in a play. Double-check the accuracy of your reference. One writer Lynne knows actually spoke of a subject's qualities as being "like Shakespeare's Cyrano." Good try, but Shakespeare didn't write *Cyrano de Bergerac*—Edmond Rostand did.

Your Own Life Experiences

The easiest research is your own anecdotal information that somehow illuminates the article. Anecdotal information typically works best as an introduction to the piece. For instance, in an article that focused on charity trends and good works and that also profiled several people who devote themselves to helping others, Lynne began her piece by describing an experience she had working on a project for a nonprofit organization. What follows is the anecdotal introduction she wrote—all the research gleaned from her own memories:

> The middle-aged, single mother of three school-age girls bubbled "thank you" repeatedly as she surveyed the work to her garden—the grass freshly cut, an array of flowers planted around the perimeter, a vegetable garden created—all accomplished in one day by Christmas in April volunteers. When the mother entered her small home and felt the new carpet under her feet, the "thank you" echoed louder and with the exuberance of Cinderella receiving her dress for the ball. Fresh paint and new decorative towels with colorful cartoon fish in the bathroom brought on giggles by the girls, while the mom clasped her hand over her mouth, suppressing even louder laughter. But when she entered the kitchen—completely remodeled and showcasing all new appliances—the woman fell silent, then burst into tears, overwhelmed by the giving and compassion of strangers. About the same time, I burst into tears, too, and hugged her. Together we blubbered, feeling wonderful about the world around us, all the bad erased, only the good shining clearly in that new, showroom kitchen.

The Phone Book

Let your fingers do the walking. The Yellow Pages may be the writer's most used reference! The phone book is to the interview as the diving board is to the pool. Between those Yellow Pages headings, copious amounts of information are available just by pushing some buttons. Remember that pet article Lynne wrote? She found virtually every source for all her informational blocks in the Yellow Pages—everything from doggie diners to pet sitters.

Credibility: A Final Note

Credibility remains the foundation of all good research. When you observe an event, take accurate, thorough notes. When you conduct an interview, take great pains to give verbatim quotes. When citing a study, give credit where credit is due. Your objective as a journalist remains reporting, not editorializing. You report on the sights, smell, taste, and feel of the experience. You give the whole picture and address all sides of an issue, accomplished only through good research. Give it.

The Straight Scoop

Want to learn more about the journalistic endeavor, reporting and ethics, and what's happening in the publishing arena? Look up the *Columbia Journalism Review* at www.cjr.org. The site also provides First Amendment links.

Dead Man Writing: Meeting Deadlines

This is it. This is what separates the winners from the losers. Meeting your *deadlines* means saving the magazine money and allowing the editor time to fine-tune your piece for publication. Not meeting your deadlines means moving on to another profession—that's the bottom line.

Deadlines remain a crucial element in the writer/ editor relationship. If you really want to freelance, commit now to meeting your deadlines without fail. In fact, commit now to turning in your first three assignments to an editor *before* deadline. You'll build a reputation within the publication as a writer to trust, someone who brings home the goods on time.

The Write Words

In case you haven't figured it out yet, a **deadline** is the final day you have to turn in an assignment. When a writer says, "I'm working on deadline," he means that the article is due that day.

Turn Off the TV

One way you can help yourself make a deadline with days to spare is by turning off the television and writing. Translation: "Don't procrastinate." Don't wait until the night before the article is due to start writing—not if you can help it, anyway. Instead, calculate how many hours, days, or weeks you believe you'll need to write the rough draft, final draft, and perfect draft. Allow yourself the time to write the project completely and flawlessly.

Dead Lines

Don't cop an attitude if your words are tweaked by the copyeditor. As professional wordsmiths and grammar police, they know what is best and correct. You'll only mark yourself as a difficult writer if you balk at the copyeditor's changes.

Take Time to Smell the Coffee

When on deadline, chances are that you'll attach yourself to the swivel chair in front of the computer, deny yourself proper grooming, and glaze over in a coffeeinduced daze. We've all been there. Up all night, plink, plink, plinking at the keyboard, hoping that the first draft emerges in a state of final-draft perfection.

We've all been there, but it isn't the best way to write. Freelancer Brooks Clark cites being tired as one of the things he least enjoys about freelancing. Reporting, writing, creating—it'll zap you of your energy. Sometimes the best thing you can do for yourself and your writing is this: Put your hands up and step away from the computer for a while. Take a walk. Play with the baby. Clear your mind. Practice your yoga technique. Just step away for an hour and rejuvenate.

Honey, I'm Late!

We just got through telling you never to be late! Yet sometimes, because of uncontrollable circumstances, you'll end up turning in your article after the deadline. What you don't want to do, however, is neglect to alert the editor that the piece won't be in on time. The moment you know the balloon isn't getting off the ground and you need more time—perhaps an interview subject critical to the piece can't accommodate the Q&A until a few days later—call the editor. He'll prove much more understanding if he has an early heads-up that the deadline needs reworking.

The Write Words

Words pulled from the text of an article and displayed boldly in quotes as a visual are called **pulled quotes.**

When a story begins on one spread and continues on another, the term to describe the layout is **jump coverage.**

Stupid People Mistakes: Copyediting and Fact-Checking

Whew! You made your deadline. Sit back and enjoy a Margarita, for now the editor is on deadline. While you sit in your armchair, we'll guide you through the maze your piece now navigates, a seemingly endless array of editors and proofreaders.

"Roger, Copy That!"

Do you remember that *School House Rock* video where the bill became a law? Well, the process that your submitted work goes through to become a printed article is roughly as complicated.

First, the editor edits your work and looks for any egregious style errors or content omissions. Next, the copyeditor grammatically edits your work, while fact-checkers retrace your steps and verify names, dates, locations, and anything else questionable. At about the same time, the art director and his crack crew of designers lay out the copy and design the visual end of the article. Elements like *pulled quotes, jump coverage, dominant photos,* and *lead-ins* are among the design staff's concerns. With the designers, your article truly takes aesthetic shape. At the very end of the process, a proofreader reads over the final proofs, checking again for spelling, grammar, and style errors.

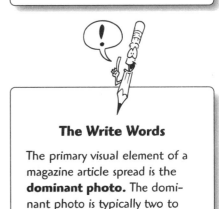

The Write Words

The first words of a story, called a **lead-in,** draw attention to the copy and are often set apart typographically for emphasis and style. The lead-in should not be mistaken for the **lead,** an opening paragraph that sets the tone and gives purpose to the story.

The Write Words

The primary visual element of a magazine article spread is the **dominant photo.** The dominant photo is typically two to three times larger than the next-size picture.

Lights, Camera, Action, Ship Out!

This is it. Your byline remains only a printing away. After everyone and their uncle have proofed and edited your piece, the article is ready for "ship out" to the printer.

Remember how stressed you were on deadline? Well, ship out is the editors' time of pressure. During ship out, vision and bottom lines converge. Time really means money for the publication here. If the editors miss their ship-out deadline, the magazine

Dead Lines

Don't assume that all magazines employ fact-checkers who will pore over your every word looking for inaccuracies. Fact-check your article yourself before turning it in, and do the legwork when your editor asks for it.

arrives late on the racks. Missed rack time translates to missed sales and lost revenue. And though the printer does provide the magazine with a final proof before those glossy pages hit the copier, magazines rarely make changes at this stage of the game. "Changes at ship out mean big bucks," confides Elena Macaluso, an associate editor with a regional glossy.

The importance of timely ship out provides another reason for the freelancer to always hit her deadlines. The sooner the magazine achieves ship out, the sooner you see your first byline. Moreover, when the magazine makes money, the editorial department garners a bigger budget for more freelance articles.

The Least You Need to Know

➤ Once you get an assignment, don't procrastinate. Make sure that you understand the assignment sheet, ask any questions you need to ask, and start writing.

➤ Write the article the editor wants, even if it differs from the article you pitched.

➤ Keep your research organized and credible.

➤ Meet your deadlines. In fact, turn in your first, second, and even third assignments early.

➤ Don't cop an attitude if your words are tweaked by a copyeditor. That's their job—to make your article better.

➤ Don't assume that the magazine has a fact-checker. Check and double-check all the facts yourself.

Chapter 10

The True Gen: Interviewing

In This Chapter

➤ Preparing for the interview

➤ Gathering your tools

➤ Conducting one striptease of an interview

➤ Staying in control

➤ Good subjects, bad subjects

Hemingway used his own term, *gen,* to describe truthfulness. When interviewing and when translating the interview into an article, gen remains of utmost importance. In this chapter, we'll show you how a good interview translates to gen in your sources. The best part? You'll find that the interview is like one long, slow, seductive striptease.

Be Prepared

Perhaps the most important part of interviewing is, in fact, preparation. Remember when Mom told you to change your underwear in case you got into an accident? Remember when she told you to keep some change in your wallet or purse—just in case you needed to make an emergency phone call? The Boy Scout motto—"Be prepared"—reverberates loudly when it comes to interviewing for a story. Before you sit down to chat with Norman Schwartzkoff, Hillary Clinton, or Harrison Ford, you need some preparation—and some really great questions.

There Is Such a Thing as a Stupid Question

How do you formulate the great questions? Research. Contrary to what your teacher told you in high school, there *is* such a thing as a stupid question, especially when conducting an interview for a celebrity profile.

Think about it. How many times does Norman Schwartzkoff want to answer how he began his career in the military? How often does Hillary want to narrate where she and Bill met? What is Harrison Ford going to think of you if you ask "What was your breakthrough role?" He's liable to look at you emphatically and say, "Duh! *Star Wars!*"

You, the reporter, sound like an idiot when you ask the simplistic, common, already-been-asked question. A writer needs to know the background of the person he or she is interviewing—whether expert, celebrity, or anecdotal source—and translate that knowledge into intelligent questions.

Let's say you're interviewing a world-renowned obstetrician about twin births. Go into the interview already knowing everything you can about labor and delivery. For instance, don't ask him to discuss the stages of labor. Myriad sources provide information on labor. Your article pertains to the significance of twin deliveries, not labor. You'll waste your time and the doc's time if you don't have probing, well-thought-out questions.

The burden, therefore, remains discovering the intelligent, interesting, as-yet-unasked questions. These questions and their spontaneous follow-up questions will provide the illuminating and colorful quotes you need for your story. Questions that show your knowledge and interest in an expert way create an intimacy that often results in the superb interview.

The Straight Scoop

We writers don't always have to move on the Information Superhighway. Sometimes an old-fashioned library works fine and holds the best background sources on a topic. Your first stop in the library should be the *Reader's Guide to Periodical Literature*. These reference books are compendiums of articles by topic and bound by the months and the year. So say that you're slated to interview Blues legend John Lee Hooker. Just look him up under his name (Hooker, John Lee) and—voilà!—any articles written about him will be listed and will include the periodical and the date.

Been There, Done That

So surf online, check out books, and look up periodicals relevant to your topic. Refer to the "All Work and No Play: Research" section of Chapter 9, "Your First Assignment," for a refresher. All good writers know the importance of research in preparation for the interview. *Roots* author and former magazine writer Alex Haley supposedly researched his subjects thoroughly before interviewing them by hanging out in their hometowns and probing the people who knew his subjects as children. Whatever you do, find out all you can about your subject or an interviewee's expertise and any important background information. Then, and only then, sit down to write your interview questions.

The Straight Scoop

Once a publication prints your article, you may wonder how the magazine gets into the racks at bookstores, supermarkets, mini-marts, and newsstands. Periodicals from *Cat Fancy* to *Mad Magazine* find their way to shelves, racks, and stands by way of a distributor. International Periodical Distributors (IPD) currently leads the magazine direct-distribution industry with annual sales approaching $200 million. That's a lot of magazine sales!

Curiosity Saved the Cat

Curiosity will save the cat when preparing interview questions. If you don't possess a natural curiosity, then freelancing may prove an unwise career choice for you. Most journalists can't stop asking questions! With this in mind, ask yourself these questions: When you immerse yourself in researching a person, topic, or event, do you find yourself asking more questions even after reading pages upon pages of information? Does there always seem to be something missing that you want to know? If you answer "Yes," you'll no doubt succeed.

Tooling Around

Formulating interview questions remains only one step in preparing for the interview. Before you ask

Dead Lines

There's a difference between asking the "tough" questions and just being a jerk. A good reporter asks the tough questions because the inquiry has relevance and remains an important element to the integrity of the story. Never torment an interview subject with intimate, irrelevant questions.

that first question, you need to gather some basic tools of the trade and make sure that they're all sharpened, juiced, and ready to go. Pens, pads, and tape recorders are small, common objects that become formidable instruments in the hands of a reporter, but only if they're accessible and in good working condition.

My Kingdom for a Pen!

Think we're stupid for bringing this up? Well, you're the one who will feel stupid if you're caught on an interview without *several* pens. Even though you'll probably tape your interviews, you'll want to jot down copious notes—observations, items you want to go back to, descriptions, and many other things. And even if you possess a briefcase of Bics, check to make sure that they work.

And one more thing: Don't drop your pens helter-skelter among key chains, lipstick, hand lotion, spare change, supermarket receipts, used check registers, and chewed gum at the bottom of the barrel. Give yourself easy access to your pen. The last thing you want to do in an interview is to conduct a treasure hunt for a writing implement.

The Notebook (Not by Nicholas)

What goes better with pens than paper? Steno pads, legal pads, college-ruled spiral tablets—it doesn't matter. Just make sure that you have several on hand with empty, doodle-free sheets. Better yet, designate one or two notebooks solely for each article you're writing.

Be Kind, Rewind

If you don't own a handheld tape recorder, go out *now* and buy one, along with some extra blank cassettes. A tape recorder ensures quote accuracy. Moreover, because you probably won't conduct all interviews in person—most freelancers don't—we highly recommend a specialized tape recorder that plugs into the telephone jack. At about $70 to $100 dollars, this recorder remains an investment, but you'll love the advantage of a clear-sounding interview with George Clooney conducted in the comfort of your bathrobe.

Freeze Frame

The fear of a subject "freezing up" when faced with your tape recorder remains relatively uncommon. By the time you sit face-to-face or call phone-to-phone, the interview will have already been arranged and approved. Your subject should be well aware of the interview and the probability of a recorder. In fact, most subjects want the recorder, as there's no chance of their being misquoted. Nevertheless, you should act considerately if faced with a suddenly catatonic subject. Your interviewee might have underestimated his or her reaction to the rolling tape and mini-microphone.

Two things you can do to get the ball rolling again and the interview going are these:

➤ Turn off the tape recorder and offer to leave it off while the two of you chat without your asking any questions until your subject feels more comfortable.

➤ Place the tape recorder unobtrusively off to the side—not directly under the interviewee's nose.

Got E-Mail?

One of the best tools of the trade for interviewing in our technological age is electronic mail. Think about the convenience. Possessing an e-mail account can save you tremendous time and a goodly sum of money. Except for your monthly flat fee, it's free. The phone company can't say the same of your long-distance phone calls.

With e-mail, a writer can send his questions any time, day or night. Any responses are already transcribed, so you've saved time there. The interviewee can answer the questions whenever convenient. Neither the journalist nor the subject remains tied to a meeting time. Moreover, there's less chance of misquoting someone when the interview occurs online. If you misquote the interviewee, he holds a copy of his responses and can easily argue your misrepresentation of him.

Granted, e-mail interviews don't work for those stories where seeing and participating in a day with the subject reveals his or her true personality and provides a full representation of the experience. They also don't work in circumstances when your subject is under investigation and his responses would surely come out guarded and even edited by a PR guy. However, they most definitely offer convenience when interviewing experts for straightforward information (such as biographical data and scientific fact or process) and receiving anecdotal information.

The one downside to e-mail interviews is the loss of spontaneity and the lack of images. You don't hear the chuckle in the responses or see the glimmer in someone's eye. Again, e-mail interviews can prove a great time-saver and an excellent interview tool,

Dead Lines

Always ask the subject of your interview for permission to tape the conversation while the tape is rolling. This way you hold documentation that the interview was agreed upon by both parties. This is especially important for phone interviews. In fact, you may go to jail if you don't 'fess up to taping a phone conversation.

Dead Lines

Always take the time to transcribe (type out word for word) your interviews from tape immediately following the meeting. Otherwise, you risk taping over the interview by mistake, thereby losing valuable information.

but use your best judgment as to what subjects will work with this technique and what subjects won't. Don't make your copy suffer later for lack of specificity in the picture you must paint with your words!

Pack 'Em Up, Move 'Em Out!

Key to your success with interviews will be your organization. Again, make sure—before you walk out the door—that your pencils are sharpened, your pens have ink, you have plenty of notebooks, your tape recorder's batteries are charged, you have extra cassettes, and you've paid your e-mail account.

Now, back to Mom. Remember when she said, "A place for everything and everything in its place" when you left something out or put it in the wrong spot? A wise woman! Make a place for everything, and put it in its place in your briefcase or bag. Your professionalism will earn you respect from your interview subject, which in turn will manifest itself in trust.

The Full Monty: The Interview

Show time! Conducting an interview can feel like opening night. Take a deep breath. It's time for you to take center stage. In this case, you won't belt out a tune or dance to a Rodgers and Hammerstein number. Instead, put on some Prince (or the Artist Formerly Known As) and get ready to bump and grind. Conducting an interview begins and ends like one long striptease. Your job is to seduce the subject into answering your questions. You need to make your subject open up and provide you with the *sound bites* for your story! So get out your boa, 'cuz here we goa!

The Write Words

In broadcast journalism, a **sound bite** is the term reporters, producers, and editors use to denote which quote should be pulled from all the tape the photographer shot and included in the visual story. Although broadcast journalists still use the term with integrity, it has taken on a more pejorative meaning today, expressing the "canned" ready-to-print or ready-to-air response from some interviewees.

Unbutton the Blouse: The Open

The big tease occurs with an open. A conversational approach typically works best on all subjects. Plan "informal time" without tough questions—or any questions at all—where you engage the subject in chit-chat. Make your source comfortable during these 5 to 10 minutes of friendly conversation. If a stripper ripped off everything immediately, who'd stay long enough to drop a dollar in her belt? Instead, she surveys her audience and slowly begins the show to entice them to stay. Likewise, you want to make your subject feel comfortable and want to stay and proceed with the interview.

In her book *Interview,* Claudia Dreifus tells a story that demonstrates the value of saving the toughest questions for later. The prominent journalist writes, "Once, while interviewing Frank Sinatra at his Waldorf Towers apartment, I swallowed hard and inquired (tactically late in the session) about his reported friendships among Mafia figures. I then quickly assumed a defensive crouch, lest the armed bodyguard seated just outside the door enter with guns blazing."

The Straight Scoop

Baltimore Sun reporter Dan Fesperman recently interviewed veteran photojournalist Jed Kirschbaum for the *Columbia Journalism Review.* Kirschbaum offered why he might shoot out a question himself when shooting a news event, saying, "Everybody has this 'Guard-all' shield around them, like in the old Colgate ad .... And nobody is going to let you past that shield if they think you're trying to steal something. The best images are when you can get past that shield people are trying to put up, especially in portraiture. You can look at a roll of film and almost see someone dropping it."

Sinatra answered Dreifus's question. Most likely, Sinatra answered the question because Dreifus had gained his trust by leading up to the question rather than opening with it. Even though the reporter knew what question she most wanted to ask (the answer to which the readers most wanted to know), she certainly didn't start off with, "So whaddabout your involvement with the mob, Mr. Sinatra?" If Dreifus had opened with that question, Sinatra probably would have showed her the door.

The emphasis on the open remains taking it slow. Establish a rapport with your subject first. Begin by unbuttoning the blouse, not ripping off the shirt.

Taking Off a Little More: The Five W's (and an H!)

Chances are, you may already have learned from your research *Who, What, When, Where, Why,* and *How* things happen, as far as these questions relate to your story. However, now is the time—just after opening with some rapport-establishing chit-chat—that you should ask or verify the facts of your story. You want to gather solid truths in this stage of your Q&A. For instance, when co-author Lynne interviewed John Lee Hooker, while still in college for her magazine writing class, she asked him to confirm the information gathered involving his birth place, age, first big hit, and so on. The Blues

The Write Words

Ever hear a reporter or journalism instructor talk about the five W's and the H questions? The five W's are **Who, What, When, Where,** and **Why;** the H stands for **How.** Asking these six questions can help a reporter provide the specific, verifiable facts for a story.

legend needed only to confirm or deny the information. Want another example? On a story covering education for a city chamber of commerce magazine, Lynne took the stats she had gathered on number of schools, enrollment, and programs, and asked the assistant superintendent of the district to confirm whether her information was correct. By doing this process of who-what-when-where-how type questions, you double-check your facts (always good!), and you also help the subject warm up with easy questions.

Take It Off and Open Up

Finally! Now you can ask those open-ended questions and encourage the source to give his own opinions. Open-ended questions don't necessarily have one pat answer. They are the "How did you feel when …" questions. These questions encourage lengthy description and discourse. In this stage of the interview, you want your source to open up. To that end, be especially careful to not lead your source in his responses. In other words, don't cut your subject off while he or she is talking to contribute yourself or interject something into the response.

Believe it or not, avoiding "leading" a subject may prove the hardest thing you do in the interview. You have to now move away from a conversation—where you naturally contribute your own insights and thoughts—and allow the subject to dominate the interaction. In this way, you gain the fullest responses. Take a note from attorneys here. Any attorney will tell you that the more a defendant chatters up in the box, the more he gives away. If you become part of the experience, you lead the subject in his or her responses.

Let your subject answer fully without interruption. For instance, let's go back to the doc delivering twins. You may ask the open-ended question, "What was your reaction when you discovered that the second child descended legs first with his head caught?" Now sit back and allow the good doctor to recreate the situation. By asking the physician his reaction, you encourage him to give an honest, emotional response concerning the potentially life-threatening birth.

Listen carefully. Opportunities will arise for spontaneous, follow-up questions from your open-ended questions. Most important, don't be afraid to ask the tough questions now. Just strategically plan and time when you'll ask the toughies.

One final note: The depth of your questioning during this stage of the interview will certainly provide your quality responses and quotes.

Take It Slow and Maintain Control

In his 1995 contemplation "The Lost Art of Interviewing," *Los Angeles Times* correspondent Tom Rosenstiel wrote, "Technology, the accelerating pace of news, the growing sophistication of sources, the increasing competition among news outlets—all conspire to make many interviews more performance art than newsgathering, often with the interviewee rather than the interviewer in control."

The Straight Scoop

In this same piece, Tom Rosenstiel wrote, "We are living in The Age of the Interview, a carnival of chat, chatter, conversation, confession, spin, sharing, and selling." He also tells the reader of the new broadcast-network name for an interview, "the Get," and describes its importance in contemporary television journalism. "Nabbing the right Get—the interview with the right member of O.J.'s family or the right celebrity in crisis—can make a show for months."

Know this: Rosenstiel's lament is valid. In order for you, the writer, to provide the reader with the best information, you must maintain control over the interview. Sometimes, you may ask your subject questions that make him uncomfortable. That's okay. It's your job. When you queried the editor and promised to write the insightful story, you didn't include a proviso that said, "… unless a question makes the target of my story uncomfortable." You promised to tell the truth. Truth telling—as Hemingway said, "the true Gen"—remains the basis of all journalistic ethics.

Maintaining control of an interview also ensures that you provide readers with good, solid information. How does one control an interview? By directing the questions back to the topic if the conversation strays off course. However, maintaining control doesn't mean missing opportunities. If the interview takes a turn that doesn't necessary follow the direction of your pre-prepared questions, pursue it.

One more thing: You, not the subject, should end the interview. It remains up to you to collect all the information you need for your article from the subject. If your subject cuts the interview short, you're out of luck and out of information. You will know when you have all the quotes, anecdotes, and information you sought when booking the interview. You should end the interview then.

That said, there may be times when you won't have control over the length of the interview, especially if you're interviewing someone famous. You may have 30 minutes or just 10. You need to be prepared for such a situation and really know how to maximize the time with the right qeustions. Some advice: Always come up with at least one outrageous question. My friend had 10 minutes with Wesley Snipes and challenged him to an arm-wrestling match. It was strange, but she got a really good interview out of it!

The Straight Scoop

If you're going to interview anyone remotely well-known, there's a good chance your main contact will be a PR rep. These people are the gatekeepers to your subject, so deal with them respectfully. Chances are, if your subject is a *really* important persion, the PR rep will be right there with you in the room attempting to control the interview; their entire job is to control and protect their client. All the more reason to come up with at least one unusual, thought-provoking question if you can.

Drink In Every Detail

Interviewing can prove both mentally and physically demanding. You need to keenly observe the surroundings, the subject's facial expressions during answers, and any other interesting aspect of the interview. The decor of an expert's home, for instance, might reveal another dimension of his or her personality, so you'll want to jot down your observations. You'll use your notes often in your article, mostly to provide background information and colorful lead-ins to quotes. Your observations enrich the final product for the reader.

Many reporters also take notes directly following an interview, detailing their overall perceptions when everything is still fresh in their minds.

Can We Do It Again?

As we mentioned, you, not the subject, should determine when to end the interview. Don't end the interview, however, without quickly reviewing your notes and clarifying any unclear information, especially if you're unsure about a subject's intended meaning behind something said. Ask the interviewee, "Earlier you said _____; did you mean _____?" By asking for clarification, you not only provide the subject the opportunity to further explain something and avoid being misquoted, but you save yourself the agony of an irate subject after print. Contrary to what many celebrities may think, the writer wants to provide an accurate representation of his subjects.

Before thanking your source, politely ask for approval to return with additional questions, if necessary. Often you'll sit down to write and realize that you missed asking an important question. With prior approval, you can easily make a phone call and gather the information. By asking during the interview, you prepare the subject for possible further questioning.

That's it. You did it. You accomplished an interview and garnered some fantastic, colorful quotes for your soon-to-be ground-breaking article in a glossy magazine. Congratulations!

Dead Lines

Always thank an interview subject after the interview. In fact, go one step further, as writer Kim Wright Wiley does, and send a formal thank-you note. Not thanking someone—who incidentally helped you make a buck and earn a byline—is just plain crass and rude.

The Straight Scoop

Of all the thousands of magazines, the title that beats the rest in circulation, with more than 13.3 million readers, is none other than *Reader's Digest. TV Guide*—yes, it's considered a magazine—follows closely, with circulation of almost 12 million. Those are pretty astounding numbers when you consider that the prominently placed weekly *People* garners slightly less than one-quarter of the readers of *Reader's Digest*, with about 3.65 million. (Source: 1000Magazines.com)

The Good, the Bad, and the Ugly: Interview Sources

In Chapter 9 we discussed the credibility of research sources—books, the Internet, and so on. Now, we must delve into the credibility of live sources—humans, Klingons, Jar Jar Binks, whoever.

Generally speaking, most interview subjects answer willingly, flattered that they are sought out for their expertise and their credibility. Sometimes, however, bad apples fall from seemingly good trees. Sometimes—try as you might—the expert offers inane and unusable answers, doesn't say anything at all, or reveals himself during the process to be less than credible. It happens. The source you excitedly lined up and researched might fail you. Dr. Hicks, Lynne's nonfiction writing professor at the University of California at Davis, called mishaps like this the "balloon not getting up off the ground." His advice to the then-fledgling magazine writer, Lynne? Abandon the source, the story, and whatever wasn't moving, and move on.

It's good advice. Even after all the initial research and work that may have been put into the source, it's always best to replace a bad interview subject with a good interview subject. Go back to square one, then, and find yourself another expert.

On a final note, good luck. Every reporter knows that no matter how much you prepare, surprises arise. It remains your job to seize the opportunities for great questions when the surprises occur. Don't feel that you must adhere to the list of questions you wrote in preparation for the interview; go with the natural rhythm of the event. Maintain control, but don't drain the life out of your subject either. Finally, enjoy. In most cases, interviewing offers a chance to experience another's life and brings the most fun to the job of writing. The experience of the story, the really great story, makes the hard work worthwhile.

The Least You Need to Know

➤ Prepare for your interviews by researching the subject thoroughly and organizing your materials.

➤ If you don't already have a tape recorder, pens, notebooks, and access to the Internet, get them.

➤ Open the interview with a conversational, comfortable approach for a few minutes.

➤ Always ask for permission to come back to a subject for clarification.

➤ If your source proves less than credible or doesn't provide you with the information you seek, jettison the interview and find another source.

Part 3

Who's Gonna Buy Your Stuff?

The more you know about the world of publishing, the better your chances of getting published. So let's take a close look at who owns what, who does what, and best of all, who buys what! Whether it's magazines, newspapers, trade journals, or something else, soon you will know how to read a masthead with the best of them.

Newspapers: What They're Looking For

Stringers, city beat, yellow journalism, penny presses, reporters who never rat out a source—this is the world of newspapers. Just the facts, ma'am. No *Mirabella* or *George* glossy glitz here. In this chapter, it's all black and white. We'll tell you how to break into the newspaper business as a freelancer. You'll learn about the major papers and what gets the attention of an ink-and-paper editor. Turn the page, because the press never stops.

Less Filling, Tastes Great!

We love waking up Sunday morning to our newspapers. Whether you find your business news in *The Wall Street Journal* or prefer the entertainment section of your town's paper, the newspaper remains an institution and the very root of mass media as we know it.

Dead Lines

In the late 1800s, when the predominant source of news for Americans was still the newspaper, many editors' and publishers' rampant disregard for objective journalism gave rise to the term "yellow journalism." Publishers ran sensationalized stories, fostered an irresponsible approach to reporting, and chose to express their own political opinions to the exclusion of other ideas. With few other ways to check out the facts, the public suffered from the tactics of yellow journalism.

The Write Words

When Benjamin Day was able to drop the price of his paper, the *New York Sun,* to one small penny, the term **penny press** was coined. Today, penny press connotes inexpensive printing of all kinds.

Though typically newspaper features amount to a fraction of the length of magazine features, we find the information they contain to be informative, charming, shocking, interesting, and helpful. In fact, more than 60 million people read newspapers daily. Not too shabby—that's one in three Americans. Newspapers, therefore, remain the major news source for most people. It's no wonder local advertisers depend on newspapers as their preferred medium—everybody reads them!

But before we talk about today and breaking your way into the newspaper world as a freelancer, let's take a brief look back at the business of print.

A Penny for Your Thoughts

Back in the 1700s, people like Benjamin Franklin used the printing presses sparingly, typically as a vehicle for religious and political expression. In the 1800s, newspapers began to proliferate with the development of continuous rolls of paper, a steam-powered press, and a means to use iron instead of wood in press construction. In fact, all these advances enabled newspaperman Benjamin Day to drop the price of the *New York Sun* to a penny a copy in 1833. Voilà! Such was the advent of mass media. For the first time in history, almost everyone could afford to read the paper.

The *penny press* was not only cheap, but it also brought about a revolution to which we owe the legacy of our current newspapers. Once the penny presses were up and running, reporters started pounding the pavement for stories, Olde Shoppes began advertising, and stories and lighter news entered the arena. With the flash of a bulb, photojournalism emerged. With the ability to disseminate thought, the Alternative Press arrived. In a sense, you could say that we owe all those wonderful sections, departments, opinions, and inserts that we pore over with a hot cup of java to Benjamin Day and his penny press.

Back to the Future

Today you can choose from more than 1,800 newspapers in the United States and Canada. The penny press, you see, spawned a $54 billion industry. Nearly 6 in 10 adults in the top 50 U.S. markets read a daily newspaper, and another 10 percent read one on Sunday, according to the most recent *Competitive Media Index*. But move over, old fuddy-duddies. Adults aren't the only readers of today's paper.

Teen Fever

Although statistics show that readership does increase with home values, education, and age, a recent study indicated that young people—one of the biggest consumer groups in the nation—read the paper each week.

The Newspaper Association of America's report, "Competing for the Markets of the Future: An Up-Close Look at the Media Teens Rely On," found that 69 percent of teenagers (age 12–17) read a newspaper in the past week, while 40 percent indicated that they read or looked at a local daily paper in the past day.

Supply and Demand

Translation for you writers: When there's a diversity of papers and a diversity of readers, a demand exists for a diversity of ideas by writers like you (yes, you!). With a strong, growing foundation and readers ranging from young to old, newspapers are fertile ground for fresh voices and new ideas. To keep readers, a paper has got to compete and offer the stories, insight, and information their readers want—often on a scant, overworked staff. Enter the freelancer.

The Straight Scoop

Contrary to popular belief, the sports pages aren't the most popular section of the paper. The most popular section of the paper remains the news of the day. Ninety percent of adult readers surveyed say they choose to peruse the news of the day each day. The next most popular section, entertainment, lagged behind, with only 68 percent affirming that they read the section daily. (Source: Scarborough Research—Top 50 DMA Market Report, 1998)

One Fish, Two Fish, So Many Fish

Again, there are 1,800 newspapers out there waiting for your writing. The sheer number of newspapers makes us stagger. And no two papers are alike: Some deliver daily, some weekly, some biweekly. You've got your local papers, your regional rags, and your national newsies. Oh, and then there are the trash tabloids, the alternative weeklies, and your community presses. Who is who? Who pays what? And where do you start? Let's start with a description of the three major categories: the national newspaper, the local newspaper, and the weekly.

National Pride

When we say national newspaper, we're talking about the likes of *The Wall Street Journal* and *USA Today;* both also hit the press and the newsstands daily. Though these newspapers showcase national and global news, they often specialize in stories for geographic areas to better serve their readers nationwide and gain local advertisers. The supermarket tabloids, like the *National Enquirer,* also serve readers nationally but print only weekly or bimonthly, at best. Incidentally, though, a city paper, *The New York Times,* is considered the paper of the nation by the newspaper world.

The Daily Grind

By far the most predominant newspaper type and the information staple of cities across the country are the daily, local papers. Smaller communities such as Pocatello, Idaho, and major metropolises such as Minneapolis, Minnesota, possess and serve their media market with a daily paper. Think *Los Angeles Times*, *Miami Times Herald,* *Boston Globe,* and *Chicago Tribune.* But also think *Modesto Bee* (California), *Mobile Register* (Alabama), *The Bristol Press* (Connecticut), and *the Maui News* (Hawaii).

Chances are, you have several daily papers within a 50-mile radius for which you could write. Whether the paper exists in a top 20 media market (such as the *San Jose Mercury News,* in San Jose, California) or offers the information of the day within a much smaller market (such as the *Cadillac News,* in Cadillac, Michigan), the presses don't stop and the stories need tellers—you!

Just because we thought you might want to know, the top 20 U.S. daily newspapers by circulation according to *Editor & Publisher* are the following:

1. *The Wall Street Journal*
2. *USA Today*
3. *Los Angeles Times*
4. *The New York Times*
5. *The Washington Post*
6. *New York Daily News*

7. *Chicago Tribune*

8. *Newsday*

9. *Houston Chronicle*

10. *Chicago Sun-Times*

11. *The Dallas Morning News*

12. *San Francisco Chronicle*

13. *The Boston Globe*

14. *New York Post*

15. *The Arizona Republic*

16. *The Philadelphia Inquirer*

17. *The Star-Ledger* (Newark)

18. *The Plain Dealer* (Cleveland)

19. *The San Diego Union-Tribune*

20. *The Register* (Orange County, California)

The Weekly Warriors

You might recognize these weekly publications as your town's alternative paper, often showcasing liberal or even outlandish stories and possibly alternative lifestyles. Many of these papers appeal to younger readers; often the writing and investigative reporting are exceptional. Unlike the daily newspapers that correspond to a particular geographical area or media market, the weeklies actually may embrace a group. One weekly might focus on and serve the African American community, while another might provide local business information. Weeklies read more like a magazine and serve a lifestyle, and they hit the racks on a weekly basis.

The Straight Scoop

Unlike magazines that describe article length by word count—like an 85-word sidebar, 1,000-word essay, or 2,000-word feature—newspapers describe article length in column inches. A column inch is $2\frac{1}{4}$ inches across (width) by 1 inch deep. Long features typically amount to about 30 column inches. Still confused? Figure that 30 column inches equals about four to five double-spaced, typewritten pages of copy.

It's Black and White: What Newspapers Want

What newspapers want isn't tough to figure out: It's news. And a long tradition dictates the process of producing a paper day in and day out. The most important thing for a freelancer to know going in is this: The newspaper business is steeped in history and can be, well, stodgy. Julie Randles, a former newspaper editor who now freelances for several papers, tells us that journalists in the newspaper biz consider it "a craft, much like a journeyman," where "generations within families" become newspapermen and newspaperwomen. This isn't to say that a freelancer can't break in; plenty do. But you must show respect for the medium and follow the age-old rules of this respected industry.

No News Is Good News

First off, don't expect to write a news story for a newspaper. Sound funny? Not really. Staff reporters write all the hard news because when it happens, you have to be there to cover it, write the story, and have it appear within 24 hours on the porches of patrons everywhere. As a freelancer, you don't have the ability to follow police scanners, arrive at fires, and tail politicians. Forget writing for the front page. Forget writing for the city section. Forget the sports pages, too. And most of all, forget the sections where a columnist or staff writer rules the roost.

Like Way Trendy

Instead, look for trends in the news and formulate a feature story idea for the lifestyle section. Features editors want to ride the wave of hot news stories and expound upon them. Perhaps you saw several broadcasts recently about women with advanced degrees opting to stay home with their children. Moreover, you know of five live sources you could talk to for the article. You may be on to a trend. Or maybe you were one of the first to realize the burgeoning Beanie Baby frenzy. You saw a trend that could've been your story in the lifestyle section of the local paper.

Although staff may write some of these trend-oriented features, they don't write them all. Sometimes an editor can't afford to lose a reporter to the hours of phone time and footwork that such features require. That's when they turn to the freelancer. Randles gave us a great example of an editor turning to a freelancer to cover the "big" story. Not big like *war* big or *Michael Jordan* big. We mean literally big—as in the biggest bra, burger, bus, and bunny in town. Tracking down the big boys took time, time that a reporter would need to devote to harder news and regular department writing.

Local Yokel

Another angle to consider when pitching a story to a newspaper is the local angle. Local papers require local angles. Don't pitch the story on highly educated women leaving the boardroom for the baby's room if you can't produce at least four to five local sources to interview from. Obviously, if you talk *USA Today* into the story, they'll want sources from around the 50 states.

Pique This

Many newspapers also include advertising-driven interest sections. These special-interest magazine-like inserts can cover myriad areas—real estate, entertainment, beauty, home decorating, bridal, and gardening. Watch for these publications. A city newspaper may offer up to 140 or more of these sections a year. Whether the sections are produced depends entirely on whether advertisers buy space. But once advertisers buy the space, editors assign stories to their small—extremely small, perhaps nonexistent—staff. These editors look for interesting pieces to put in the insert. Be forewarned, however—not all editors hold to the same high editorial standards for these inserts that they do for the paper proper.

If I Were a Rich Man

Now we have to talk about something important. Okay, yes, we've avoided it, but it's important nevertheless: money. The truth of the matter is that newspapers pay very little compared to magazines. That's partly because a tradition exists for paying your dues within the business, and partly because the budgets just aren't there to support freelance pieces. Heck, cub reporters on staff barely make enough to survive.

Remember those advertising-driven inserts? Randles told us that her budget for freelance pieces when she edited an insert didn't exceed $200. A freelancer might receive $75 for a bridesmaid checklist and informational piece within the bridal insert. Thirty-inch column features for the lifestyle section— like the really big story mentioned previously— garner a tad more, in the low hundreds. But before you scream "Chump change!" consider the intrinsic benefits of writing for newspapers.

Dead Lines

If you want your story canned and your body strapped to the press, argue with the copyeditor over cutting words from a newspaper feature you've written. Space translates to ink and paper, which all costs money. Moreover, time means money, too. Copyeditors on papers typically must prepare up to 40 stories in four hours for print in the next edition. So, turn in the cleanest, tightest copy you've ever written, or buck up and lose some of your baby!

R-E-S-P-E-C-T

Like it or not, the newspaper business prides itself on exceptional journalism. Newspaper people (reporters, editors) tend to have a we're-better-than-magazines-and-television attitude. It's a snobby attitude, as if we're talking journalism vs. pop (TV) journalism. Granted, newspapers have a long tradition—who can argue? In good papers, you receive the real goods—hard news and investigative reporting. So, although a snobby attitude exists, it possibly is warranted.

You can't imagine the benefit of a clip from a respected newspaper. Here's where it benefits the freelancer. Different newspaper groups—Scripps, Gannett, and McClatchy, for starters—all know what papers rock and what papers don't. Even a clip from the *Sacramento Bee,* a small California paper compared to the *LA Times,* commands respect for you as a writer within the newspaper biz. An editor at the *Chicago Tribune* won't sneeze at the clip because the McClatchy papers possess a reputation for excellence. Magazines also look highly upon good newspaper clips, although the reverse isn't necessarily true. There goes that snobby attitude again.

With all this said, just understand that you won't make a living freelancing solely for papers. Look upon your newspaper clips as a few extra hundred bucks or so a month and a collection of prestigious clips for your writing portfolio. Often you might not even make any money, but you'll get paid in copies. Your real pay, however, remains your byline in the respected paper.

There are other good sides to newspaper writing besides the byline and the clips. First, because a newspaper turns around every day, payment arrives quickly—typically within 10 days! It's fast cash. Also, when you earn credibility as a freelancer for a paper, you may just find yourself offered a staff position in the future.

Great Ways to Get Inky Without Squeezing a Squid

According to several editors of papers and freelancers whose bylines appear frequently in newspapers, here are the newspaper departments you have the best chance of breaking in to as a freelancer:

➤ **Lifestyle section.** This is the place for those trend stories and timely essays. For instance, co-author Lynne earned a great newspaper clip in the prestigious *San Jose Mercury News* by writing an essay during the spring on gardening with her grandfather in the Silicon Valley as a child. She received pay only in the byline and copies, but it was well worth it, she says. "When people see my clip from the paper, they respect the clean writing and the reputation," Lynne says. "I always include it with any pitches." Pitch trend stories, but submit essays.

➤ **Opinion/editorial.** The editors of this section buy only a smattering of freelance offerings a year but are always on the lookout for compelling pieces. You must submit the completed opinion piece.

➤ **Neighborhood inserts included in the paper.** These sections are staff-written for the most part, but editors do look for personal and human-interest pieces devoted to the suburbs within large metropolitan areas. Sometimes they offer "My Story" departments and will pay a minimal amount for each one they publish. Or, you might offer to write an interesting column each week. A broadcast reporter Lynne knows from the NBC affiliate in Sacramento, Tim Hererra, wanted to try his hand at print journalism and pitched a couple column ideas to the neighborhood insert of the *Sacramento Bee*. Hererra now frequently writes a "Dad" column for the suburban addition to the paper.

➤ **Advertising-driven inserts.** Keep your eyes peeled for these sections, which pop up regularly in papers. Better yet, call the advertising department and ask what sections are slated to appear. Perhaps you wrote a great massage therapy article that might fit in a beauty and salon insert.

The Straight Scoop

The Associated Press (AP) remains the oldest and most respected press organization in the world. Begun in May 1848 when 10 men representing six highly competitive New York newspapers met to discuss pooling resources to collect the latest news from Europe, the Associated Press now boasts 48 Pulitzer Prizes, provides up-to-the-minute stories across wires from around the world, and dictates the style that journalists adhere to in their writing. To find out more about the organization, go online to www.ap.org. You'll also find an order form for the journalist's bible, *The Associated Press Stylebook and Libel Manual*. Word to the wise: If you don't own one, buy one.

Let Your Fingers Do the Pitching

Remember earlier when we emphasized the importance of pitching your ideas to magazines in writing? Throw that advice out the window when pitching ideas to a newspaper. Above all, newspaper articles must be timely, so sending a pitch in writing wastes precious time for everyone. Chances are that someone will "scoop you" if you don't push the buttons on the phone and call the editor today with the idea. That's right—we said, "Call!" This sense of urgency is unique to newspapers.

Here's what you do:

1. When you get the editor on the phone, say, "First, let me ask if this is a convenient time to talk with you." With the time crunches constantly propelling newspaper editors to put those sections on your porch by 5 A.M. the next day, he'll appreciate the courtesy—especially when he must say, "No." You'll ingratiate yourself for a subsequent call, as he's likely to remember the polite journalist who understood his crazy schedule.

2. When the editor responds with, "Yes, I have a minute," introduce yourself and offer the trend you've been noticing or a brief—*brief*—description of your piece. Include the number of sources you can line up and offer to send clips. If the editor shows an interest, he'll ask for a proposed lead, perhaps an outline, the sources listed, and the clips—probably faxed to him within hours. Make sure you send clips showcasing succinct and pithy writing that adheres to AP standards.

That's it. And that's another benefit of the newspaper's hectic pace: No waiting for weeks on end to hear from the editor. You'll typically know within a day if your idea works for the publication.

So call with those story ideas. Comment on trends that deserve an article. Fax over a lead, and you may find yourself writing for the papers.

The Straight Scoop

The Newspaper Association of America, NAA Foundation, and the American Society of Newspaper Editors join with their international counterparts, The World Association of Newspapers and the International Press Institute, to promote World Press Freedom Day every year on the anniversary of the Windhoek Declaration (May 3, 1991). On that day, a statement of principles was written in Southern Africa by publishers, editors, and journalists from throughout the African continent to preserve and extend freedom of the press around the world. Each spring, the NAA distributes a package that includes opinion pieces from leading press freedom advocates from around the world, a copy of the Charter for a Free Press, and a variety of quotations on press freedom.

The Least You Need to Know

➤ The newspaper business is the mother of all mass media; it demands and deserves respect for its rich role in our history.

➤ Your best chance of breaking into a newspaper is at the local level with a timely, trend-oriented piece.

➤ Make sure that you adhere to AP stylebook rules. You can't write for the newspapers without this foundation of expertise.

➤ Don't expect big bucks from newspaper gigs. Instead, look upon the work as the garnering of prestigious, respected clips and possibly fast-food money for the month.

➤ Only in the world of newspaper writing is it acceptable to call, rather than write, the editor with a quick, rehearsed pitch that offers at least four sources.

Chapter 12

The Glossies: What They're Looking For

In Chapter 11, "Newspapers: What They're Looking For," we looked at newspapers—their history, how to break in, what works, and what doesn't work. In this chapter, we explore the *glossies,* the large circulation consumer-interest magazines. We also look at the glossy gods that run them—the editors. Take a peek at the history behind the advertising-driven, lifestyle-enhancing, celebrity-profiling publications that you want to write for. Learn what editors want and what will get you drop-kicked out the door.

Flash in the Pan: A History and Overview

When did all this glitz and glamour begin? One thing is for sure: Americans have embraced magazines since the 1700s. Readers have been loyal to *The Saturday Evening Post* for more than 270 years now. *Harper's* magazine debuted in 1850 with a print run of

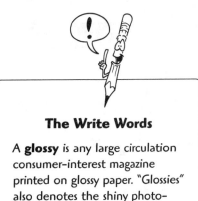

The Write Words

A **glossy** is any large circulation consumer-interest magazine printed on glossy paper. "Glossies" also denotes the shiny photographic prints used for sharp reproduction.

7,500, grew to 50,000 within six months, and introduced Americans to great writers such as Horatio Alger, Stephen A. Douglas, Mark Twain, and Jack London. From flappers and jazzers reading *Vanity Fair* in the roaring '20s to your mother enjoying Betsey McCall in your grandmother's copy of the popular women's magazine *McCalls,* generations continue to subscribe and love magazines. Just how many out there couldn't live without *Sports Illustrated?*

You get the point. Magazines invaded our land a long time ago and took hold. Could *The Saturday Evening Post* have launched a thousand ships? Yes. Now it's time to launch your career as a magazine writer.

A Mag Is Born

Each year thousands of new magazines hit the newsstands. Some magazines launch with the backing of big bucks, like the Tina Brown entry, *Talk.* Others enter the glossy arena with little more than a personal loan from an uncle. The amount of upfront money doesn't necessarily make or break the magazine. A magazine's survival depends upon a sustainable market within a specialized community. Magazines sell lifestyle and strive to keep their fingers on the pulse of groups of people.

The Straight Scoop

The Top Ten Magazine Categories, according to the Magazine Publishers of America, are ...

1. Business and industry
2. Health
3. Education
4. Computers
5. Travel
6. Regional interest
7. Automotive
8. Entertainment
9. Lifestyle
10. Women's interests

Advertisers win with this arrangement. Let's look at *Sail* magazine. Who reads *Sail*? People who love to feel the wind on their faces and taste the saltwater in the air, who want information on technique and how-to. Advertisers of boat equipment and gear companies can target accurately within the pages of *Sail,* with no wasted circulation, an attractive prospect. Thus, *Sail* gets revenue from the advertisers and stays afloat in world of 1,000 launches a year.

It's a simple concept, but one no freelancer should underestimate. Cat people read *Cat Fancy.* Craft people read *Martha Stewart Living.* As a freelancer, your job is not just to be aware of your audience, but also to analyze the personality that the magazine hopes to encapsulate on glossy paper.

What's Happening to Our World?

Merrill Panitt, a longtime editorial director for *TV Guide* (always a top magazine in terms of circulation), once said, "Magazines are creative work. You can't put a scale or measure to what or how a magazine is created. It's all in the creative world of its editors and publishers."

A creative world, yes. But it's also a world that follows the trends of the time to meet the needs of a variable, and even eccentric, society. So what are the trends in magazines lately? According to Dr. Samir Husni (a.k.a. Mr. Magazine), who every year wades through the thousands of emerging magazines and analyzes them in an annual guide, magazines relevant to baby boomers, such as *Bride Again* (focusing on remarriage and the encore bride); family heritage publications, such as *Family Tree Magazine;* and teen glossies, such as *Cosmo Girl,* top the magazine marketplace.

Here Today, Gone Tomorrow

Just because a magazine starts out with gusto is no guarantee that it will survive. True, an average of 10 new magazine titles launch every week, all aimed at filling a per-ceived void or need among consumers and covering topics ranging from cooking to computers to media personalities to music. Still, many magazines close each year.

In 1998, for instance, the revered and irreverent *Spy* magazine shut down, among countless others. And though some titles reemerge with new publishers—*BBW* (*Big Beautiful Woman*) reappeared in late 1999 after shutting down presses in July 1998, and venerable magazines *Vanity Fair* and *Life* have also had their experiences with shutting down and restarting—more don't.

All That Glitters Isn't Gold: What the Glossy Gods Want

Now that you know a little about the history of glossies and can tell others over cock-tails about the diversity of publications fitting "niche" audiences and advertisers, what about what the editorial gods want from you, the writer? Isn't that why you bought this book, for goodness' sake? It is. So let's get down to it.

The Straight Scoop

Looking for new launches? Interested in magazine trends? Then check out www.mr-magazine.com, the Web site of Dr. Samir Husni. His definitive annual *Guide to New Consumer Magazines* can be ordered from the site as well.

In a nutshell, the editor wants a writer who can deliver the lifestyle that the magazine's readers aspire to and can translate that lifestyle in the articles she writes. Translation: Write what the editor wants because it's what the reader wants.

To convey the personality of the magazine, you have to do several things. All these things help the editor. In fact, consider everything you do from here on out in servitude to the god or goddess within the editorial office that houses the magazine for which you want to write.

Pick a Magazine, Any Magazine

Your first step to determining what an editor wants is finding the editor. So, pick a magazine, any magazine. What magazine do you want to write for? Heck, pick two that you've got ideas in mind for. Got them? Good. Keep them in mind.

Stack 'Em and Rack 'Em

Ever roam the stacks at a university library? Ever sit with one of those old bound books full of back issues of old magazines? If you haven't, do it. Go to your nearest local university or college, and look up the earliest issues of the magazine you just chose. Scrutinize the fonts, the articles, the advertisements, and the editor's page. Study the evolution of the magazine from its beginning to its present-day "voice." Know the magazine like an old friend.

We know. We've told you this before, but it bears retelling. You can never "know" the magazine too well. We recommend going back 12 issues (at least 6) and studying the content. Commit the covers to memory. Think we're going overboard? Don't. Not one editor we spoke with appreciated a pitch from a writer unfamiliar with the magazine. Editor's know—by the tone, by the inappropriate topic for their publication, and by many other things—when a "generic" pitch was sent. And you won't receive an assignment from a generic pitch.

138

Exam Time

Now that you've studied the magazines, ask yourself several questions about the titles you've chosen:

➤ Is the tone conversational? Formal? Analytical?

➤ What age group does this writing most appeal to?

➤ Do the writers use first person, third person, or both in their articles?

➤ Are the articles information- or entertainment-based?

➤ What are the lengths of the features and the departments?

➤ Who are the major advertisers?

➤ Most important, can you see your article within the publication's pages?

Now armed with the information gleaned from these questions, it's time to pitch.

The Straight Scoop

Go online to www.magazine.org, the official site of Magazine Publishers of America. You'll find the latest news about the business; calendars of seminars, trade shows, and conferences; awards; resources (such as hotlinks, guidelines, and fact sheets); newsletters; and sales information. We highly recommend checking out this site to stay current about the glossies if you intend to write for them.

Curve Ball, Knuckle Ball, Change Up, Fast Ball, Slider, Fork Ball—Pitch!

Fact: Editors want great pitch letters. If your pitch comes in like a Sandy Kaufax fastball, you'll blow your editor away. Knowing the magazine inside and out will better prepare you to write that winning, innovative pitch that catches an editor's eye. We know. We've discussed this before. But hey, it's too important not to drive home again. Glossy gods want great pitches. A great pitch can't be written without understanding the personality of the magazine. So you can either wear the uniform or turn in your gear. Case closed.

Going Up: In the Door and Up the Elevator

Congratulations! Your pitch garnered your first glossy assignment. Now what—besides writing the gosh darn thing? This section answers how to ingratiate yourself with the editors and gain a better chance of having the great assignments thrown your way. Wouldn't it be nice to have an editor call you and ask, "Would you be interested in writing ...?" It can happen.

Meet with the Editors

One of the best ways to become a "frequent contributor" remains building a rapport with the editors. Very simply, drop an editor you've worked with recently a note with a cool clip they might not have seen—without a pitch for a story! Or, even better, if you find yourself in the same town as the editorial office of the magazine, offer to take the editor out to lunch. Give the editor a face to the voice and the words. During lunch, pick the editor's brain. Let the conversation orbit the editor. What is he interested in seeing in the magazine? What is her vision? How did he get his start? What advice does she have?

Dead Lines

When your great idea garners an assignment with a glossy, don't go pitch a similar story to its direct competition; for instance, don't pitch and accept a story at *Child* if you've already been assigned the same thing at *Parenting*. Have some loyalty! That's not to mention that neither the competition nor the original magazine to which you pitched the assignment will be pleased to learn that they're carrying the same editorial content within a month or so of each other, courtesy of you!

Yes, Sir, Thank You, Sir

Make yourself available for assignments. Don't refuse assignments right away—unless, of course, you truly believe that you can't handle the subject. Otherwise, tackle anything the editor throws your way and prove yourself. Say, "Yes." Then say, "Thank you."

Hurry Up!

Turn around your initial work for a glossy quickly, cleanly, and accurately. Build a reputation as a fast writer and a good writer. Lots of writers can write well. Differentiate yourself as the writer who writes well and quickly—without sacrificing precision.

Johnny on the Spot Meets Girl Friday

When you acquire a reputation as a writer that an editor can depend on to provide good copy quickly, chances are that the editor will call upon you to "fix" a botched article or turn around something under a crunch. You've arrived. Smile and live up to your reputation. You are now a commodity—a hot commodity.

The Straight Scoop

For more than three decades, the ratio of advertising pages to editorial pages of magazines on average has not changed. Fully 50 percent of glossy magazines are composed of advertising, while the other 50 percent encompass articles and editorial content.

Think about it. You not only provide the magazine with great ideas, but you also fix things and make them right in the hectic, fast-paced world of publishing. When you take a little of the burden off the overburdened editor, you're on your way to writing your ticket as a freelancer. You've gotten in the door, up the elevator, into the office, and into the break room, too. Enjoy.

Stalkers Will Be Prosecuted: Ten Ways to Turn Off an Editor in Seconds

Okay, now you really, really know what editors want. We've practically beaten it into you in the span of several chapters. But what do they hate? There are ways to turn off an editor completely to you as a writer. Avoid the following 10 items like the plague to ensure your success as a freelancer:

1. **Be a stalker**. That's what editors call writers who pester them about story ideas, upcoming events, anything. These writers "stalk" the magazine in an attempt to break in. Continue these tactics, and you'll have to break *out*—of jail!

2. **Misspell the editor's name in a pitch**. Editors say that misspelling their name is a sure sign that you'll be sloppy on the research and content of any article you're assigned. After all, you didn't care enough about accuracy to check out the proper spelling of their name.

3. **Write longer than the assigned word count**. Do this deed, and plan on not having another assignment from the magazine. Editors hate it when you 1) don't follow directions, and 2) expect them to cut your wordy rough drafts down to size.

4. **Don't meet deadlines**. Nothing more needs to be said here. Meet your deadlines or be doomed.

5. **Balk at editorial changes or edits to copy.** Hey, you're not the boss. Trust that the editor or copyeditor knows best. After all, they exist to make your article better.

6. **Tell an editor what she should do regarding the content of the magazine.** Just don't.

7. **Turn in a different article than what was assigned and developed on the assignment sheet.** Again, the editor wants what the reader wants. It's your job to please them both.

8. **Pester the editor with numerous, unnecessary phone calls about the assignment.** Editors don't want to hold your hand.

9. **Don't call with genuinely important questions.** Editors would rather have you ask a question than guess wrong and turn in something they can't use.

10. **Send a pitch without a SASE.** Don't do it if you want to get a response.

The Least You Need to Know

➤ Magazines sell a lifestyle and appeal to people's desire to be someone or belong to some group.

➤ Your job as the writer is to deliver through your articles the image and information the editor strives to evoke and exhibit.

➤ Thoroughly research the magazines for which you want to write.

➤ Build a reputation with an editor that you can turn around an article quickly and accurately in the voice of the magazine.

➤ Don't stalk the editor, misspell a name in a pitch, write too long, miss your deadline, balk at copyediting changes, tell an editor what to do, turn in something the editor didn't ask for, pester the editor with questions, neglect to ask the editor *good* questions, or forget to send a SASE.

Chapter 13

Trade Magazines: What They're Looking For

Welcome to the approachable world of what you just might know like the back of your hand—trade magazines! If consumer glossies serve the general reading public, trade journals serve focused groups of professionals. It might be helpful to think of the glossies as the "civilian" style of magazine and the trade journal as the more specialized "Army" type of publication. So strap on your boots and press your fatigues, because we're going to lead you through the obstacle course to some of the best writing gigs out there. You'll learn why the trade magazine's smaller staffs mean work for you. You'll also learn why trade publications can prove more open to new writers and why their editors could be more open to your calls. Attention!

The Army Wants You!

You won't find trade publications displayed among the racks of glossies in the super-market checkout line. Publisher's Clearing House won't offer you a subscription to them, either. Though packed full of information and employing outstanding journal-ism, the trade magazines aren't aimed at the general population. Trade magazines—technical journals, professional journals, they go by many names—appeal to specific groups. These are the magazines of doctors, dancers, and executive directors. Salon managers, salespeople, and school teachers all read their respective professional magazines to stay on the cutting edge of their industries.

Perhaps you never knew that a world of magazines outside of general consumer pub-lications existed. Well, it does. You might even read one monthly at work but have not considered the possibility of writing for it. With the nature of the publication, a misconception persists that the magazines are only staff-written. This assumption per-sists for many reasons. First, because the readers of trade magazines are a specialized group, it might seem that the magazine would staff only a few writers specializing in the field. Or, you might think that perhaps a smaller publication with a circulation a fraction of the size of a glossy can't afford freelancers. Finally, these magazines don't rest on the checkout stand rack next to the myriad magazines that we all want to write for. We know they hire freelancers. But those out-of-sight publications? Who knows whether they hire freelancers? Well, they do, and they probably offer you a better chance at a byline than *Modern Maturity* or *Rolling Stone*.

The Straight Scoop

The Washington Post Company not only owns the revered *Post, Newsweek* magazine, and several broadcast stations, but it also owns the Dearborn Publishing Group, Inc. Dearborn, a publisher and provider of licensing training for securities, insurance, and real-estate pro-fessionals and Post-Newsweek Business Information, also produces several trade magazines and trade shows.

What Do You Know?

Many freelancers earn bread-and-butter bucks by writing for trade publications. One of co-author Lynne's first articles appeared in *AirBeat,* the journal of the Airborne Law Enforcement Association. The article was about a new surveillance aircraft. Lynne is neither pilot nor peace officer, so the idea required some research. For other writers, an article in a trade magazine could be as easy as pulling information from the recesses of their own brains. For instance, consider the elementary school teacher who aspires to freelance write. She might pitch a story to *Wonderful Ideas,* a professional journal for elementary school teachers that offers great ideas to use in the classroom. The teacher's years of experience make her the perfect candidate to pen an article or two.

The Straight Scoop

You might be asked to provide your article one of several ways—on disk, electronically, or as a hard copy. Most editors now ask for your assigned article submission on a floppy disk or as an attachment electronically via e-mail. It's faster than receiving a hard copy in the mail, and no one has to retype the manuscript.

Don't Pigeonhole Yourself

Don't pigeonhole yourself into writing for only the technical or trade journals that match up with your past career path. *Writer's Market* lists more than 100 pages of trade magazine opportunities. Sit down on a slow afternoon and go listing by listing through *Writer's Market.* Read the guidelines of each magazine and conjure an article idea that you could write for the journal. You'll probably be surprised. Who'd have thought that your brother-in-law, an engineer for Boeing, may prove the perfect profile for *Military Space,* a biweekly newsletter covering space technology?

Another great place to look for different trade journals is the *Columbia Journalism Review* site that we've mentioned in previous chapters. Just double-click on Magazines on the home page listing to the left. You'll find yourself at a search page. Enter a category of magazines—like entertainment or teaching—and list the magazine category as "trade" in the box under the search box. Pages upon pages of trade publications will appear, listing the phone numbers, addresses, and even Web sites for each journal. Just like you've got a million and one ideas for the consumer glossies, you'll find as many ideas for the pages of trade publications, too.

What the Trades Buy

Now that we've reviewed the many categories and publications under the trade umbrella, just what the heck do they want? Well, really, they want the same thing that the glossy consumer mags want—to serve their readers. But whereas consumer magazines appeal to a lay population of people, trade journals often require a level of technical expertise in the writing. The trades buy just about anything and everything that pertains to their readers and offers their readers information. The formula is the same here as with consumer glossies. It's all about the reader, and these magazines remain intent on helping and maneuvering their readers through their many careers with success.

The Straight Scoop

Just as many consumer magazines fall under one larger publishing umbrella—like Hearst or Condé Nast—several publishing groups cater to the trade magazine community. One of the biggest trade journal publishers is Intertec, a division of Primedia. Intertec publishes 90 magazines, supplements, and newsletters on professional subjects ranging from real estate to retail, to rescue, and everything in between; it supports more than 3.8 million subscribers. Check out either the Primedia Web site at www.k3.com or Intertec's Web site at www.intertec.com.

We hate to sound like a harpy here, but study your *Writer's Market* and research the magazine. The only way you'll learn about the specifics of what kinds of articles the trade magazines require is by doing the same thing you did with the consumer magazines.

Call the journal. Although trade editors often are equally as busy as their consumer counterparts, they are generally more approachable. You'll probably find it refreshing to talk with them about the writing possibilities at their publication. Just go into the phone call having immersed yourself in the magazine. Talk the talk from the confident standpoint of knowledge.

Getting Your Foot in the Door

Because trade editors are typically more receptive to phone calls, convincing the trade editor could prove less intimidating than convincing an editor at, say, *Self*—as long as you've got a great idea that's factually based and that fits the magazine. Finding strong writers with an interest in a narrow field of topics isn't easy. Trade editors diligently look for unique ideas. When you call a trade editor up expressing an interest in the magazine and professional area of expertise and offering a great idea to fill the pages of the magazine and better inform the professional he serves, well, you've just made his day easier. Couple your sound journalistic skills with your enthusiasm, and guess what? You may find yourself on assignment for a trade magazine.

In fact, Perry Bradley, Editor-in-Chief of *Business and Commercial Aviation*, told us that the ability to write is a good starting point, but even more important is "subject-matter knowledge, an ability to report, knowledge of the conventions of journalism, and enthusiasm" in garnering an assignment with his high-end, glossy trade. "You'd be amazed at the number of freelancers who don't show any enthusiasm," laments the veteran editor and pilot. Speaking personally, but echoing what we've heard editors say over and over again, Bradley also told us that he looks for "writers who do their homework and take the time to understand the audience our magazine serves and the type of stories [*Business and Commercial Aviation* runs]."

Who You Know

What do all the career counselors tell you is the most important thing in landing a job? Networking, right? Well, then doesn't it make sense that you need to network within the fields of trade publications if you want to publish in them? In trade magazines, you might be able to earn an assignment by establishing relationships with insiders. Heck, Lynne will come clean now about the *AirBeat* article. Her father just happened to manage the air program that used the unique surveillance craft. He is also a member of the Airborne Law Enforcement Association. Lynne took the cool idea, researched the plane, and then networked her way to the writing gig. (Something Lynne admits now that she should have done in this situation, however, was use a *pseudonym,* as her father—same last name—is quoted in the article.)

Dead Lines

Even though you need to possess a level of expertise on the subject you're covering, don't think for a second that you're the professor and acquire a cocky attitude—especially during interviews. Keep in mind that many of your readers and most of your sources know a heck of a lot more than you could hope to know on the subject. You're the reporter, not the professor. Be prepared, but be humble, too. Use your knowledge to inform and enhance the article, not to dominate it.

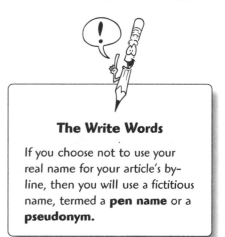

The Write Words

If you choose not to use your real name for your article's byline, then you will use a fictitious name, termed a **pen name** or a **pseudonym.**

Perry Bradley recommends trade shows as the best networking opportunity for writers. You'll come in contact with insiders within the industry, increase your source pool, and place yourself as a writer in the center of the action.

The Straight Scoop

Trade journal writing might make you a global commodity. Because of the service-oriented nature of the publications, many possess readers and advertisers overseas and are true international magazines. *Business and Commercial Aviation,* for instance, boasts a third of its subscribers outside the United States. Even *Today's Image,* a tanning industry mag, sends copies outside the United States to readers. So, go ahead, feel like Fitzgerald and Hemingway. Rub elbows with the international crowd. Write for a trade journal.

I'll Call You

The power of the phone call works with trade magazines as a networking tool, too. You don't have to call these guys with a pitch. Remember how Mom told you to show an interest in your date and ask about his day, his work, and his life? Mom's advice applies to trade editors, too. They genuinely appreciate when someone shows an interest in their area of expertise, whether it's pet supplies or waste management. So, don't be afraid to call and discuss the magazine's article needs and throw yourself out as a writer looking to add fresh ideas and fresh blood to the publication. Just remember to inquire whether your call comes at a good time. A good way to begin the conversation? "Hi, Mr. Bradley, I'm a freelancer hoping to talk to you about writing opportunities with your publication. But before I begin, let me ask, have I caught you at a deadline or an inconvenient time?" By asking the preceding question, you tell the editor that you appreciate his busy schedule. Most likely, he'll lend you his ear, and if he's busy, you'll hang up with a good time to call back.

The Best Things in Life Aren't Free

So you've snagged an article with a trade? Now the most obvious questions pertain to money. Not to burst your bubble here, but few trade journals possess the budgets of national, consumer glossies. Relatively few pay $1 per word or more for a feature of 2,000 words. Some, including *Managed Care, A Guide for Physicians* and *Commercial Investment Real Estate,* do, however. More pay anywhere from $150 to $1,500 for a 2,000-word feature. And plenty pay nominal sums of up to $150 or make payment in copies. But like the newspapers, look to the trades to earn your first clips—some great, detailed, journalistically sound, impressive clips. Moreover, build up your contacts, and you could make a goodly sum each month on trade writing.

Q&A with Amy Hamaker, Executive Editor, *Today's Image*

Amy Hamaker rose up through the trade ranks. She began her editing career as an editorial staffer (a.k.a. Private First-Class) and over her five years at Creative Age Publications rose to executive editor. She now runs the show for Today's Image *magazine, a trade journal for the tanning industry. Here's the inside information she gave us about freelancing in the trades.*

Q: What do you enjoy most about your job?

A: I probably enjoy networking with the different people in the industry the best. You really get to know the personalities within the industry when you work for a trade. I also like learning new things. You get to know subjects in depth because it's really focused.

> **Dead Lines**
>
> Granted, one of the best ways in the door of a trade mag is skill in the job area, an expertise. Don't ever lie about your expertise to pump up a pitch, however. If you're not the Glass King of Queens, don't tell the editor of *US Glass, Metal, and Glazing* that you are. It's guaranteed that when he starts talking technical, you'll prove yourself *glassless* and right out the door!

Q: What do you enjoy the least?

A: In trade publishing, it's a delicate balance of readers and advertisers. With consumer books, advertising comes from a broad base. With trade, you're more closed in. Battles can occur over what the reader wants and [what] the advertisers [want]. I don't like that. But I'm also really lucky with *Today's Image*. I haven't come across those battles. So far, so good. [*Today's Image* had recently been sold to Creative Age, and Hamaker took on editorship in September 1999.]

Q: Describe your typical day.

A: The pace is pretty fast. It's my job to not only plan what is going on, but also to do the nuts and bolts, everyday work. My staff is only about $1^1/_2$, and I produce about 60 to 70 pages of editorial each month. That's why I depend so much on freelancers. My typical day usually involves editing a story, proofing pages from galleys, scouring on-line sources for information, assigning articles to freelancers, and approving or finding artwork for subsequent issues. It's busy.

Q: What do you look for in new freelancers?

A: I look for people who send writing samples ... a cover letter or a query letter ... because I know that clips have been edited by someone else. I want to see the clips, too. The query letter should show an understanding of our readers and our subject. Then, if the writer seems like a fit, I have to know whether they'll work within my budget.

Q: Can you give an example of an article you'll be assigning, the pay, what you expect the writer to do, and what you may provide as help?

A: For example, for the April issue, I'm running a story on choosing independent contractors over staff in a salon. The tanning salon owner may choose to contract space out to someone who does nails, for instance. Independent contractors are prevalent in the business. The article will deal with renting space, the legal differences between someone on staff and a contractor. Those legal differences could get our readers in trouble. I could assign that story to a freelancer. The length should fall between 2,000 and 2,500 words. Any shorter, and I'll have trouble filling the book. I would generally pay $300 to $500, depending upon the subject matter, sources, thought necessary, and footwork. I would generally try to give as many sources as I could. I might know of a tanning salon. I would also include information on the tanning industry. I try to give at least a month's notice from deadline.

Q: Even though it's great to have industry knowledge, it sounds like you'd take a strong writer and journalist over someone who knows the industry?

A: Generally, yes. Subject matter competence I can help fill in.

Q: What do you look for in a pitch letter?

A: A great pitch letter tells me who the writer is and what experience he or she might have. The letter tells me about the story idea and how it relates to my industry. I used to work on NailPro, and someone sent us a pitch letter meant to be a funny story about going into a "Little Shop of Horrors" to get your nails done. Obviously, the writer didn't know our audience—the salon owners. Trade magazines are highly specialized. A writer needs to show that she knows the audience in the pitch.

Although Hamaker listed the standard things that freelancers shouldn't do—such as miss deadlines without telling the editor what's up—she ended our conversation saying, "The most valuable freelancers to me are those who send me story ideas … freelancers that keep in contact with me and help me shape ideas are an enormous help. I depend upon good relationships with freelancers. It's like having a second staff."

The Straight Scoop

Don't fear the professional certification, education, or badge behind a trade magazine if you've got a great story to pitch. Writer and teacher Tamara Givens achieved her first published clip by pitching *The Highway Patrolman*, the journal of the California Highway Patrol, and a story about Friday Night Live, a high school program emphasizing teen sobriety and responsibility. Givens was the program sponsor. The editor not only paid Givens pretty well for her smart article, but she also paid the school yearbook photographer for his pictures!

The Least You Need to Know

➤ Trade magazines cater to professionals in most every area and seek articles backed with knowledge of the subject area.

➤ Like everything in the business world, networking plays a key role in garnering the trade gigs. Attend the trade shows and talk to people in the industry.

➤ As in the consumer glossies, know your publication and know the reader. In a word: research.

➤ Though few trade pubs pay big bucks, many offer reasonable pay and great clip opportunities.

➤ Because many trade publication staff size is limited, trade editors really appreciate and depend on the great ideas and dedication of their freelancers.

Part 4

Online: The Newest Frontier

The Web is one big writer's market. What do Web sites need more of all the time? WORDS! And you know how to write them. So learn what you need to know in order to take your old-fashioned writing skills out into this bold new world. Who are the big players, and what kind of material do they buy? How can you get them to notice you? And best of all—who pays what, and when?

Chapter 14

What's on the Web

For 13 chapters you've read about the world of print publications. Sure, sometimes we've tossed in a quick reference to the onscreen world of the Web, but for the most part we've been talking about paper publications. This is the old-fashioned kind you can read on the bus and crumple up before you toss 'em in the trash—magazines and newspapers.

But, hey, you're well-informed. You're on top of things. You know that the biggest thing to happen at the end of the last millennium was the development of the World Wide Web. So when are we gonna get down to business and tell you how to develop your freelance career online?

Answer: Right now!

Welcome to Web World

Make no mistake—the online world has come of age. From its earliest days of geeky-looking type on a page to the real-time streaming video now available on some sites, the Web is officially where it's at. And it is where you as a writer need to be, too.

Let's look to see what kinds of folks are on the Web and what they are doing there:

➤ **Women.** Women are on the Web in growing numbers, and countless sites cater to their interests and needs. What are women doing online? They're chatting with other women and reading about cooking, gardening, finance, hobbies, children, and all manner of other topics. Women are on the Web for networking and for community-building. Sites that target women, such as iVillage and women.com, now rank among the 50 most visited sites on the Web. And these are content-rich sites.

➤ **Seniors.** Older Americans are now logging on in record numbers, too. Folks over 55 now make up 7.5 percent of all Web users. And these are folks with very particular health needs, travel needs, and other special interests.

➤ **Travelers.** The Web is a veritable wonderland of information for folks on the go. Here people can learn about new destinations, search out bargain rates, and scope out fresh information from recently returned travelers. Some sites even have "Web cams" that let visitors actually see what is going on at a resort 24 hours a day! Web content targeted to travelers is a fast-growing area.

Everyone wants a special hub that speaks to their own needs. Mountain biking, European camping, wine, cigars—you name it and there's a Web site (and a loyal following) devoted to it.

Business-to-Business

"I love it!" says Priscilla Huff about writing for the Web. "And I definitely see the demand for writers growing." Huff writes about small business issues and is the iVillage home-based business expert. "I started out writing articles just on women's home business topics and have expanded to writing on small business in general. And now one other site wants me to write about home office technology. There is an ever-growing need for business-to-business content. It is a big market and getting bigger all the time." (*Business-to-business* refers to goods and services marketed directly to businesses instead of the general consumer market. Business-to-business commerce on the Web is predicted to dwarf general e-commerce in the coming years.)

So there are Web sites for women, seniors, men, business people, college students, self-employed folks, job seekers, gossip hounds, music fans—the list just goes on and on.

Dead Lines

Do *all* writers need to write for the Web now? Certainly not, but ignore this trend at your own peril. Just as professional writers once transitioned from typewriters to word processors, after a while, everybody did it. And the few who didn't looked like dinosaurs.

Why Web Sites Need Writers

In Chapter 2, "The Modern World of the Freelance Writer," we touched on the topic of the critical role that writers play in the success of Web sites.

Web sites are made up of two things: pictures and words. The pictures come from a Web designer, and the words come from a writer. Even e-commerce sites that are all about selling products are heavy on words. Take Amazon.com, which has descriptions of books, reviews of books, and articles about writers. That's words, words, and more words.

The success of a Web site depends primarily on one thing—the ability to get visitors to come back to the site. Repeat customer traffic is what it's all about. And once you have someone on your site (or *back* to your site), you want them to stay there and to spend time wandering from room to room, from one part of your site to another.

How do you get visitors to come to your site and stay? With content, pure and simple. Web sites need writers to do two different things:

➤ To develop the initial content that is found on a site

➤ To continually update and provide new material

You have to keep your visitors coming back with something new, compelling, and interesting. If your Web site looks the same every time, why would anyone come back again?

Ellen Reid Smith is an online marketing consultant who works with many big-name Web sites to help them improve their customer loyalty. Here's what she told us about the importance of written content to a commercial site: "It's all about selling something. An e-commerce site might also have articles their visitors could read in order to build context around the items they are selling so that they can sell more. For instance, on a health site, a visitor might read what looks like an article on arthritis that happens to use a particular product as a reference point. That's not quite as blatant as the *advertorial* approach that print magazines take, but the point is none the less to sell the product."

Dead Lines

The Web is all about what is new and fresh. And the way to keep it new and fresh is to constantly change the information on a Web site. You need to follow this dictum in your own writing life, too—keep your contacts, ideas, and style new and fresh.

The Write Words

A combination of editorial and advertising pitch is called **advertorial.** This is the sort of article that is always identified as "a special advertising section" at the top of the page. Advertorial looks and sounds just like the rest of the magazine, and is frequently written by the magazine's staff.

The Straight Scoop

Online columnist Nick Usborne writes a weekly column for the marketing site ClickZ.com. Here's his take on the role writing plays on the Web: "Sharing information will take words. To do it well will take the skilled use of words. And if you want those words to generate direct and immediate sales, the level of skill required takes a sharp turn upward. Right now, you can surf the Web and begin to separate the sites that recognize the value of words from those that don't."

"We've got to wrestle control of Web sites away from the geeks and place it in the hands (and pens) of writers," observes longtime freelancer Jim Brown. "Just because some Web design geek can make a logo spin around and throw flames on your screen doesn't mean that folks will come back to that Web site."

Brown is right. Dazzling as computer graphics can be, unless it is a computer game, the Web is all about words. The words come from writers like you.

The Straight Scoop

Even e-commerce sites use articles. In a recent *Wall Street Journal* article evaluating online jewelry sites, the highest-ranking site won not for the fancy earrings it sold, but for its content. "We liked the site's 'Luxury Reports' articles on gardening and real estate," the review read. And where would articles come from? Writers!

Just How Big Is This Market?

How big is this market? *Very* big. New sites open up at an astonishing rate. Unlike the time and expense involved in starting a new print publication, new online publications can get started quite inexpensively. And so they do, in record numbers. Most start small and cheap, and then hope to be discovered and go big like Nerve.com. (We'll take a close look at some of the players in the next chapter.)

Unlike paper publications or even daily newspapers, Web sites need to change their content continually. Thus, their need for freelance material is even more acute than for traditional publications.

Remember, it isn't only online publications that need fresh, fast material—commercial sites do as well.

The Straight Scoop

How can you keep up with all the new sites that debut? *The Industry Standard* is both a magazine and a Web site that focuses on the Internet community. You can find in-depth news about start-ups, failures, and high-tech trends. Find it on the newsrack or online at thestandard.com.

Shameless Commerce Division

Commercial sites that sell some sort of service (as opposed to publications totally devoted to articles) need help from writers, too.

Jennifer and her husband, Peter, are under contract to develop content for a large women's financial site that is currently in the pre-launch phase. "This is not a publication in any sense," Jennifer says. "But these folks know that in order to compete with the other financial sites that are targeting women, they've got to have a content element that is both informative and fun to read." In addition to being paid to write, Jennifer and Peter have also been named to the site's editorial board.

"If you are doing enough work for a site, ask for some sort of title," Jennifer recommends. "Perhaps you could call yourself a weekly columnist or the senior content provider or the California correspondent. Any kind of credential can help you land your next online gig, and also help you look more professional to traditional print editors. I love telling editors that I am a weekly columnist for USAToday.com, or that I am on the editorial board of a major money site. It sounds so impressive."

Keep abreast of who is opening what by reading *The Industry Standard* or some other net-focused publications, and keep your ears open. It might sound far-fetched now—that someday you might find yourself developing original content for a brand new site under construction—but if that's what you go looking for, you'll find it.

Help Wanted

This all sounds great, but how are you going to find out who needs writers? In Chapter 17, "Build It and They Will Come," we give you the lowdown on the Web sites that will help you get freelance work. Does it surprise you that the information you need is on the Web?

Persnickety Editors

Freelancer Sally Richards found another way to make money on the Web: She edits other folks' work.

"I began looking for business sites such as corporate home pages that had obvious grammatical errors. I printed out those pages and made the needed corrections. Then I faxed the page and a cover letter to the business, explaining who I was and how I could help. I began charging $70 per hour." Sally set up an online merchant account so that even her clients's payments could be handled online. "I have my clients sign a contract, pay half up front, and make the rest due upon completion."

Could you do something like this? Just start visiting Web sites with your copyeditor's eye. The big guys won't be interested in your help, but plenty of mom-and-pop Web sites out there could use the services of a professional wordsmith.

By getting the word out about your copyediting services, you could also find yourself in the position of helping a new site develop original content. You just have to plunge in and see what you can find.

The Straight Scoop

"Freelance writers around the globe are realizing the financial opportunities available via the World Wide Web," freelancer Sally Richards asserts. "And I am a great testimony to that. My freelance income connected to writing on the Internet increased my bottom line by $30,000 in 1998." What's more, Richards says she never once sent out a packet with clips, mailed a disk, or even enclosed a SASE. It was all done with e-mail.

No Special Language Required

Do you have to know how to use *HTML* to write for the Web? Most often, no. You write and turn your work into the site's editor or producer, who then prepares it to appear on the Web.

You might want to learn a bit about HTML, though, if you plan to put up your own Web site as a way to develop your clips. We'll give you some examples in Chapter 18, "The Parts of the Article," of some unknowns (including a young guy named Matt Drudge) who turned themselves into writers and journalists overnight just by starting their own news sites. That's sort of a "let's sweep out the barn and put on a show" mentality.

The Write Words

HTML stands for Hypertext Markup Language, the computer coding by which text appears on a Web page.

Start on the Web and Move on to Print

In addition to unknown writers finding fame and fortune with their own Web sites, there are also many instances of freelance writers who used the Web to break into print publications. It was easier to get a break on the Web, and that gave them their first clips to send to print editors.

Mary Ellen (she doesn't use a last name) didn't even start out to be a writer. She just wanted to share some of the miraculous things that had happened in her life. So, she created an e-mail newsletter about the miracles that have happened to her and sent it to family and friends. Then they passed it on, and they passed it on ....

"After I'd been doing it for just a few weeks, I heard from a charity organization affiliated with The Artist Formerly Known as Prince," she says. "They asked if they could post my stuff on their site. Of course, I said yes. And then I heard from another big-name organization that wanted to do the same thing. Before you knew it, my site, www.angelscribe.com, was linked all over the Web. And then I heard from a book publisher! My first book, *Expect Miracles,* came out in 1999, and I am hard at work on a second." That's not bad for someone who never intended to write commercially, but just to share information with friends.

Building up a body of work online will help you get print work in one other way: You can easily e-mail your clips to editors at magazines. Jennifer uses her column on USAToday.com as a hook when e-mailing the editors of "land-based" publications looking for work. "I can easily attach a link that will take an editor straight from my e-mail message into my *USA Today* column. That's much easier than following up with a batch of clips in the mail."

What's Next?

Now that you have a better handle on this whole Web thing, what can you do with this newfound knowledge?

In the next chapter, we'll take a closer look at what kinds of publications exist on the Web and what kind of material editors are looking for. So try to stave off your urge to put down this book, and jump online to surf around. Read on!

The Least You Need to Know

➤ Both online publications and commercial sites need the services of writers.

➤ Writers do two things: develop initial content for new sites, and write updates and articles to keep sites updated.

➤ Developing original content for a new site pays more than writing an article for a Web publication.

➤ Writers also can find work online copyediting and improving existing Web sites.

➤ Once writers get online clips, they can use these to try to get print assignments.

Chapter 15

Online 'Zine Scene

In This Chapter

➤ Online 'zines: an overview

➤ The major online 'zines

➤ Does virtual writing pay actual money?

You should now be well and properly convinced that writing for the Web lies in your future. But just who *are* all these publications on the Web? Are the online magazines just electronic versions of the magazines you see at the newsstand, or are there publications that exist only in cyberspace? A little bit of both, actually. Let's start with the newbies—the cyber mags.

A Brief History of 'Zines

Who was the very first magazine to exist only on the Net? Them's fightin' words for many of the old-line *'zines,* the folks that have been out there since the mid-1990s.

The earliest online magazines were generally pretty scruffy affairs compared to the jazzy stuff on the screen nowadays—just plain text on the page. They were simple in structure and appealed to a very particular subgenre, in most cases. A 'zine might be aimed at the fans of Anne Rice or followers of particular punk bands, for example. The online 'zine scene was just a high-tech morph from the magazine scene in general.

Originally 'zines were called "fanzines." Fanzines were cheaply produced labors of love by the devoted fans of alternative rock bands, movie stars, or any lifestyle choice that lent itself to sort of an outlaw feel. There were 'zines devoted to tattooing and body

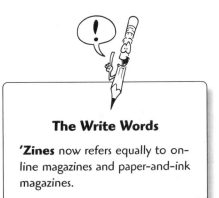

The Write Words

'Zines now refers equally to on-line magazines and paper-and-ink magazines.

piercing, animal rights activists, and even 1960s sitcom reruns such as *Gilligan's Island*. Anyone with access to a copy machine and an automatic stapler could put a 'zine together.

So, when desktop publishing became popular, 'zines became easier to create. When the Web allowed any-one with a dial-up connection to create his own little cyberspace world, a 'zine frequently became part of that world. And as Web design became more sophisticated, 'zines also became glossier and more commercial than during the old days of Kinko's and a staple machine.

Commerce Intrudes

Paper-and-ink 'zines are still distinct and separate from the full-scale commercial publications of media conglomerates such as Time Warner or Condé Nast. And in the early days, so were Web 'zines. But on the Web these days, everybody is trying to make a buck, and that includes the 'zines.

Online 'zines such as Salon and Nerve, which were started as hip alternatives to staid publications such as *Time* and *Newsweek,* are ironically becoming big commercial players on the Web.

Meet the Major Players

Why do some publications exist only on the Web? Wouldn't it make sense to do both a paper version and a Web version? In fact, many (if not most) Web publications are defiantly Net-only affairs.

Publishing online has real advantages over print—the speed with which changes and updates can be made, the fact that graphics can move on the screen, and mostly the fact that there is no stiff print bill to be paid every month!

Publications appear on the Web with blinding speed—and sometimes disappear just as quickly. So let's start off by taking a close look at the big players in the online publication scene, the ones that have been around a little while and promise to still be around by the time this book is printed.

Salon.com

Salon.com was founded by a cadre of veteran newspaper writers in San Francisco. Taking a chance on the new media long before others did, these folks really broke new ground. Thankfully, it has paid off for them. On occasion, Salon has made the news itself because of the stories that it runs on politics and the media.

So what kind of material will you find on Salon? You'll find a fairly wide gamut, everything from breaking news to book reviews, political commentary, and health articles. The site is updated daily, with some sections updated several times a day.

Does Salon deal with freelancers? Yes. It buys feature articles and short pieces on a wide variety of topics. To get the full flavor of this site, you should spend a considerable amount of time wandering around from section to section to absorb the style and tone.

Here's a snippet from Salon's writers' guidelines:

> Salon welcomes article queries and submissions. The best way to submit articles and story pitches is via e-mail.
>
> We ask that you please send the text of your query or submission in plain text in the body of your e-mail, rather than as an attached file, as we may not be able to read the format of your file.
>
> Also please note that Salon does not solicit fiction or poetry submissions and will not be able to respond to such submissions.

Go online to get complete guidelines at www.salon.com/contact/submissions/index.htm.

The Straight Scoop

Salon.com is not only a market for freelance material, but it is also a frequent topic of conversation among writers on the freelancers' chat room Byline on The Well (www.thewell.com). Salon.com owns The Well, which is one of the oldest online communities, and Salon editors are sometimes participants in the discussions on The Well. So, the discussion board discusses its corporate owners and at times the very editors who are lurking either onscreen or offscreen, reading the discussion thread. Who said the media isn't free? Check it out.

Slate

Established a few years after Salon.com, Slate has the backing of a big pocketbook—Microsoft. Slate also has the talents of longtime political magazine figure Michael Kinsley, who shocked the established media world when he traded in his Washington, D.C., dark suit for the flannel shirt and hiking boots of Redmond, Washington, when he took the job of editor.

What will you find on Slate? Slate's interests are varied, from up-to-the-minute politics to pop culture and the media. A recent feature article was a close-up look at "Life at $6.15 an Hour in a Telemarketing Boiler Room."

Slate does accept freelance material. Oddly enough, staff wants to receive freelance submissions in the mail, not online. Go figure. *Unsolicited* submissions can be sent to this address:

> Slate
> 1 Microsoft Way
> Redmond, WA 98052

Submissions should contain a SASE for your manuscript's return. Slate also will take poetry submissions; its poetry editor is poet laureate Robert Pinsky. Send poetry to this address:

> Slate
> Robert Pinsky, Poetry Editor
> Boston University
> 236 Bay Street Road
> Boston, MA 02215

Dead Lines

So you just found a cool-looking site on the Web and think it might be open to your writing. What you really like about it is that the screen isn't cluttered with all those junky banner ads. Well, just remember—no advertising, no money to pay you.

The Write Words

When you send an editor your entire article that hasn't been asked for, you've sent an **unsolicited manuscript.**

Word

Established in 1995—practically a hundred years ago, as far as the Web is concerned—Word is a general interest online publication targeted to the 20s and 30s set. "Irreverent" and "insightful" seem to be the watchwords here. Word's slogan is "Issues, Culture, Webzine–R–Us!" It is a pretty edgy Web site, with lots of jumpy graphics and wacky artwork—it's not for those over 25 whose eyesight might be failing them. A recent story was described this way: A Valentine's Day Diary: A romantic love story that is not in the least bit depressing.

From this site's guidelines, we learn the following:

> For the most part, Word does not publish fiction, poetry, "news-feature" journalism, commentary, or opinion pieces, anything dealing with celebrities, or anything mainly focusing on the Internet.

> Due to our very small staff, circulation of submissions can sometimes take quite a while. Please don't take our slow response as a reflection of our level of interest.

What kind of stuff does Word publish? When you access the submissions guidelines through www.word.com/yhome/submit.html, designers have thoughtfully embedded links to "This Kind of Stuff" that will take you directly to samples of what they are looking for. Kinda cool, really.

The Straight Scoop

Several online magazines have tried—and mostly failed—to sell subscriptions to their sites. Slate tried it for a while and then pulled the plug. An online financial publication called TheStreet.com seemed to be doing it successfully, with upward of 100,000 readers paying $9.95 a month to access the daily (sometimes hourly) insight and commentary of its columnists. But TheStreet.com has just announced that its site will now be 100 percent free. At the same time, however, it announced that it is shifting all its popular columnists over to a new site, www.realmoney.com, which will cost subscribers twice as much as before.

Cybertimes.com

This is the online publication put out by *The New York Times*. This is not simply *The New York Times* online edition—that's a different Web address that recycles all its material from the printed newspaper.

Established in 1996, up to 70 percent of the articles on the Cybertimes comes from freelancers. You can query the editor, John Haskins, but do spend as much time as possible absorbing the site to get a real feel for it.

Epicurious.com

Epicurious is a wonderful site created by food-and-travel people for food-and-travel people. It is an original online publication created by Condé Nast under its Condé Net division, and is an amalgamation of several Condé Nast publications. *Gourmet*

Dead Lines

The surest way to introduce a virus into your computer is to open an attached file from a stranger. So, what makes you think that an editor will open *your* attached file, then? Put your pitch in your e-mail, and cut and paste any short clips into the body of the e-mail, or provide URLs to sites where your work can be seen. Even assigned articles often must be turned in this way.

magazine contributes to the site, as does *Bon Appétit, Condé Nast Travel,* and other upscale magazines. Most of what you'll find on the site is connected with one of the other magazines, but this 'zine also does take some work from freelancers.

Epicurious readers will find a delicious combination of food articles, wine and restaurant reviews, and travel pieces.

The folks at Epicurious told us that the best approach for freelancers to take is to contact the appropriate editor with a story pitch and their credentials. You can access the masthead and find editors' names at www.epicurious.com/a_home/a03_staff/who/who_we_are.html.

ParentSoup

Originally started as a chat room by a few parents, ParentSoup grew quickly and was absorbed early on by the folks at iVillage. This site uses some freelance material in the general areas of health, technology, holidays, education, parenting, and other topics of interest and concern in the lives of today's active parents.

Send your submission to PSeditor@mail.ivillage.com. We weren't able to find out whether or what they pay.

The Straight Scoop

We've received mixed messages from freelancers about how much they are being paid. Developing new content for Web sites, particularly commercial sites, can pay very high hourly fees. But writers have found that some Web publications pay 25¢ a word, or 50¢ a word. And some do pay the standard $1 per word. As with other publications, rate of payment has more to do with your level of experience and your reputation. As both develop, you put yourself in position to ask for more.

Shewire.com

Shewire is a women's news site owned by Gen X media company Snowball.com. Shewire does accept freelance writing—as a matter of fact, it relies on freelancers for most of its content. The news focus on this site is issues that affect women's lives—from marriage rites to human rights, and tons of topics in between. Check out the entire site at www.shewire.com before you submit anything.

Send your story idea or completed article to submissions@shewire.com, and include the name of the section to which you are submitting in the subject line. If you haven't received a response from the editors in three weeks, send a reminder by e-mail. Shewire does pay freelancers (co-author Jennifer knows because she freelances for them!). The rate varies, but it is around 20¢ a word.

The Straight Scoop

Inquiring minds need to know, and inquiring writers might get paid for what they know. *The National Enquirer* on the Web pays up to $500 for story ideas. Just summarize your story idea and e-mail it. You can even submit photos, but as the site warns, "when submitting photos, please do not submit phony photos from the Internet"—like those cool shots you have of Elvis and Princess Di. Check out www.nationalenquirer.com.

Travel Magazines on the Web

Travel writing is the most hotly contested area for freelancers. Everyone and their mother wants to write travel pieces. So what is going on the Web? Mostly big glossy magazines that are simply making their print version content available online, too.

So, does that mean there aren't any markets for travel writing online? Never say never—that's the first rule of freelancing!

We visited a number of travel sites on the Web to see who was open to freelancers. Here's what we found:

➤ **Bigworld.com.** This is the online version of *Big World* magazine. In its "Write for us" section, the site cheerfully admits to currently looking for columnists and writers: "We're a good starting point for someone just breaking into writing—or someone who's always wanted to try it. To be upfront, we can't pay much." Alas, "not much" turns out to be $35 for a feature story ....

Send your queries to:

Heather Buettner
Submissions Editor
Big World
P.O. Box 7656-H
Lancaster, PA 17604

➤ **Islandsmag.com.** Guidelines are accessible online. A beautiful glossy travel magazine, *Islands* focuses on islands around the world. You may send online queries to Editor@islands.com.

➤ **Tripsmag.com.** "The magazine for active, adventurous travelers who are looking for travel information in an unusual, offbeat, irreverent voice." Does that sound like *your* voice? If so, online submissions guidelines request a short query via e-mail.

➤ **Transitionsabroad.com.** In printed form, this magazine has long been the standard for cheap student travel. Its Web site does encourage freelance submissions about "active involvement rather than passive tourism." Payment method depends on the actual size of the article, $1.50 to $2 per column inch (which is about 50 to 55 words, or 3¢ a word).

Hot Stuff

Much is made about the popularity of adult material on the Web. From porn sites to chat rooms, the Internet is a pretty sexy place. So what if you want to write sexy stuff?

Most of the sex stuff on the Web is—surprise—in picture form. But a few brave sites are trying to titillate and arouse through well-written stories rather than with pictures of bosomy cheerleaders.

Nerve

Nerve.com is the best known of the literary erotica sites. Submission guidelines are as follows:

The best (and pretty much only) way to submit writing or photography to Nerve.com for consideration is to post it on your own NerveCenter home page. Simply sign up for a free community membership on www.nervecenter.com, go to the home page section, follow the simple instructions for building your own site and uploading text or images, and send the URL of your new home page in the subject line of an e-mail to the appropriate address: meredith@nerve.com for photography submissions, isabella@nerve.com for writing submissions. Due to the high volume of inquiries we receive, only submissions posted on NerveCenter home pages will be considered.

Got that?

genrEZONE

genrEZONE is a quarterly electronic publication that does include erotica, but it is not limited to it. Check this out at www.genrezone.com. Although the site encourages freelance submissions, its rate of pay is quite low: $1/4$¢ per word, to a maximum of $25 per 10,000-word novelette. That's not going to keep groceries on the table for a serious freelance writer.

The Straight Scoop

Where can you get the rundown on all the erotica sites out there? An e-book that covers this field, *It's a Dirty Job: Writing Porn for Fun and Profit!* You can order it online at www.writersweekly.com/index-dirtyjob.htm. It includes a chapter on "Paying Porn Markets." Good luck!

Instant Gratification

One thing to keep in mind about writing for the Web is that, unlike a magazine assignment in which you might have months to research, write, revise, and polish, you might have only days to bang out a story for the Web. It's more like writing for a newspaper than for a magazine. Sites with a gnawing need to keep their content fresh and ever-changing might say yes to your query—and ask you to send it in tomorrow!

Jennifer took an assignment from the online version of *Fortune* magazine to cover a women's high-tech conference in the Silicon Valley. She drove down the night before, was at the conference at 7 A.M., interviewed and scribbled notes all day long, drove four hours home, and upon arriving sat down in front of her computer to write the story. She filed it at 10 P.M. that night.

Proud to have turned in a story so quickly, she went to bed—only to wake up the next morning to find an e-mail from her editor asking that the story be cut and pasted into an e-mail rather than sent as an attached file. The point is, as quickly as Jennifer wrote the story and turned it in, an editor was just as quickly pouncing on her e-mailed submission.

Tight as the deadlines are, the payoff and the publication come just as fast. Stories submitted and accepted by magazines could be months in the works, with long periods of pins-and-needles anticipation of seeing your well-crafted story (and your name) on the pages of a finished magazine. Equally long periods can drag by while waiting for the check.

But when writing for the Web, you turn it in and—bingo!—there it is. Most stories appear online within days—sometimes within hours—of being turned in by the writer. (Longer feature pieces probably will not appear as quickly, as the editors are dealing with a more complicated editorial calendar, in those cases.)

The Least You Need to Know

➤ Most major monthly publications recycle material from their magazines for their Web sites, with little new material, but plenty of online 'zines need fresh freelance material.

➤ Salon.com and Slate, two of the major Web 'zines, are good markets for free-lancers.

➤ Queries, clips, and most submitted articles should be cut and pasted into e-mails instead of sent as attached files.

➤ Pay for online writing ranges from nothing or $1/4$¢ per word, up to the standard $1 per word.

➤ Writing for the Web often brings both faster publication and faster payment.

Chapter 16

Contentproviders.com

In This Chapter

➤ You, too, can be a content provider

➤ The Web style of writing: short, informative, edgy

➤ Live on in syndication

➤ Using the Web to find work on the Web

Well, who would have imagined that never before in the history of the printed word would words themselves be in such demand! And so are the people who write them. In this chapter, we'll learn more about the style of writing for the Web and how to use online sites to find assignments.

"Content" and Other New Words for Words

Words are words, most places anyway. But on the Web, words are "content." Words are what fills an attractively designed page and keeps customers coming back again and again. Remember what writer Jim Brown said about the spinning logo—a hot design alone isn't enough to keep folks coming back to a Web site. There has to be something there beyond bright colors and moving banners—and that something is content, or words.

If words aren't always called words, writers aren't always called "writers," either. If you want to work on the Web, you need to know the other new words for writers:

➤ Content developer

➤ Content provider

➤ Interactive writer

➤ Marcom writer

➤ Technical writer

➤ Marketing writer

These terms are taken directly from job listings for writers on the Web. The strange thing is, some of these writers do the same thing (like a marketing writer and a marcom writer).

But what do these writers do? Let's read the description of just a few:

➤ **Marcom writer.** "You will be expected to tackle a wide range of projects—crafting everything from engaging Web copy and cutting-edge marketing materials to crisp proposals and straightforward documentation. Qualified candidates will be versatile, multivoiced writers who are comfortable composing for both traditional and new media outlets."

That's a cool-sounding job, but what the heck does *marcom* mean, anyway? It's a high-tech term that means "marketing communications."

➤ **Technical writer.** "Write and edit end-user manuals, and create user guidelines, online help directories and Web sites. Needs 1–2 years of solid post-graduate academic or professional writing experience, and the ability to work independently."

Amazing! Even academic writers can get high-tech jobs nowadays!

But are all these companies looking for people who can *write,* or people who can *write for the Web?* Is there a difference? Yes, there is. But don't panic—you can learn how to do it.

The Write Words

Anyone who provides the content for a Web site is a **content provider,** another word for a writer. It's also sometimes called a content developer.

Web Style Writing

You've been perfecting your writing skill for years, so why should you have to do anything different now to get work on the Web? The short answer is: because the Web is different.

Although we've been waxing poetic throughout this book about how the Web is really all about words, the real truth is that it is about *few* words. We're talking punchy sentences and information presented in a straightforward way—fast.

Very early in the history of the World Wide Web, Web designers discovered that although the folks who spent time cruising the Web were happy to read, they wanted to get straight to the point. What has developed is a style of writing and a style of Web design in which the short paragraph rules. Bulleted points are king. Sidebars are royalty. And the phrase "click here for more" is what enables readers to bring up other screens to pursue a topic more deeply—if they want to.

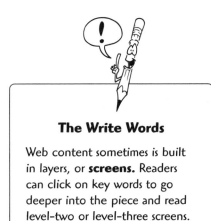

The Write Words

Web content sometimes is built in layers, or **screens.** Readers can click on key words to go deeper into the piece and read level-two or level-three screens. Screens are also called pages.

A Real Live Example!

Want to get a good sense of Web writing without actually having to turn on your computer? Surprise— you're holding it in your hands! That's right, the *Complete Idiot's Guides* are actually a good way to introduce yourself to the basics of what writing for the Web is all about. Notice how the page is broken up by punchy headings in big, dark type? You'll see the same thing on your screen.

And notice how the potentially monotonous printed page itself is broken up with short sidebars that explain nuggets of information? That's totally Web style.

"It's like writing haiku," says Elaine Pofeldt, who runs the small business site for *Fortune* magazine's Web site. Haiku, the famously spare Japanese poetry style, aptly suggests the elegant brevity of the typical Web screen. Just as the haiku condenses a lot of ideas into a small, three-line package, the Web piece must condense a lot of information into a small package with a powerful punch. "Space is limited, so learn to use your words wisely," Pofeldt advises.

What Does It Take?

A longtime magazine writer before moving to the Web, Elaine Pofeldt believes that the most important skill any writer can bring to the Web is the ability to research. "Writing for the Web is all about research skills," she says. "You must develop the best [information] sources available because you will then have to use your words well. There is only room for cutting-edge information …. Writing for the Web is also about being a time manager."

Pofeldt points out that the folks who are going to the Web for news and information are fairly well-informed to begin with. They don't want to read the same kind of information that they could learn in their daily newspaper. So to position yourself as a reliable freelancer for Web sites, you need to develop a reputation for delivering new and mind-expanding information.

The Straight Scoop

Here is a bit of Web haiku to help you imagine the process of writing Web pieces:

> *Bright words dance with type*
> *The screen flickers before me*
> *To improve, remove.*

That's 17 syllables about writing and editing. Write what you want, and then cut out most of it, leaving only the good stuff.

Dead Lines

Most pieces written for the Web are just a few hundred words. Think twice about selling your 4,000-word essay about biking through the French countryside on the Web. It can be done, but your best chances are with short pieces.

Other than trying to keep your pieces short, researching intensively, and trying to use the best sources of information possible, what else is there to writing for the Web? Sometimes, there is an *attitude*.

One reason the Web is attracting so much attention is that much of what is written there has a bit of an attitude, an edge, or a stronger viewpoint than is found in other kinds of writing. Don't be afraid to put your own point of view, your own stamp, on what you're trying to write and sell to the Web. It can be your own viewpoint that makes you a successful Web writer. In the next chapter, you'll meet a couple of Web writers who became successful because of their iconoclastic attitudes.

Read, Read, Read

The best way to learn how to write for the Web, though, is to spend a lot of time reading what's already out there. Take a look at the top news sites such as USAToday.com and CNN.com. Notice how brief the headlines are and how condensed are the articles.

Cruise through sites with longer pieces as well, including Salon.com or Nerve.com (you'll find pretty sexy stuff, though, so be warned) to see if you can spot the differences between how a piece is written for the Web versus a printed publication.

You will see a few style tricks over and over: lots of bulleted points and eye-catching sidebars where key phrases are repeated or "called out."

The more familiar you become with the finished product on the Web, the greater the chances you will soon see your work there!

The Straight Scoop

When Jennifer and her husband, Peter, both veterans of several personal finance books, first began writing for the Web, their articles often ended up being too long. Is such a thing possible? On the Web, it is. Web users don't want to read page after page—they want short pages with key points that communicate information quickly. Jennifer and Peter still write for the Web, but it doesn't take nearly as long as it used to!

Sell, Sell, and Sell It Again

One tried-and-true way to increase your income as a writer is to resell your articles. After you sell an article to a magazine or newspaper, you can always refocus and re-cast it to appeal to another publication. You can continually refocus it for lots of other markets, too. In fact, it's possible to sell one piece of writing 3 or 4 or 10 times. That's very efficient and very profitable. Can you do this on the Web? You betcha.

Say you've written a short travel piece about the most romantic spots in Paris. What can you do with it?

There are hundreds of travel sites on the Web. Most of them make their money by selling travel books (they have affiliate links to big online booksellers such as Amazon.com and barnesandnoble.com and get a small percentage of the price). But how do you get a Web site visitor to decide right then and there to buy a book about touring France? By giving them a taste of France, as in your piece on Paris.

First try to seek out the biggest potential buyer of your piece. Get the writer's guidelines for the big commercial travel magazine sites, and hit them first. If that doesn't work, try smaller sites such as Sallys-Place.com, which is a wonderful culinary travel site, or charming personality-driven sites such as TWENJ.com (Travel with Ed and

Dead Lines

Who owns your Web work? It depends on what kind of contract you sign. Some sites want writers to sign a "work-for-hire" agreement that assigns all rights to the site. With a work-for-hire contract, you are paid but can never sell the piece again. Professional writers frown on this, as does the Writer's Union.

Julie). Travel sites run by travel book publishers such as Lonely Planet and the Rough Guides also look for content by freelance writers. The smaller sites aren't going to pay you, but if your article is posted there, it does give you that critical first clip you'll need to go on and be published elsewhere. It might not have the same cachet as a clip from a glossy magazine, but if it's good, any published clip counts.

Jennifer has learned a bit about self-syndicating on the Web. She writes a weekly column for USAToday.com called "On Your Own" about being self-employed. *USAToday* pays her $100 for a 500- to 700-word piece. That's not exactly a dollar a word, but she's free to sell the piece to other business sites after it has appeared on the *USAToday* site. So, by offering it to other small-business Web sites for a syndication fee of $25 per column, Jennifer hopes to build up the amount she earns on that one weekly piece to well above a dollar a word.

Finding Work on the Web

If you want to write for the Web, you also must learn how to use it. Use it for research, use it to conduct interviews, use it to query editors, and use it to find work.

Many of us graduated from college with stars in our eyes, imagining that our English degrees would enable us to grab highly sought-after positions. Ummm, it didn't happen—at least, it didn't happen then. But it is actually happening now—there are jobs listed all over the Web for which writing ability is required. Hard to believe? We knew you'd be skeptical, so we visited many of the top sites and have included actual job listings for freelance writers from the top job boards.

Craigslist

One of the premier sites for freelancers with a yen to write is craigslist.org—as in, a guy named Craig who started a list. That's exactly what founder Craig Newmark did. Craigslist is based in San Francisco and has many sections for goods and services in the Bay Area (such as apartments and personal ads), but one of the most visited parts of craigslist is the section on writing and editing jobs. Here are just a few short snips from the jobs we found listed on January 23, 2000:

➤ **Freelance writers.** WetFeet.com, a career and work portal, is looking for talented freelance writers to contribute content to our award-winning Web site. Specifically, we need writers able to write fast and well about companies in a variety of industries. Pay equals about $20 an hour, but if you're really fast you'll earn more.

➤ **Bay Area—Freelance Music Writers.** SF Gate, the leading Bay Area news and entertainment Web site, is in search of music writers to cover the local concert beat. We need short (200 words), informative and engaging blurbs about musicians and bands performing around the Bay Area.

➤ **Freelance Health Research/Writing Opportunities.** SavvyHEALTH.com, a consumer health Web site, is looking for freelancers for ongoing, temporary, in-house projects.

Don't contact these companies—these jobs will be long gone by the time you read this book. But we suggest that you fold down this page to mark your place, put down the book, fire up your computer, and see what kinds of opportunities are on craigslist today! Don't be shy, just apply.

Help Wanted

In addition to Craigslist.org, you'll find help wanted listings for freelance writers at the following sites:

➤ www.inkspot.com

➤ www.higherminds.com

➤ www.content-exchange.com

Imagine how your life as a freelance writer might change if you could just get past those first few clips. Screw up your courage and apply!

The Straight Scoop

A great place to find out more about where freelance writers can find leads on all sorts of things is on the Byline conference on The Well. One of the oldest chat rooms online, The Well does require a monthly membership fee. Check it out at www.thewell.com. You'll find writers from around the country happily swapping information on topics such as "Who is the contact for Oprah's new magazine?" and "Did that deadbeat magazine ever pay you?"

Free for Nothing

Along with the job listings for freelance writers, you'll occasionally run across Web sites that offer nada, zip, nothing, as payment to freelance content writers. These are usually Web sites that are just getting started and don't have any money to spare. Should you do it?

This is not how you want to spend all your writing time, of course, but why not write a few pieces for free to get that first batch of clips going? If the site does find success and (even better) some financial backing, you might be in a great position. As one of the first writers who was willing to take a chance and work for free, you might be looked upon quite favorably now that there's money to throw around.

If you do a bit of content writing for free, at least try to get the site to give you a big byline. You might even ask to have your picture or a large author bio included. Look for anything to help you build up yourself as a professional.

Sitting on the Dock of eBay ...

Clever heading, isn't it? No, you can't really auction your talents off on eBay (a few engineers tried, but nobody bid), but there are several sites where freelancers can sit on the dock and auction off their talents, or at least let the world know what they can do—and how much they'd like to be paid to do it.

Monster.com has a section called Monster Talent Market where you can post your skills and talents and let potential employers bid on you. Alas, when we last checked the board, the folks who were auctioning off their skills as "freelance writer—general business" and executive writer—speeches, op-eds, reports, and more" had not received any bids in their auctions.

eWork.com lets you register your skills for free in a giant online matching service. The system then matches you up with employers in its database. For instance, Jennifer signed up and described her skills as "business writer" and quickly got a match with a company that was looking for freelance articles on the health care industry. Although it's free to register, you can enter a dollar amount that you're willing to pay for a match, which moves you to the front of the line. Check it out.

A Word to the Wise

One bit of warning, though—not everyone has been pleased with the way their Web work has turned out. At least two longtime writing professionals that we know of took a chance on Web upstarts, were given many promises of future riches, and ended up with zip.

One writer based in the Northeast had this to say: "I was never paid by the Web site launch I worked for. And neither were the other writers I brought in to write pieces. Three or four other writers are pretty pissed at me for convincing them to do the work. It was a crummy experience, and I will ask the next Web site that comes along to 'Show me the money!' before I get involved." Not only did he end up with nothing, but with fewer friends and contacts as a result.

Are you light-headed from the possibilities we've presented here? It is truly astonishing how big a difference the Web has made in the life of the average unsung writer. Read on to learn about how a few otherwise unsung writers created their own Web sites and became very well known. It might be a strategy that's perfect for you!

The Least You Need to Know

➤ Web sites have a tremendous need for content and content providers—that is, words and writers.

➤ Writing for the Web requires a shorter, punchier, and more to-the-point style than traditional journalism.

➤ You might be able to sell one piece to many different Web sites if you retain the rights to it yourself.

➤ Some Web sites post opportunities for freelance writers and help writers match their talents with positions available.

➤ Writing for free might be a good way to get your first online clips.

Chapter 17

Build It and They Will Come

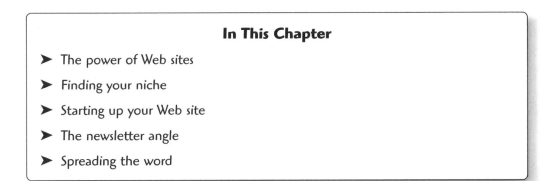

In This Chapter

➤ The power of Web sites

➤ Finding your niche

➤ Starting up your Web site

➤ The newsletter angle

➤ Spreading the word

It's too cool, all the opportunities for freelance writers on the Web. But is there a way you can take advantage of the way of the Web to really launch yourself as a writer, as a mini-celeb yourself? There is. Sit back while we regale you with tales of the previously unknown who took advantage of the Web and built themselves a reputation, quite literally.

These crafty folks found a way to get editors to call *them*, to get the media to pay attention to *them* without the benefit of years of work and reputation. Some even found book contracts at the end of the Web rainbow.

Matt Drudge and Other Web Celebs

Ever heard of Matt Drudge? Wait, let us modify that. Had you ever heard of Matt Drudge before his Web site, The Drudge Report, broke the news that *Newsweek* was sitting on a story about President Clinton and an intern named Monica? Chances are, you'd never heard of him.

Matt Drudge was not a longtime writer who had toiled anonymously for years, building up his skill and his contacts until the fateful day when he broke through into the big time. No, Matt Drudge was a young guy with a battered felt hat, a computer, a Web site, and a dream—he wanted to be a journalist.

The Straight Scoop

Just because you're popular doesn't mean that people like you, as Matt Drudge found out at his appearance at the National Press Club in June 1998. During the question-and-answer portion of his talk before that august body of journalists, the questions became more than a tiny bit mean-spirited. Here is an example: "With all due respect [Mr. Drudge], in the past half-hour you have been inaccurate 8 to 10 times—about history, government, the media. You said there were no suits approved by a president, no profits in early newspaper and radio. Do you think journalists should have any minimum educational requirements?" Ouch!

So how did he do it? How did Drudge go from managing the gift shop at CBS to being a featured guest on the Sunday morning news shows in just a few short years? He built it, and they came. What he built was a Web site.

Drudge skipped college and went straight to Los Angeles. A voracious reader and watcher of news, he attributes his site's popularity to being in the right place at the right time. Here's a quick overview of how Drudge explained his rise to the members of the National Press Club:

> "[Growing up in Washington, D.C.] I used to walk ... by ABC News ... stare up at the *Washington Post* newsroom ... knowing I'd never get in—didn't go to the right schools ... didn't come from a well-known family—nor was I connected to a powerful publishing dynasty.

> So, in the famous words of another newsman, Horace Greeley, I ... went West.

> But my father worried ... he dragged me into a Circuit City store [and bought me a computer].

> And as they say at CBS studios: Cut, two months later."

Drudge described how he learned to post messages on the Net, messages about secret stuff he'd learned while working his menial job at CBS. He started sending out e-mails, and the list grew and grew; he named it The Drudge Report. "One reader turned into five, then turned into 100," Drudge says. "And faster than you could say 'I never had sex with that woman,' it was 1,000, 5,000, 100,000 people. The ensuing Web site practically launched itself."

Do we encourage you to take this approach? While it worked in a big way for Drudge, we would heartily encourage you to work hard on your Web site to earn the respect of the journalism world—and to take great care with fact-checking.

Ain't It Cool?

Matt Drudge isn't the only young, untrained journalist to put up a site and create a name (and hence a writing career) for himself. Harry Jay Knowles created a movie gossip site called Ain't It Cool News (www.aint-it-cool-news.com) in his mid-20s, while still living at home with his dad.

He created the site when he was 24 as a time-filler while he was recovering from an accident that had left him partly paralyzed. Early on, his site drew heat from the big studios because of the negative tone of his reviews. But when Knowles sent spies to advance screenings of *Titanic* and circulated early reports of the big hit it would become, the tide turned: "Hollywood began to see that not only could I negatively affect film, but I could also change word for the better," he explains.

Knowles does take a pro-Hollywood approach to his writing: "I never talk about who's sleeping with who. I never talk about drugs. To me, the negative backside of Hollywood does nothing but diminish the dream." And through his own initiative, Knowles has realized his own dreams of a writing career.

Playing the Links

In addition to these examples of young writers who created their own careers online, there have been those who, rather than writing, simply created big information clearinghouses.

Douglas Gerlach created a site called Investorama that contained 1,800 different money- and finance-related *links* to sites on the Web. In 1995 (practically the Stone Age, as far as Web history goes), Gerlach recognized the enormous power of the Internet and came up with an idea of how the World Wide Web could help investors. He set

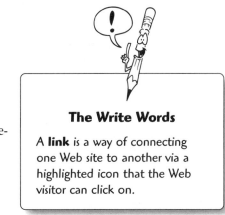

The Write Words

A **link** is a way of connecting one Web site to another via a highlighted icon that the Web visitor can click on.

about building the site that grew into the link-crazy Investorama. It didn't hurt his career, either; now Doug is a published book author as a result of his Web site. He was able to establish himself as an expert on online investing and has written two books on the topic.

Can you see the potential for establishing yourself and igniting your writing career?

Small-Town Success

Smaller, less splashy examples are two travel sites that we mentioned in the previous chapter: Sally's Place, and Traveling with Ed and Julie. These folks created Web pages as extensions of their personal interests—travel and food. Their sites have now grown into full-fledged online publications from which they can launch their own writing elsewhere.

Sally, and Ed and Julie, now have something that could lead them to book contracts—they have a *platform*. Many publishers are looking for writers who have a platform, literally a place from which they can speak. Whether it's a radio show, a newspaper column, or a Web page with high traffic, a platform can get you noticed.

The Write Words

The author's proven ability to sell work through a Web site, a public speaking forum, a radio show, or a newspaper column is called a **platform.**

What Do *You* Have to Say?

Drudge had behind-the-scenes information to disseminate. Knowles had the inside scoop on a few things, too. If you were going to put up a Web site and build your career that way, what would *you* have to say?

It's not just information on sex, politics, and the movies that people look for on the Web. Countless people log on every day looking for hard information in other areas. Is there a topic you hope to specialize in as a freelance writer? Food? Travel? Health? Building your own Web site gives you the opportunity to establish yourself as an expert in those fields, and you'll have lots of people looking for you.

Like Douglas Gerlach, you might establish yourself simply by building a site that links to thousands of other Web sites on the topic that is dearest to your heart. A site with thousands of links to other travel sites, or a site with links to other sites about travel to Paris, will win you scores of readers—and fans!

Niche Player

Finding a niche to specialize in is your best approach. At this point, it's safe to assume that Drudge has political gossip pretty well covered and that Knowles owns the Hollywood gossip angle. But it's a big, big world out there. What do *you* want to say?

The most successful small sites focus on topics that are of deep interest to a large number of people. Let's look at two women who found their Web niche in their own health challenges.

Two women have built Web sites based on their struggles with eating disorders. Amy Medina turned her problem with anorexia into a site called The Something Fishy Web Site on Eating Disorders (www.something-fishy.org) to tackle the subject head-on. It provides page after page of explanation, analysis, and support. Medina receives 150 e-mails a day from readers.

Colleen A. Thompson also has built a site about eating disorders. Hers is called Eating Disorders: Mirror Mirror (www.mirror-mirror.org). Like Medina, Thompson has struggled with this issue; she wrote the first installments of the site from her hospital bed.

Both of these women now have a pretty good chance of writing articles and books because they have a platform that they created themselves in the same way that you, too, can create your own platform: on the Web.

Why did the same topic—eating disorders—work for both of them? Because no two people approach things the same way. Through individual voice, or a different emphasis of some sort, many players can be in the same niche. Once you decide on a niche, look carefully to see who is doing what, and find a way that you can be different.

The Payoff

Sound expensive? It isn't really, and the payoff in terms of your writing career can be tremendous.

Co-author Jennifer is the author of well over a dozen books. She also has a weekly column on the *USAToday* Web site. But how many actual articles has she written and had published over the past few years? "Maybe 20, all together," she admits. "I'm kind of shy when it comes to pitching stuff—real shy." So how has Jennifer managed to get over her reluctance to approach strange editors with article ideas?

She explains: "I built a Web site all about encouraging women to go out and build up their own personal net worth, a money motivation site for women called Goals and Jewels. It's pretty swanky-looking, with lots of glittery jewels on the page. But it really only cost a little over $1,000 to get it designed and up and running."

How has having a financial Web site helped Jennifer with her freelance writing career? She now can e-mail editors with pitch ideas and build a link to her site right there in the e-mail. The link takes the editor right to an article on the Web site that Jennifer has written. For personal finance and money ideas she's pitching, the Web site helps her show off her writing skills.

Jennifer built her Web site around a specific niche—money motivation for women. Medina and Thompson built their sites around a specific niche—eating disorders. Is there a niche for you on the Web? Build it, and they will come—editors, that is. And they will come with assignments for you.

Setting Up Your Web Site from A to Z

Let's follow the process that Jennifer used to get her Web site up and running.

First, you must register a *domain name*. A domain name is the words that follow the "www." part of your Web address. If your plan is to establish yourself as an expert and freelance writer in a particular field, you would be wise to register a word or phrase that somehow evokes the topic. For example, if you want to become the pre-eminent expert on hanging out and drinking coffee in literary cafes in Paris, you could be www.literarycafes.com. (This name wasn't registered at the time of this writing, but it might be by the time you read this book!)

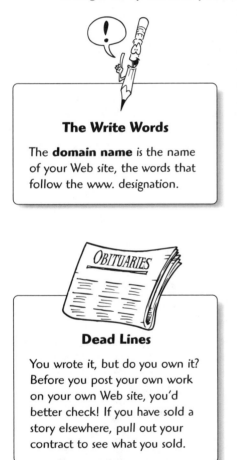

The Write Words

The **domain name** is the name of your Web site, the words that follow the www. designation.

Dead Lines

You wrote it, but do you own it? Before you post your own work on your own Web site, you'd better check! If you have sold a story elsewhere, pull out your contract to see what you sold.

Registering a domain name costs around $100. Log on to www.verio.com and follow the instructions. You also can go to www.register.com to register a URL.

Second, you must design a Web site. Yes, there are books you can read and courses you can take, but if your goal is to build something that will give you instant credibility as a Web writer, we say bite the bullet and hire a professional. You will go much farther much faster with a Web site that looks professional. Remember, this is something that you will want to publicize, something that you want magazine and newspaper editors to visit. If you plan to use this site as your online professional resumé, will visitors be impressed if the site is a hack job done by your 12-year-old nephew?

Having said that, we want to discourage you from spending a fortune on a Web site. Don't go too cheap and shabby, but don't mortgage your house, either. This is by no means a slam-dunk, guaranteed way to build a freelance writing career. We don't want you to go into debt to try it. A great book to read is *The Complete Idiot's Guide to Creating a Web Page, Fourth Edition.*

Third, fill your Web site with content. You already know what content is—words, words, words! This is your chance to strut your stuff as a writer. If you have clips from previously published articles that pertain to the topic of your Web site, add 'em. If you haven't been published before, here is your chance to write and post pieces that you think best display your skills, the pieces you would be proud for an editor to review.

You also can add links to other Web sites and articles, or condense pertinent news stories. One of the features on Jennifer's Goals and Jewels site is a section called Women and Wealth in the News. In this section, she collects major news stories in newspapers and magazines about women and their hard-earned money, and writes a short summary of the story for her Web visitors to read. She then provides links to the news sites if they want to read the entire story. As a writer, you need to sensitize yourself to copyright issues. Web sites can't reprint an entire, actual story without contacting the copyright holder for permission.

Web Style? Which Style?

One thing to consider when designing your Web site is how you want to present your writing. We've suggested that if you want to write for the Web, you'll need to adopt a brief and to-the-point writing style. That includes lots of bulleted points and short items. If you plan your Web site to be a showcase for your Web journalism and a launching pad for your own career as a Web journalist, you should write that way.

On the other hand, if you want to position yourself as a freelance writer of full-length magazine articles, full-length magazine articles are what visitors to your Web site should find.

There are ways for you to accomplish both. Discuss this with your Web designer, so that the home page has short items that link to full-length pieces on other screens.

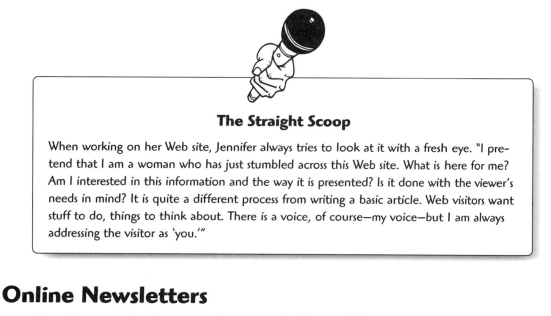

The Straight Scoop

When working on her Web site, Jennifer always tries to look at it with a fresh eye. "I pretend that I am a woman who has just stumbled across this Web site. What is here for me? Am I interested in this information and the way it is presented? Is it done with the viewer's needs in mind? It is quite a different process from writing a basic article. Web visitors want stuff to do, things to think about. There is a voice, of course—my voice—but I am always addressing the visitor as 'you.'"

Online Newsletters

There is a somewhat less expensive way to build up a following as a writer on the Web. You can create an e-mail newsletter. This was the way Matt Drudge started out, sending an e-mail full of gossip to folks who had requested it.

We've mentioned Mary Ellen before, the woman who started an online miracle newsletter that eventually grew into a Web site and then into a book called *Expect Miracles*. Starting an e-mail newsletter was her first step toward success as a published writer.

Business writer Azriela Jaffee sends out a free online newsletter called "The Entrepreneurial Couple's Success Letter," an offshoot of her books on the topic. She has thousands of subscribers around the world, not a few of which work in the media and are reporters and editors themselves.

If you develop a business-oriented e-mail newsletter, you certainly could e-mail it to members of the media that you think might be interested in it. Be warned, though: Send it only once with a friendly "Thought you'd like to know about this" message attached. Then let them decide to sign up to receive it on their own. You won't gain admirers and supporters in the publishing world by bombarding people with unrequested e-mail newsletters.

How do you start up an e-mail newsletter? Compose a few paragraphs and e-mail them to friends and family. Ask for feedback and criticism before you move on to the next step, which is to ask your friends and family to forward it on to *their* friends and family. And so it grows. You'll need to let readers know that they can request a subscription. This usually is accomplished by asking them to send a blank e-mail to you with "subscribe" in the subject line.

Two companies (and no doubt there will be more in the future) can help you run an e-mail newsletter—for free! Check out www.onelist.com or www.egroups.com.

Dual Approach

Elle McGirt, a financial journalist, has combined both Web approaches. She has a financial Web site for women called www.cassandrasrevenge.com that's filled with her writings on a variety of money-related topics. She also sends out a free e-mail newsletter to 30,000-plus readers. Where has it gotten her? She now has a regular gig with Oxygen Media's Web site and also with *Ka-ching*, its money show for women.

Getting the Word Out

What if you built a Web site and nobody came? It wouldn't do you much good at all, particularly if your not-so-secret purpose is to launch a career. So how do you get traffic on your site? There are several ways to do it.

The most tried-and-true method is an old-fashioned press release. If you've built a Web site that offers interesting and quirky information on an obscure topic, or a behind-the-scenes peek at something that a vast number of people wonder about, you stand a fair chance of getting some media coverage.

The Web portal Yahoo! now has a magazine, *Yahoo! Internet Life* that features hundreds of quirky Web sites every month. Most general-interest Web magazines also have columns or sidebars that review or mention Web sites of interest.

Built a Web site about food and cooking in hopes of building a career as a food journalist? Write a press release about your Web site and send it to food editors around the country.

Radio exposure also can help you gain visitors. You can launch a full-scale publicity campaign that includes ads in a publication called *Radio and TV Report* (call 1-800-989-1400 for more information). Ads run several hundred dollars and can help generate interview bookings. This publication is sent to radio and television producers around the country who are on a continuing search for interesting guests. So, if your topic might be of interest to the general public, why not try to talk about it on the radio? Again, this kind of approach goes a long way toward establishing yourself as an expert in whatever niche you've chosen.

Dead Lines

One thing that a Web site should not be about is ... you. Why would a visitor want to spend time at your Web site if it is written in such a way that the focus is always about *you* and *your interest?* Keep the content always focused on what the visitor is going to get out of the experience. Always ask yourself, "What is the reader getting out of this?" Don't build a vanity site; build a site that offers something of value to visitors.

Building on Your Web Site Success

Don't forget why you built your Web site in the first place—to become a freelance writer and to sell magazine and newspaper pieces! So get to work pitching story ideas to editors.

If your Web site is a real hit, what else can you do? If you can establish yourself as an online expert on a valuable topic, you can do all manner of things:

➤ Write books

➤ Make speaking engagements

➤ Teach classes for The Learning Annex or a similar adult education organization

➤ Develop a column and try to sell it

All these also contribute toward your success as a freelance writer. So why not get busy and learn how to make the Web work for your freelance career?

The Least You Need to Know

➤ A Web site can be a valuable tool in establishing yourself as a writer and expert on your chosen topic.

➤ You can become well known and regarded as a topic expert simply by building a large link library to other Web sites.

➤ Starting an online newsletter that grows into a large free subscription base has led to writing success for several Web writers.

➤ Successful Web sites always offer something to the reader; they are not just vanity sites for one person's opinions.

➤ Publicize your Web site with press releases and radio interviews.

➤ A successful Web site not only can help your freelance career, but it also can lead you into writing books, giving talks, and teaching classes on your topic of expertise.

Part 5

A Short Course on Writing Effective Articles

Polish up your writing skills to sell all your new knowledge. Learn how to hook the reader right away, and how to write short, punchy pieces that appeal to today's reader. Learn the difference between a sidebar and a feature-length article. And learn how to assess every writer's biggest hope—should this article really be a full-length book instead?

Chapter 18

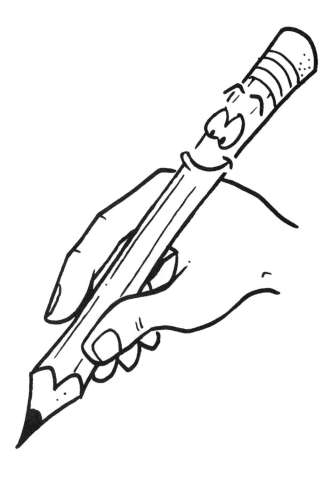

The Parts of the Article

In This Chapter

➤ The write stuff

➤ Opening up to the reader

➤ Leading the reader on

➤ Sculpting the body

➤ Closing words

You've come so far. With an assignment sheet in hand, your interviews complete, and your research finished, it's time to write. In this chapter, we give you the basic components of all articles, the pieces of the puzzle. We also introduce you to some stylistic devices and even grammar tools to make your copy sing. Writing is indeed a craft. Craftsmen continually work to refine their art, don't they? So prepare yourself, because sitting down at the computer to churn out your article may prove the hardest part yet. Consider this your quickie course in magazine writing.

Everything Organized and Ready to Write

What's the secret of a really great party (besides liquor)? Answer: preparation. The best parties result from a host or hostess who has prepared in advance for all the guests' needs. The china glistens, the crystal sparkles, the food tastes wonderful, the conversation energizes the room, and the atmosphere feels comfortable. Likewise, the best articles result from thorough preparation and organization.

The Host's Checklist

Make sure before you sit down to write that all your dinnerware—er, writerware—is ready to go:

❏ **Do you have ink in the printer?** Don't laugh. Before you send off that article by e-mail, you may want to proof it the old-fashioned way: with a pen on a hard copy.

❏ **Do you have paper for the printer?** Like we said before, you just may want to proof your creation like Hemingway did before the technological boom.

❏ **Do you have a disk with free space available and ready?** We recommend a clean disk for each article. You can keep Internet research, transcribe your interviews, and write the finished product on it. Make sure you have a label, too.

The Straight Scoop

Writers employ "literary device" to enhance their writing. Just what is literary device? Alliteration, allusion, pun, simile, hyperbole, metaphor, paradox, symbolism—these are a sampling of the literary devices that authors use. If you aren't familiar with these terms, we recommend that you take an introductory class in English literature, or concentrate on some of the glossary entries in the back of this book. We guarantee that the understanding of device usage will actually make crafting an article easier.

❏ **Do you have your transcribed interviews and your research ready and available? Have you highlighted the quotes you plan to use?** If you highlighted those great quotes, you won't have to get out your pith helmet and search for them during the writing process.

❏ **Are any reference books you plan to use—*AP Stylebook, Chicago Manual of Style, Roget's Thesaurus, Bartlett's Familiar Quotations*—by your side?** When you have to know if you're dangling a modifier at 3 A.M., your writing professor from college won't appreciate the call. Go to a reference book instead.

❏ **Where are your notebook and pen?** Chances are, you'll find that you need an answer to a question while writing. You'll need to call up a source and jot down the information. It never hurts to prepare. Incidentally, you may want something on which to jot down a few notes for the editor. The pad works both ways.

❑ **Do you have your assignment sheet?** You'll want to have the assignment sheet handy to make sure that you've answered all the editor's questions within your article. Tape it to the wall, your body, the chair, whatever. Make the assignment sheet readily available.

❑ **Is the coffee brewing?** Just a suggestion. Both co-authors Jennifer and Lynne find caffeine the muse of all muses when writing.

We suggest using these questions as a checklist the first few times when writing on assignment. Modify the checklist, of course, to suit your particular needs and style.

Forget-Me-Nots: An Outline

Now that you've arranged your disk, pen, paper, and reference materials, you just start writing, right? Not exactly. Before you write the whole shebang, you need to give some thought to how you plan to tackle the article. You do this in the form of a *prewrite,* or outline.

An outline need not take the classic Roman numeral format that you learned in school, nor stick to *MLA Handbook* style. Anything that works for you will work for your article. Lynne likes to draw several boxes on a piece of paper, with each box representing a theme/source/key idea within her article. Within each respective box, she lists items that she wants to cover and the first few words of pertinent quotes. "I just check off the items in the boxes as I get to them," says Lynne. Sometimes she also writes a rough lead and lists items she wants to hit within the piece.

Some other prewriting organizers include bubble clusters and spider diagrams. Whichever prewrite you plan to use depends upon how you "see" your article visually. The outline helps ensure that you don't forget anything as you drill away on the desktop.

Now—armed with all your materials and a plan of action—you're ready to write.

The Write Words

A **prewrite** is any number of ways to organize your article. The most common prewrite is an outline. Other prewrites employed are bubble clusters, where you bubble ideas around one central theme on a piece of paper, and spider diagrams, where you use lines moving out from ideas with brief descriptions to organize your thoughts.

Serving Appetizers: Brief Openings and Titles

The brief opening is the teaser, usually bolded in large, stylized font, to give readers in one or two sentences a glimpse of the content and entice them to read the article. It is also called the "dek." Technically, the brief opening isn't usually part of the writer's

Dead Lines

Don't bail on an assignment citing writer's block as the excuse. There is no such thing as writer's block in the nonfiction, freelance arena. Buck up and write. To quote a major ad campaign written by a writer without writer's block, *just do it!*

Dead Lines

Don't overuse adjectives in your copy. The unlucky, opinionated, overworked, persnickety editor will think that you don't know your subject well and are grasping at anything to describe the person if you use too many adjectives. Who is this person? Who knows? There are too many adjectives bumping up against each other to make sense of the personality behind the words. So use your adjectives appropriately and sparingly.

assignment; the editor writes this. But you can do the busy, overworked editor a favor by suggesting your own opening. So go for it. You're closer to the piece anyway. You should be able to sum up the whole thing in a sentence or two, right?

Here's what you do. Grab a glossy, any glossy. Find a feature article. More than likely, along with the byline, the title, and the introductory paragraph will appear a sentence or two teasing the reader into the article. Let's take a look at an example from one of Lynne's articles. Assigned to write an 1,800-word feature on "Wrangling Managed Care," Lynne wrote this brief opening, or dek, for the editor that was indeed used as the teaser:

> Today's health care organizations profess quality medicine but remain businesses—where the bottom line ultimately regulates the care we receive. Here's a look at a few ways you, the consumer, can take control of your health care.

In two sentences, Lynne summed up the gist of the article.

Go ahead, try it. Read several features, without sneaking a look at the teasers. Try to sum up the article in two lines. Use this trick: Imagine that a million bucks rides on whether you can describe your article and entice someone to read it in two sentences. That, my friends, is a brief opening.

Soup's On! A Winning Intro/Lead

So you hooked the readers with the brief opening. Now you need to keep 'em reading. You accomplish this by a winning introduction. Statistics show that if you can't hook readers within the first few sentences, you've lost them. But relax, you managed to hook the most elusive fish swimming in publishing waters—the editor of the magazine that put you on assignment!

Introductions remain so important, in fact, that the next chapter is devoted to hooking your readers early and hooking them hard. Stay tuned—we'll lead you through the treacherous waters of winning leads in Chapter 20, "Machine Gun Writing." For now, let's look at the introduction for "Wrangling Managed Care." You'll see the lead again in the next chapter—a direct quotation lead. Simply put, you begin with (or use within the first few sentences) a quote. Here is the lead and introduction for the story on health care:

> On my way to see a doctor about some foot pain, I passed a young woman as she left the large medical complex and overheard her complain to her mother: "I was about ready to strangle that doctor," she said. Hoping that the doctor she saw wasn't the same physician with whom I had an appointment, I stopped the woman, who then recounted her story. She'd been in a car accident, and for months the doctor continually prescribed various narcotics, even though the woman repeatedly told him that she had to drive long distances to work and that the pain killers made her sleepy, and even though she professed on a number of occasions that the Vicodin, Tylenol with codeine, and other pills were making her sick and masking her injuries. "If he hadn't given me the referral to the physical therapist today, I don't know what I would have done," she said.

> Unfortunately, in today's world of medicine, her story remains all too familiar. As this article goes to print, the U.S. Senate continues to debate—at great lobbying efforts from the American Medical Association—a Patient's Bill of Rights. In a statement released to the press regarding the AMA's efforts on behalf of the bill, Dr. Nancy Dickey, a trustee on the board of the associations, says, "People are most vulnerable when they're sick, and patients need to know they can trust their physician. If the patient has to wonder if their physician puts them first or the plan's profit's first, the trust in the patient-physician relationship is already eroded."

The lead and introduction hook the reader, in this case, with several startling quotes and facts. But this is only the introduction. What the article really addresses are ways the consumer can take control of his care. We give the information in the body of the piece.

For the Meat-and-Potatoes Man: The Body of the Piece

The body of your article serves to answer all the reader's questions, provide solid information, and illuminate the subject. In "Wrangling Managed Care," Lynne sought to provide readers with information in the following areas:

1. Skating past voice mail

2. Avoiding passive treatments

3. Securing referrals, second opinions, and tests

4. Researching a diagnosis

5. Gaining empowerment and speaking up

The body of the article covers all five issues, but let's just look at the first of those body subheads, "Skating Past Voice Mail."

Skating Past Voice Mail

> "Your call will be answered in the order received."

> "My father was a pediatrician. The kids came to the office. He made house calls. Parents called the house. I just don't know how we got to where we are today," says Dave Hosseini, the executive director of the regional office of Patients' Rights, a consumer self-help organization specializing in mental health concerns.

This first paragraph of the body opens with a strong quote from a professional in the field of patients' rights. He echoes the concerns of millions of patients—lack of phone/personal attention by doctors of managed care.

The next paragraph sets up the contrast of the way things used to be before managed care and shows how things are today:

> Today, we don't call our physician at home—physicians are now part of a larger, more complex medical system. Often, we phone a huge call center and first confer with an advice nurse. Countless mothers will nod in unison about the frustration over holding on the line, listening to Muzak, as the toddler cries from an ear infection.

Now, to add objectivity to the piece—to be fair and maintain journalistic ethics by giving both sides—a doctor who directs managed care for a university system speaks:

> Dave Ormerod, M.D., the medical director of managed care for the University of California, Davis Health System, says, "Most physicians are sensitive to the patients' needs for closer communication and desire to facilitate that as much as possible."

The quote shows both sides of the issue—sure, we all want to talk to our docs, but look at the demands placed upon *them* in the managed care system:

> He goes on to explain that "more and more demands are being placed on the physician's limited time, such as federal regulations requiring much more documentation of a visit and some pressure by their organizations to see more patients in less time."

Finally, Lynne ends this section of the body with exactly what the body of an article should provide the reader—information! Again, the body remains the meat and potatoes of the article feast:

> The ability to screen calls by office staff or an advice nurse enables the physician to deal with several nonemergency concerns during selected times of the day. Ormerod offers these suggestions to help alleviate patient frustration regarding the system:
>
> 1. Don't expect to speak directly to the physician when first calling the office. Be prepared, rather, to leave a clear and concise message.
>
> 2. Sometimes the advice nurse will be able to address your concerns completely. Please trust that—even if the nurse handles the call—your doctor will receive notification of the encounter.
>
> 3. Provide a specific callback time that is convenient for you. Understand that most return calls are made during the lunch hour or at the end of the day. Please allow a 60-minute time frame where you will be at a certain number at which the doctor may reach you. It's also good to have an answering machine on—just in case the doctor is unable to return your call during the specified time frame.
>
> 4. If you have access to electronic mail, determine whether your physician would be amenable to receiving correspondence, questions, or updates by this route.
>
> 5. If communicating via e-mail, keep your messages concise. For instance, if you have pain, tell the doctor, "I have pain in my right shoulder, which I believe I pulled while playing basketball. Should I have an X-ray done, and what can I take to lessen the pain?" Allow a reasonable time for the doctor to respond—at a least 24 to 48 hours using this mode. Also, do not use e-mail for medical emergencies.

We won't bore you with all the subsections of the body of this article; however, look at what we listed above. The body featured information-packed sections, everything from getting a second opinion to securing special tests. Once more, if we haven't impressed this upon you enough, the body provides the detailed information of the article.

Some Additional Pointers

These important items will help you produce the best possible writing of your body—or any section, for that matter. In fact, you'll see these tips again in subsequent chapters because they are important components of good writing.

➤ Sit down and write all the questions you'd want to know about your subject. Answer them in the course of the body.

➤ Incorporate any quotes, statistics, or research that back your findings within the appropriate paragraphs. If you write, "Childcare continues to cost parents more and more each year" in the course of your piece, and you found a recent study giving the percentage of the increase, cite it. Likewise, if an interview source provided you with a biting or hard-hitting quote, use it. Lynne actually wrote an article on the state of childcare where a former daycare provider lamented the low pay, saying, "You can make more at In-n-Out Burger." She incorporated the quote into the body of the copy.

➤ Use *active verbs*. Try not to use *is, am, are, was, were, be, being,* or *been*. These verbs make for dull copy. Look at the next two sentences:

1. She is a writer.
2. She writes.

And let's try it again …

1. The tired writer is sitting at the desk.
2. The tired writer sits at the desk.

The active verb provides better, more visual copy because it is shorter and gets to the point more quickly. This isn't broadcast news. We've already told you that shorter is better. When you finish writing a piece, go back over your article and try to rewrite with this in mind. Don't sacrifice meaning for an active verb, but more than likely an active verb will better showcase your meaning anyway.

The Write Words

The verb tense shows the time of an action or the time of a state of being. Writers of magazine features generally employ **active verbs** in present tense. Active verbs are more colorful. Present tense places the reader at the time of the event and is more engaging.

The Straight Scoop

As a writer, you describe in words everything the reader needs to see, feel, taste, and hear. So document your observations in as much detail as possible. As you write, you'll use those items to make richer, more meaningful copy. For instance, if the celebrity you're interviewing popped open a Budweiser, write, "He popped open a Budweiser" instead of "He popped open a beer." The difference may speak volumes about your subject.

➤ Employ transitions. When you move from one idea to another within sentences of paragraphs or between paragraphs, you must transition. Otherwise, you lose the reader and mark yourself as an immature writer. Although sophisticated writers know that the careful arrangement of words can act as a transition, they nevertheless also use standard "transition words." Reacquaint yourself now with common transition words and phrases:

Besides	Still	Consequently
First	Meanwhile	Moreover
Later	Therefore	Then
For example	However	On the contrary
For instance	Accordingly	Again
In addition	Afterward	Yet
Indeed	Beyond	Likewise
In fact	Rather	Eventually
On the other hand	Nevertheless	Furthermore
Though	Nearly	In other words
Then	Of course	Specifically

➤ Read your article aloud to yourself, to someone else, to the dog—it doesn't matter. You'll pick up awkward sentences and unclear references when you hear your work. We highly recommend the "someone else," too. Your "proof-listener" may hear something awkward that you missed or ask a question that you forgot to answer.

➤ Join a writers' group and continue to take writing classes. All good writers will tell you that their writing constantly evolves and that the input of other writers helps make them better writers. You never arrive at one culminating place as a writer. Writers work at their craft and appreciate the constructive criticism of other professional writers. You'll become a better writer by studying writing. We guarantee it.

Dessert: The Perfect Closing Paragraph

Yummy. The perfect closing—like a really great dessert—tastes great. Basically, the closing paragraph gives your article a feel of completion. This may mean or require ending on a strong, fantastic quote. It may mean commenting on your subject, a little editorializing.

A closing should complement, not outdo, the overall article. Often the closing re-states key ideas from your introductory paragraph and also sums up the entire piece.

The closing comes full circle. In the final analysis, ask yourself this question after reading your work: Does the article feel finished?

What follows is the closing paragraph to the "Wrangling Managed Care" article. This paragraph comes directly after discussing the need for patients to educate themselves and, most importantly, speak up.

> And Hosseini, who likens our new HMOs to "giant Targets of medical care," closes with this: "As in everything in life, we have to learn to be a consumer. Most times when you go shopping, you don't go without a list. You prepare for a shopping trip. The same goes for health care. Make a list. Shop for the best policy. Then bring a list of your concerns to your physician."

Lynne let the expert close the piece, which is often a good device to use. If an expert sums up the gist or theme of the article, end on it. Let the expert talk! The story also came full circle. Lynne began the body of the article on Hosseini's words about his father, the pediatrician, and ended on Hosseini's advice to the health-care consumer. A continuity of characters reinforces the closing.

These comments don't suggest that you must use the same expert in your closing as you may have used in the introduction or beginning of the body and then use only quotes to close. *Au contraire!* Other times, you will need to determine what the overall idea of your article may be. You will need to tell the readers the last idea they should know. Closings are toughies, and there is no right way to close an article. You must determine yourself whether you answered the questions and finished the piece. As we discussed before, reading the piece aloud may help you determine whether your ending falls flat or finishes.

Writing Headlines and Titles

Even though editors may not require the teaser copy of a brief opening, an editor will want a title for your piece. Don't get us wrong—he'll probably mold it to his own liking, but he wants to have some clay to work with, you know.

Sometimes the title may already have been conceptualized when the pitch moved from letter to assignment. In those cases, great. But when you need to come up with a successful title on your own, keep the following points in mind:

➤ A title identifies the content of your article.

➤ A title gives the reader an idea of the significance of the article.

➤ A title attracts the reader—it hooks 'em in, baby.

➤ A title reflects the tone of the story—happy, irreverent, funny, solemn.

There's no formula for a great title. Think catchy but significant. You don't want to lose your reader in some surreal reference. Think clever, not cluttered. Omit unnecessary words. Do your best, but don't fret over the title. Again, just give the editor something to work with or think about.

You already saw the title of the piece we've examined: "Wrangling Managed Care." Here are some examples of other titles to study, so that you, too, can "feel" what makes a good title.

➤ **"No Baby on Board."** This article discussed women who choose not to ever have children, and profiled four "childfree" women.

➤ **"Off the Court."** This article covered the nonprofit and charitable work being accomplished by a team in the WNBA.

➤ **"In the Garden of Earthly Delights."** This essay showcased the relationship a young girl nurtured with her grandfather while gardening together.

➤ **"Ethnic Eats!"** This title ran as a coverline (on the cover) for a roundup piece on restaurants serving up international flavors.

Titles are tricky. Again, much like everything else—the dek, the hook, the opening, and the introduction—the title draws the reader to the story. In a fragment or extremely short sentence, you tell the readers what they can expect to find in the article.

The Least You Need to Know

➤ Before you sit down to write, organize your materials. Make sure you have disks, paper, ink, and even coffee if you can't write without it.

➤ Prepare an outline for your article in which you jot down key items you want to cover. You'll be less likely to forget them with an outline.

➤ Make the editor's life easier; take a stab at writing the two-sentence teaser for your article.

➤ An article is made up of a hook, body, and conclusion.

➤ The use of transitions, literary devices, and active verbs will enrich your copy and set you apart from amateur writers.

➤ Good titles attract the reader, are concise, and reflect the tone of the story.

Hook 'Em Early, Hook 'Em Hard

If we haven't impressed upon you in the chapter about pitch letters (see Chapter 8, "Writing a Winning Query") the necessity of hitting hard upfront and grabbing the reader's attention, we hope to do so here. A strong lead hooks the readers and keeps them reading, just as your pitch letter hooked the editor. You sold the editor on the story; now it's time to sell the readers on it.

In this chapter, we show you some tricks for accomplishing great leads. We also give you more "devices" to create better copy. Yawning readers don't result in more assignments for you—or more sales for the magazine. Didn't think this gig would be about sales, did you? Guess again—and follow our lead.

We're Following the Leader, the Leader, the Leader

The lead of your article is none other than the beginning—the *introduction*. The lead, well, leads the reader into the body of the story, essay, feature, or whatever you're writing. Now, a dry, lifeless lead causes readers to flip the page and seek another story. To retain those readers, your introduction must sing!

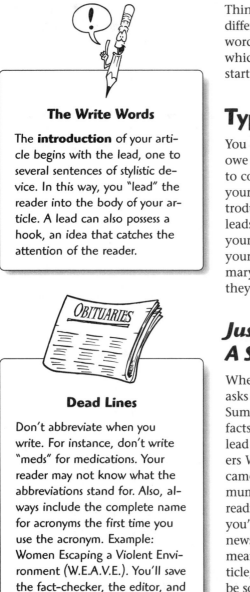

The Write Words

The **introduction** of your article begins with the lead, one to several sentences of stylistic device. In this way, you "lead" the reader into the body of your article. A lead can also possess a hook, an idea that catches the attention of the reader.

Dead Lines

Don't abbreviate when you write. For instance, don't write "meds" for medications. Your reader may not know what the abbreviations stand for. Also, always include the complete name for acronyms the first time you use the acronym. Example: Women Escaping a Violent Environment (W.E.A.V.E.). You'll save the fact-checker, the editor, and the copyeditor time lost coming back to you for a definition of the acronym or abbreviation.

Think about it. If you saw the first paragraph of three different stories side by side, and each started with these words, respectively—"Murder," "Cats," "Education"— which story would you read first? Probably the one starting with "Murder."

Types of Leads

You can choose from eight primary types of leads. You owe it to yourself to be familiar with all of them and to consider carefully what type of lead you choose for your article. By using the stylistic devices in your introduction, you develop style in your writing. Also, leads serve to emphasize something and add color to your copy. One more thing: Use what works best for your article. Don't try to force one of the eight primary leads into your introduction; use them only if they work for your story and make it better.

Just the Facts, Ma'am: A Summary Lead

When a crime investigator begins an interrogation, he asks for the facts, the story stripped of interpretation. Summary leads offer up to the reader right away the facts of the story you have to tell. It's the same type of lead you find in newspaper stories. You give the readers Who, What, When, Where, Why, and How things came down. You entice the readers with the bare minimum in the hopes of engaging them and keeping them reading. You'd want to use this type of lead if the story you're writing transcends the five W's and one H. In a newspaper story, a summary lead provides a practical means of quickly giving the facts. But in a magazine article, the facts alone, dispensed right at the outset, can be so titillating that the readers want to keep reading to find out just what type of circumstances could produce such facts.

Steinbeck Is as Steinbeck Does: A Descriptive Lead

Steinbeck earned the kudos of critics worldwide for his lush descriptions of the Salinas Valley and his intricate characterization. The images and Steinbeck's ability to transport the reader into the scene kept the reader progressing through novels such as *East of Eden*. The following is Steinbeck's description of the character Slim in *Of Mice and Men*.

A tall man stood in the doorway. He held a crushed Stetson hat under his arm while he combed his long, black, damp straight hair back. Like the others he wore blue jeans and a short denim jacket. When he had finished combing his hair he moved into the room, and he moved with majesty only achieved by royalty and master craftsmen. He was a jerk-line skinner, the prince of the ranch, capable of driving ten, sixteen, even twenty mules with a single line to the leaders. He was capable of killing a fly on the wheeler's butt with a bullwhip without touching the mule. There was a gravity in his manner and a quiet so profound that all talk stopped when he spoke. His authority was so great that his word was taken on any subject, be it politics or love. This was Slim, the jerkline skinner. His hatchet face was ageless. He might have been thirty-five or fifty. His ear heard more than was said to him, and his slow speech had overtones not of thought, but of understanding beyond thought. His hands, large and lean, were as delicate as those of a temple dancer.

> **Dead Lines**
>
> Don't use slang unless the magazine regularly or readily employs it. Most don't! In the glossy women's magazine *Allure*, for instance, slang in the fashion industry was covered in the March 2000 issue ("delish" for delicious, and "ramen" for permed hair that looks like Ramen noodles), but the features certainly don't use "delish" in the copy. More often than not, you'll turn off your reader and your editor if you employ slang.

Don't fret. You don't have a novel to write, just a paragraph—one descriptive, engaging paragraph called, appropriately enough, a descriptive lead.

In a descriptive lead, your writing provides the reader a mind movie, projecting across the brain's screen the five senses of the experience. Check out the following few sentences and ask yourself if you "see" anything:

> While the rain splattered in bulb-like bursts on the cement, the cool chill tickled us as we sat down to talk under the umbrellas at the court of a pink and pretty hotel in Beverly Hills. The actress wore little makeup, but the condensation reflected on her smooth skin brought an angel-like and playful appeal to her.

The Write Words

Foreshadowing is a device by which the writer creates suspense and also hints at what may come later in the story. For instance, if you describe the red curtains, the red dress, and the red door sign, and red, red, red seems to be emphasized over and over again almost ominously, you may be foreshadowing more red to come in the form of blood, hinting that a murder may play a part in the article later.

Dead Lines

Don't repeat key words in the copy. Repetition shows a weak mind and a feeble writer. Get out your thesaurus, and use it!

Then she began to talk about her next film, and the thunderous clap overhead *foreshadowed* the bad picture.

We see torrential rain, a pink hotel, an angelic creature, and the comings of a horrible movie. Again, a descriptive lead engages the reader visually. Pretty incredible, huh, when you consider that you're actually painting pictures with words? It sets the reader in the scene. Whether you're covering a movie star or a parade, by describing the scene you automatically engage the reader in the action. Really fantastic writers—such as Steinbeck—actually transport the reader with a descriptive lead into the fictional world of their novels. Your goal in using the descriptive lead, therefore, is to transport the reader to the scene of your feature. If you're interviewing Spielberg at his Beverly Hills home, let your reader know what the digs looked like, how the cushions on the couch felt, and what the aromas wafting through the halls smelled like. Get out your palette for the descriptive lead.

Good Golly, Miss Molly! An Astonishing Lead

An astonishing lead shocks the reader with an unexpected event, word, or anything that grabs his interest. For example, if you open an article with the phrase "Walk here and die!" the reader will want to know where not to walk and will read on.

Statistics typically provide the fodder for astonishing leads. For example, consider these opening lines: "Count the first eight women you see at work today. One will contract breast cancer." The lead astonishes because the writer brought the statistic home to a personal level for the reader.

But not all astonishing leads relay a sad or horrifying message. Take, for instance, a lead that may appear in a parenting magazine: "The baby you're carrying is actually two." That leading sentence may provoke pregnant readers to read more. What could such a statement mean?

You get the idea. Make the readers' eyes bulge in disbelief, dread, anticipation, or curiosity. Do that, and you've successfully hooked 'em.

Short Work: A Staccato Lead

Remember when your high school English teacher told you not to use simple sentences or fragments? Throw her advice out the window for the staccato lead. With a staccato lead, the writer uses fragments and short sentences.

Here's an example: "The best of times. The worst of times. We didn't know what the millennium would bring."

Here's another: "After the tests. After the surgeries. After the chemotherapy. After the radiation. After cancer, one must learn to live with the disease."

Go ahead, frag away and simple-sentence it up. Your old English teacher will be none the wiser—or she'll take credit for nurturing the writing wizard that you've become.

Dead Lines

Make sure that you don't over-use commas. Keep a good grammar book by your side, and check it! You won't impress the editors with comma splices.

Play with Me: A Parody Lead

People love parody leads. Parody leads play on songs, lyrics, literature, and any cultural item that is easily recognizable. Parody leads take puns one step further.

Example:

> "Take me out to the mall game. Take me out to the store!" Perhaps it's the new cry of thousands of women nationwide, as recent statistics show that shopping is the favorite pastime of the fairer sex.

Dead Lines

Don't shift your point of view during a piece. You'll seem flaky, and your reader will be confused if in one paragraph you express one opinion and in the next express another. You risk receiving a kill fee instead of payment if you go schizophrenic in your article.

The writer used a parody of America's favorite pastime, baseball, and its traditional song, "Take Me Out to the Ball Game," to lead readers into the story about shopping. The familiarity of the song instantly engages the reader. The shopping "twist" furthers the hook. Congratulations—the reader is hooked into further reading.

"I Did Not Have Sexual Relations with That Woman": A Direct Quotation Lead

One of the most forceful leads available is the direct quotation. You immediately offer your reader an eavesdropping opportunity because quotes are someone's actual words. The reader gets to be "a fly on the wall" and listen in on intimate details. And when the quote hits hard—voilà!—you've hooked yourself a reader.

The Straight Scoop

Ann Patchett, the author of *Patron Saint of Liars* and *The Magician's Assistant,* and a regular contributor to various magazines, was signing copies of her books at a nonprofit event. With each person who approached the table and asked how to get published, how to take an idea and move it to paper, Ms. Patchett responded, "Write. Write it." Good advice. Becoming a writer requires more than just talking about it or planning to do it "when you get the time"—it requires that you sit down and actually write.

Co-author Lynne likes using the quotation lead. "The reader becomes part of the dialogue from the get-go," she says. You don't even need to begin the first line with the quote. Doing so within the first two lines works just as well. Remember that "Wrangling Managed Care" feature? The second sentence read, "I was about ready to strangle that doctor!" These were the words of a wronged patient. Perhaps readers of "Wrangling Managed Care" continued reading to find out why the patient wanted to strangle her doctor.

The Straight Scoop

Need a nudge to get you pitching? Taking a writing class may just prove the bridge between unpublished and published for you. Many writing professors motivate their students by offering an A if they get a magazine assignment during the term. That's another great reason to take a writing class! Remember writer Tamara Givens, who wrote the piece on Friday Night Live for the CHP serial? She earned that byline and an A because of it from her college instructor.

What Is a Question, Alex? A Question Lead

When you ask a question, you expect an answer. By asking a question in a lead, you've personalized the lead to the reader by asking her a question. It's as if you wrote the piece with the reader in mind. The questions serve to lead to the answers, of course, probably something the reader will want by the time she finishes reading the questions.

Let's pretend that the writer's assignment is to unveil the world of career counselors and advise readers how to make a career counselor work for them. The lead might begin, "Tired of your job? Having a hard time getting up out of bed each morning? Lacking career satisfaction? Well, maybe a career counselor can help." By the time the reader answers the questions, she just may want to know how a career counselor can help her get out of her dead-end profession. She keeps reading.

But the question lead doesn't have to be a direct address to the reader, either. In a question lead such as "Why would a man who has everything—a great job, a beautiful family, an exciting lifestyle—throw it all away to become a goat herder?" you pique the readers' curiosity by asking a question that they just have to have answered.

The Straight Scoop

Want to read a funny, insightful, and inspiring book about the writing process? Pick up or check out Anne Lamott's nonfiction work, *Bird by Bird: Some Instructions on Writing and Life*. In the book, Lamott tells readers that the secret to being a writer is to give yourself "short assignments" and expect "shitty first drafts," and expresses how "writing turns out to be its own reward." Though geared for the creative writer, helpful lessons for all writers appear within the pages.

Extreme Sports: A Contrast Lead

A contrast lead points out extremes. Opposites attract in the contrast lead. Essentially, you also obliterate a stereotype or the perceived idea in a contrast lead. Here's an example:

> Despite the fact that advertisements and magazines glamorize modeling and showcase their world as one big party, insiders tell us that drugs, unattainable standards of thinness, and long work days result in burn-out and even death among America's favorite supermodel sweethearts.

Here's another example:

> Short days, summers off, ahhhhh, the life of a teacher, right? How about insulting pay, long hours correcting papers, and no respect!

Somewhat like an astonishing lead, a contrast lead shocks the reader with the opposite thoughts and extreme differences. Contrast leads are best used to make a point.

On a final note, leads remain perhaps the most important part of your article. With a really great lead, you retain the reader. Guess who your first reader is? The editor. In fact, a lead must be so perfect that editors will often tell you to go back to the writing board if the introduction doesn't hit the mark. With Lynne's first feature in a glossy, for instance, the editor came back and asked her to rewrite the introduction—specifically, the lead, the first few sentences.

So, work on perfecting your leads. Make 'em sing, or count yourself out of the free-lancing arena. Leads are that important.

The Least You Need to Know

➤ The opening sentences of your article constitute the lead. The lead should arouse the readers' interest and keep them reading.

➤ Your lead may well be the most important aspect of your article. After all, if the reader stops reading, what's the point of having written?

➤ There are eight types of leads: summary, descriptive, astonishing, staccato, parody, quotation, question, and contrast.

➤ Don't underestimate the importance of a strong lead.

Chapter 20

Machine Gun Writing

In This Chapter

➤ Fast writing for fast reading in a fast world

➤ Machine gun writing—fast, powerful, and sure

➤ Quotes, verbs, and tense

➤ The importance of editing yourself

In our fast-paced world, people crave their information quickly, and editors know this better than anyone. In this chapter, we show you the difference between a feature and a flashy, 250- to 500-word burst of information. Get out your flak jacket and your totally hip prose because we're entering an MTV-like combat zone. Where once there were motion pictures, now videos reign. Well, the same goes for writing. Because in order to write these crisp, cutting-edge "video-like" features, you'll need some refined editing skills, too.

We're All Part of a Ritalin Nation

Today's lifestyle is all about speed. We purchase gas at the pump, make deposits at a machine, and shop online. We wolf down dinner out of Styrofoam box while working on a project due yesterday. We juggle careers, soccer practice, car payments, and edge maintenance in cyberspace. Life is fast—and so is our need for quick information.

Dead Lines

Avoid the word *very* at all costs in your writing. You can convey degrees of difference by choosing a better, more efficient word. For instance, instead of writing "He was very happy," write "He was overjoyed."

The Write Words

When a feature article is broken down into many subarticles, editors sometimes describe the approach taken as a **breakout.** What you, the writer, do is break out all the different concepts or mini-stories into separate sidebar-like boxes of information.

Break-Dancing for Dollars

To respond to the reader's need for short bursts of news and information that packs a punch, print media have responded by breaking up stories into mini-stories. Instead of a long feature, with interviews of several people woven into 2,000 words, a magazine may break up the profiles within the feature into several short, vignette-like bursts of 250 to 500 words. Instead of a feature on one wide topic such as "pets," magazines now may break up the topic into a multitude of interesting subtopics or substories. This division of stories allows the reader to read those sections he wants and avoid those that don't interest him.

Let's take the "pet" story that Lynne wrote. Here's the actual breakdown of the feature:

➤ A 300-word introduction

➤ Six 200- to 350-word pet/master profiles with a large pictorial focus

➤ Nineteen two- to three-line pet/master profiles

➤ A 200-word story on rescue societies

➤ A 100-word story on pet bakeries

➤ A 150-word story on a pet grieving hotline

➤ A 200-word story on pet sitters

➤ A 500-word story on choosing the right pet for your family

➤ Eleven pet trivia questions (example: Are ferrets really illegal?) with answers

The editor assigned Lynne one feature on pets but chose to make it a *breakout,* to divide the feature into short, attention-grabbing profiles and informational pieces. When you have short pieces that are outlined for you, you don't have to worry about the transitioning of thought to thought in one long piece. Roundups and breakouts are easier to write but generally are more time-consuming because there are more components.

The Department Store

Like feature articles being broken into combinations of shorter pieces, magazine *departments* are undergoing a similar transformation, covering multiple subjects within the same department. Just as a department store breaks up shoes into women's, men's, and children's areas, magazines may divide a section, such as "Beauty," into short pieces of copy all relating to the theme of beauty, geared for quick reading with maximum information payoff.

Let's look at the "Beauty Front" department in *Shape* magazine. A recent issue showcased six different items on one page—everything from shiny nails to gemstone use in skin care products. The copy was short and sweet—and must have been written by someone.

Once you embark upon a freelancing career, chances are good that you'll write these pithy, information-packed pieces often. So let's look into machine gun journalism.

Ratatatatat: Machine Gun Writing

Do you feel like Bruce Willis in *Die Hard* right about now? What the heck do we mean when we say machine gun writing?

Well, think about it. The machine gun empties bullets quickly and hits hard. Machine gun writing accomplishes the same thing. But instead of bullets, the writer shoots fast, hard-hitting words. Every word packs a "meaning punch."

Machine gun writing—writing articles that are short and information-packed, and that belong to a larger feature or magazine component—is probably the most challenging writing a freelancer will do.

Just cranking out something, writing fast without really thinking about word choice or sentence structure, requires little skill. But careful writing, using the right words and arranging them for maximum effect (as in poetry) takes time. Machine gun writing seeks to accomplish this kind of mastery. Gaining the skill of this level of writing for the masses of MTV-ers, boomers, and Gen X-ers should prove a never-ending challenge.

Now this isn't to say that feature writing (for long pieces) is ineffective and less carefully crafted. In essence, all writing requires carefully "attacking" the piece and using the best word choice, active verbs, and cleanest prose possible. The difference here is that it's good writing taken up a notch. The difference lies in the length of the piece,

The Write Words

Sections in a magazine devoted to one area each issue are called **departments.** For instance, if a magazine covers health, beauty, and finance every issue, each topic is termed a department (as in, "Beauty" department, "Health" department, "Finance" department).

Dead Lines

Never say *less* people, *less* dogs, or *less* objects of any kind. Write *fewer* instead. *Less* refers to an amount and means smaller in actual size, whereas *fewer* means smaller in number.

217

not the quality. With a longer piece, you can include more and take your time to develop your subject. But in a short profile, for example, you've got 250 words—that's it. You must tell someone's whole life (or the components of his life that matter most to the reader) in 250 words. One page, double-spaced—that's it. Situations and people tend to be far more complex than 250 words allow. But for the good writer—the artist with his flak jacket on—250 words can accomplish miracles.

With "Rambo writing," as with anything in life, practice makes perfect. To master this kind of writing, you must practice it daily, in your letters, notes, and e-mails. Concentrate on using the most informative words and the most visually arresting verbs. Incorporate any quotes that back up your meaning. Don't just crank out any old message. Practice your art in everything you do.

The Straight Scoop

At the dawn of the new millennium, nine magazine experts—from former and current editors to media moguls—chose the "10 best" magazine editors, with the results published in the *Columbia Journalism Review*. Here are the winners:

1. Tina Brown, *Talk*

2. Graydon Carter, *Vanity Fair*

3. Gregory Curtis, *Texas Monthly*

4. Barbara Epstein and Robert Silvers, *The New York Review of Books*

5. John Huey, *Fortune*

6. Walter Isaacson, *Time*

7. Michael Kisley, *Slate*

8. Lewis Lapham, *Harper's*

9. Adam Moss, *The New York Times Magazine*

10. Jann Wenner, *Rolling Stone*

Just think, some day soon you may write for one of them!

Let Me Speak! Using Quotes

You'll want to learn to pull the best quotes from your interviews. This isn't an easy task, but here are some questions you can ask yourself about the quotes you plan to use in the article.

➤ **What do I want to tell or convey to the reader about the person I'm interviewing?** Ask yourself questions such as "Do I want to show this person's funny bone? Tenacity? Laziness? Work ethic? Strength? Hardships? What?" Then answer and stick to it. You can't cover everything!

➤ **Do any of my quotes reveal for the reader the message I want to convey?** In a piece on a producer for public television, Lynne wanted to express the woman's sense of humor and brash, larger-than-life personality. Therefore, when the woman laughed and told Lynne that beyond watching PBS they should "send a check," Lynne ended the profile on the quote. The producer's sincere yet humorous approach to her livelihood's survival was what needed to be conveyed. One quote served that purpose.

➤ **Do I have too much of the quote? Do I really need all the lines of the quote to express my intent?** Let's say that the subject told you, "My dog is my best friend, a real pal, a sidekick. We are compadres. I'd die without him." Perhaps you want the reader to know the subject loves his dog, but you don't have the space to give the whole quote. Instead, you say, "My dog is my best friend. I would die without him."

➤ **Can I *paraphrase* any of the quote to accomplish a fuller, tighter piece?** For example, suppose that your subject gives a longwinded quote expressing how she voted on each issue in a recent election. Each vote was way on the liberal side of politics. Instead of using her quote, you may write: "Jane Doe professes to have voted on the extreme left of all issues in the recent election." Hence, you paraphrased the quote.

The Straight Scoop

All writers sometimes confuse the use of *who* and *that*. Just remember that *who* refers to people, as in "Diego is the one who dove off the board." You wouldn't say "Diego is the one *that* dove off the board." *That* refers to animals or objects (that don't have specific names), as in "Here's the house that I built."

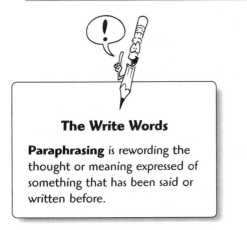

The Write Words

Paraphrasing is rewording the thought or meaning expressed of something that has been said or written before.

➤ **Is the quote striking? Does it have a purpose?** Let's say that you're covering an educator, for example. You decide that the colorful aspect of the educator is her poor beginnings in the rural South, and now she helps poor children overcome their adversity. Would you quote the educator talking about her favorite hobby ("I relax by playing golf")? Absolutely not. In 250 words, you have to give your reader her story in her words and use the quote in which her father told her, "When you walk to school, you walk proud, Lillie!"

➤ **Would the piece seem less interesting without the quote? Stay the same? Be more interesting?** Take the quote out of the story and read it aloud. Does the story sound better? Is it less interesting? Answer the question and move on.

The other important facet of quoting is placement. You'll learn in the next section where to place your quotes in machine gun writing, as well as where to place other information.

Placement of Your Information or Word

You get only one chance, baby. In a machine gun piece, you don't have room for a lengthy buildup or for gradual development of ideas. Take aim and fire. Don't bury important statistics, information, or quotes. Put the heart of your subject into the paragraph or two in which you have to do it. Give the thrust of your piece—the voice of your subject, a recent ground-breaking study—front and center access to the reader.

Dead Lines

Wordiness reeks! Learn to write uncluttered articles with the most appropriate active verbs. Don't say, for instance, that someone "proceeded to turn left." Instead, write that someone "turned left." Clean out the messy word closet during the writing process.

If you procured a fantastic quote from a person you're profiling (or anyone else), lead with it, don't bury it. Remember the quote from the last chapter, about the woman who wanted "to strangle" the doctor? That quote was moved from the body of the paragraph to the beginning because it spoke volumes about the frustration of patients receiving managed care. Suppose the woman had said, "I went to see the doctor today." That quote holds less relevance to the subject.

Let's look at an example of a machine gun profile with quotes front and center.

This profile is taken from a roundup covering up-and-coming women in a city. Each piece needed to convey why the woman should be watched and what she currently is doing to warrant the attention. Look at the quotes chosen for this piece, too. Interestingly, they are not from the mouth of the person profiled, but from her supporters.

Michelle Ray Davis

"I want to change coaches—to Michelle," Shannon Pauls tells her mother, "because Michelle makes me do it, and I want to do it." Pauls knows that Michelle Ray Davis coaches with a passion that will take the young skater to the Olympics one day. Skate parents speak of the teacher who involves herself in every aspect of their children's sport—the music, the costumes, the choreography, even transportation. Davis, for instance, picks up Ed Lee's daughters from school once a week to get them on the ice. "Michelle is a very accomplished, aggressive skater," says the father. He appreciates that the coach "shows them—doesn't tell them—what they can be."

While an amateur skater, Davis trained under the same coaches as Debbie Thomas and Kristi Yamaguchi. When her alcoholic father abandoned the family, Davis turned professional to send income home to her mother. The professional skater toured the world, starring in ice shows from South Africa to Mexico.

Dead Lines

Never say that a person or pet "sustained" injuries. Live beings "suffer" injuries, whereas nonliving things, such as chairs or cars, "sustain" damage.

Dead Lines

Writers who know style rules never use the percent sign in writing (%). Spell it out instead. Example: Twenty percent or 20 percent.

With more than twice the coaching load of most instructors at Roseville's Skatetown, Davis's fervor for champions remains unparalleled. She anticipates taking four of her private students to Nationals in the next five years. In May, five of Davis's students took medals at a regional competition in the Bay Area—two received golds. "Out of all the coaches," says Skatetown owner Scott Slavensky, "Michelle stands out. If she hooks up with someone as talented and committed as she is to the sport, I don't doubt that she'll coach an Olympic star from this facility."

Use It or Lose It: Keeping Active

Ask any editor what stylistic trait differentiates a weak writer from a great writer, and he'll probably respond, "Verb choice." An editor Lynne worked with once told her that she rates new writers by circling the verbs in their clips. If the majority are passive, colorless verbs, the writer loses out on an assignment—even if the pitch is positively wonderful.

When we say active voice, we mean that the subject of the sentence performs the action. Let's take a look at a sentence written actively and then written passively.

➤ **Active:** Patrick pets the purple hippopotamus.

➤ **Passive:** The purple hippopotamus is being petted by Patrick.

Notice that using passive verbs makes a sentence longer and therefore takes up more space. When every word must hit like a bullet in these short pieces, why write a long sentence when you can write a short one by using the active voice?

Colorful verbs vividly show the scene and paint the picture in action. Active verbs are less tedious and less boring. If every word of your writing must hit hard and pack punch, why tolerate boring sentences?

Take a look at the profile of Michelle Ray Davis, after changing some of the active verbs to passive verbs and after exchanging more colorful verbs for less vivid ones. The changes have been italicized.

> "I want to change coaches—to Michelle," Shannon Pauls tells her mother, "because Michelle makes me do it, and I want to do it." Pauls knows that Michelle Ray Davis is a coach with passion who *is going* to take the young skater to the Olympics someday. Michelle *is involved* in all aspects of her students' sport according to parents. Davis even picks up two students from school each day so they *can skate*. "Michelle is a very accomplished, aggressive skater," says the father of the girls. He *is appreciative* that the coach "shows them—doesn't tell them" what they can be.
>
> While an amateur skater, Michelle *took lessons* under the same coaches as Olympic stars Debbie Thomas and Kristi Yamaguchi. Michelle's father *is an alcoholic* and when he *left* the family, she *became* a *professional skater* to send income home to her mother. The professional skater *went* all over the world, starring in ice shows from South Africa to Mexico.
>
> Michelle *has* twice the coaching load of other coaches. She *has* a fervor for champions. She *is anticipating* taking four of her private students to Nationals in the next five years. In May, five of Davis's students *won* medals at a regional competition in the Bay Area—two received golds. "Out of all the coaches," says Skatetown owner Scott Slavensky, "Michelle stands out. If she hooks up with someone as talented and committed as she is to the sport, I don't doubt that she'll coach an Olympic star from this facility."

The profile stinks! And it's got more words, proof enough that more isn't necessarily better.

As the reader, which profile do you find more vivid, more alive, more interesting? The active paragraph! In your writing, use active, colorful verbs.

The Tension Is Killing Me!

Besides using active voice, remember to write in the present tense, as if it's happening as the reader reads the copy.

Let's look at the difference between past and present tense of verbs.

➤ **Past:** She ate cookie after cookie, all the while talking about her film.

➤ **Present:** As she talks of her film, the actress eats cookie after cookie.

By keeping the tense present, you enable the reader to become more involved in the story, to step into the action. Your writing unfolds like a movie on a screen. Keep it active, keep it present, and you'll succeed in writing for a Ritalin nation.

The Straight Scoop

Even in copy, numbers can baffle us "word" people. When a number pops up in your next article, remember this simple rule: Spell out one through nine. Use the symbols for all numbers above nine. But be forewarned, exceptions exist (kind of like those confusing theorems of math classes past), so check either the *AP Stylebook* or the *Chicago Manual of Style* if you're unsure.

Off with Her Head: Editing

Now that you've put together a machine gun piece, don't assume that you're done. Have you answered all the questions the editor may have put forth on the assignment sheet regarding this profile or that informational box? Now, count the words. Are you within limits? Are there sentences you don't need? Perhaps you could delete them and add more pertinent information. To provide your reader (and your editor) with the tightest copy, you must edit the piece yourself before turning it in.

"But," you may protest, "I'm not an editor!" We understand. Editing remains a talent that eludes many a writer, but you've got to try. Bear in mind that this isn't the official edit. A professional editor will do that task for you. But you want to turn in the best copy you can. Try to look at the following steps as less "editing" and more "cleaning." At the least, this process will make editing an easier task for you.

➤ Read your story one sentence at a time. Ask yourself, "What isn't pertinent to the story? What can I delete without sacrificing vivid, colorful copy or meaning?"

➤ On a separate piece of paper, write down all your verbs. Are they boring? Can you think of better ones? Are they in the passive voice? Change any instances of passive voice to active voice, and make that copy even tighter.

➤ Read your piece aloud. The ear could pick up awkward phrases that the eye might have missed.

➤ Have someone else read your story—your mom, your dad, your sister, your best friend, anybody. If you know another writer willing to edit your work, go for it. Ask the person to give you feedback.

Dead Lines

Know what peeves a source and an editor the minute the mag hits the rack? A misspelled name. Always, always double-check the spelling of an interview subject's name, and make sure you get it right in the copy. You'll save the editor a nasty call—and yourself a reputation as a sloppy writer.

Now, after accomplishing what Lynne likes to call "tidying up the piece," or editing, count your words again. Then turn it in and relax. Although the editor might tweak the writing here or there, you'll know that you did your best and turned in the cleanest, most colorful copy possible.

The Straight Scoop

Another way to improve your machine gun writing is to improve your vocabulary. If your store of knowledge includes a wider-than-average range of verbs, your writing benefits; you'll always pluck the best verb for the job. So, pick up a power vocabulary book or two. Purchase a word-a-day calendar. You'll be surprised at how much your writing will improve.

The Least You Need to Know

➤ Our fast-paced world has given rise to the need for short articles packed with information. We call these short pieces "machine gun" pieces because each word hits like a bullet packed with meaning.

➤ Even though you may be assigned a 2,000-word story, the editor may choose to break up the story into several mini-stories. Be prepared to write in this style.

➤ Use only the most vivid quotes. Never throw a meaningless quote into your copy.

➤ In short pieces especially, use colorful verbs in the active tense.

➤ Don't forget to edit your piece.

Part 6

The Business of Freelancing

Now that you've learned the nuts and bolts of writing, you'll need to know how to sell your writing, and how to keep track of what you sell. In this part, full-time writers share many a secret about how they stay on top of their writing, and on top of their income! Learn professional systems for tracking your work, getting paid, paying your bills, and paying your taxes (the freelancer's badge of honor!).

What if only one magazine covers that topic? Is that an indication that your specialty might be too small? Not necessarily. Developing a strong relationship with only one specialty magazine is a great way to establish your career. And who knows? The size of the market may well expand as interest in that topic grows. Just remember the days when there was only one computer magazine on the market ....

The Straight Scoop

What might seem like a niche market today could someday grow into a strong mainstream market. Just think: Years ago there would have been only a handful of writers who were writing about this crazy new thing called the Internet. And now how many specialty magazines cover the field? That's not to mention major features in *Time* and *Newsweek*. Even glossy magazines such as *People* have Web site columns these days. So, had you been one of the handful of writers who got in early and established yourself as an expert, you now would more than have your hands full of assignments.

Learn the Editors

Focusing on one field or specialty makes it that much easier to learn who the gate-keepers are, what they like, and how to best approach them. With a smaller cast of characters to keep up with, you can better keep on top of who comes and goes in the world of magazines and other publications. A magazine that you have had trouble breaking into might suddenly have a change on the masthead—and here is your chance to become friends with the new editor!

Learn the Competition

Once you choose a particular field, you also will begin to notice who else is writing in it. You will start to learn other writers' styles, tones, and approaches. This will help you develop a style that won't seem like something that is already out there—a product that is already on the market, so to speak. Are these people your enemies? Heavens, no. You might actually want to seek them out. Professional writers are not threatened by the presence of other writers in the field, but often are pleased to have the company. They also may be willing to help you and share contacts.

Looking for Holes

You've discovered all the possible markets for this topic, learned who the gatekeepers are, and scouted out which other writers are out there. Now what do you do with this information? You analyze.

What you are trying to do is spot the holes in the market, the opportunity for you to pitch a new idea for an article that hasn't been written.

"The more you know about your topic, the more you keep up with what is changing and what is on the horizon, the more article ideas will occur to you," says Jim Brown, whose specialty is writing about government and the health-care industry.

A Niche of One's Own

This sounds pretty good, doesn't it? The idea that you can rocket to the top of free-lance writing success in record time by specializing in one topic. But the question is, what topic? The world is your oyster, but which one is the pearl?

The best first step is to look closely at your own life. What are your passions, your hobbies, your interests? Are they passions, hobbies, and interests shared by millions of other people, too?

"Do what you love, love what you do," is the advice Cynthia Stewart Copier gives those who want to follow their dreams. Are you involved in hang gliding? Gourmet cooking? Wine making? Quilting? Parachuting? Specialty publications cater to all those hobbyists. Do you collect first-edition, leather-bound books? Old movie posters? You name it, there is a magazine or a Web site devoted to it.

Start with your own life and work outward. Ask your friends what kinds of things most absorb them. You might well discover an emerging niche. Certainly the writers who first noticed the growing interest in the Internet were the ones best positioned to become experts in that topic—or Beanie Babies, or day trading, or emerging trends. Be there first, and be rewarded.

Should you develop a specialty only in a topic that moves you to your core? No. Plenty of working writers are experts in topics that bore most of us—health regulations, governmental regulations, and so on—and still get steady work. They might not be too interested in the topic, but they spotted an underserved market that they knew they could break into. Once you have a few writing credentials under your belt, you can hitch it up and move on to another topic.

Dead Lines

Once you establish yourself with the editor of a specialty magazine, don't ever grow too comfortable. Change happens. The day you pick up the phone to call your longtime pal with an article idea and a new voice answers the phone, you'll have to start over again. Keep your clip file together, because you might have to prove yourself all over to this new guy.

Should you stay away from areas in which there already seem to be a few established experts? Not necessarily. If you truly believe that you have a different spin on things—a new way of thinking about wine, for instance, or an unusual education or background that will bring something new to a field—then go for it.

Building a Reputation

How do you go about building a reputation in your field? Slowly. One query letter at a time. One editor at a time. One article at a time.

When trying to break into a particular specialty that has only a limited number of publications, you must be professional in your approach. Follow the freelance etiquette rules as you've learned them in this book, do it to the letter, and try very hard not to get on an editor's bad side—if you do, bing! There goes one potential buyer for your work.

"Over time I have developed a reputation for turning in work that is 100 percent pristine," says Lynn Pribus. "I also fact-check tirelessly, particularly when it comes to quoting sources for medical articles. You do not want something published that can have life or death implications and have it be wrong. Editors know how much care I take, and they appreciate it."

You can even build a reputation for persistence by consistently sending queries that have thoughtful ideas targeted to your chosen publication. If your ideas are solid and your writing style passes muster, eventually you will get the nod from an editor.

The Straight Scoop

"I never set out to write about women's issues," co-author Jennifer admits. "But gee, ever since I graduated from a women's college in the early 1980s and worked as a lobbyist for the National Organization for Women, it has sure turned out that way! Sometimes it bores me—why am I pigeon-holed into looking at things from a woman's point of view all the time? But other times I do feel like I am making a real contribution." In the 20 years since she graduated from college, Jennifer has written about women and small business, women and self-employment, women and personal finance, and women and wealth-building.

Writers Talk About Their Niches

Dena Amoruso worked for many years in new home sales. "It looks like kind of an easy, Vanna White type of job—the smiling woman wearing the nice suit showing the model home—but in fact it is pretty hard work," she says. "You never get weekends off, and forget Mother's Day!" So Amoruso decided to try something else: freelance writing. "Working in the new homes world, I knew that it was an underserved market. Despite the fact that most people buy this kind of a home nowadays, there was very little being written on the topic."

So now Amoruso writes about new home construction. She has a syndicated newspaper column, a Web-based column, and a healthy base of public relations clients for whom she does unsigned pieces. "Someday I'd like to make money doing the kind of writing I love—writing about the things in life that matter to me—but until then, this is paying the bills. HGTV Radio just called me this morning. They want me to do an interview on a 30-station syndicate." Who knows who will be listening? Could be a book editor who will track her down for a book, or a TV producer who will want her to host a show ....

The Straight Scoop

Dena Amoruso went from real estate to writing in record time. "Because I specialized, because I sat down and started writing on a topic that I not only knew well and understood but also knew was a large underserved market, I was able to build a successful freelance writing career in a matter of months rather than years," she says. Yes, it truly does pay to specialize.

In three short years, Cynthia Stewart Copier went from having written nothing to having written a dozen articles and three books. Her stories have also been included in four best-selling gift books. Copier even has made a guest appearance on the Barbara Walters's television show *The View*. How? She began writing about what she knew best. Copier is a successful multilevel marketing distributor. She and her husband have built up an enormous downline of distributors that stretches around the world. As Copier built her business, she began to notice that many of the old prejudices against multilevel marketing companies were falling away. Her passion is helping women build their businesses, and her passion led her to wonder if perhaps there was an undiscovered market for writing on the topic.

"I wanted to help all these women build up their businesses, and so I started out writing the things that I needed myself," she says.

It has worked for Copier in a big way. In addition to her success as a writer, she now receives regular requests to speak to women's groups, where she receives a speaking fee that dwarfs any pay a writer could hope to get for an article.

Judy Zimmerman always loved to travel. "If I had extra money come into my life, I always chose to spend it on travel," she says. So when she and her husband decided to take two months off to travel through Europe, Judy decided to try to sell some articles about their experiences.

Well, she intended to write the articles, but she didn't really expect that anyone would buy them. She knew that in order to write off some of her expenses, she'd need to have a record of how she'd tried to sell the work. "I never took a writing course," she says. "But I did take a class called 'How to Market Your Nonfiction Writing.' Before we left on our big trip, I sent out plenty of queries, fully expecting that they'd all come back as rejects. Lo and behold, a few came back with assignments! And that is how I got started as a travel writer.

"I sell about 35 articles a year, mostly to newspapers. Travel editors are a fairly stable lot, with not too much job hopping. So, they have seen my name over and over and over on pitch letters. And eventually, they buy from me. Every January, I call the papers and ask for their editorial schedule. That way I know what kinds of topics they have coming up, and I can target specific issues. If the Denver newspaper is doing a cruise issue in May, I know not to send an article about spas.

"Even with my success record, it is getting even more challenging to market travel pieces. It is so competitive, and it really doesn't pay that well—it always surprises fledgling writers when I tell them that a lead story in a Sunday newspaper travel section, a big story with big photos and everything, really only pays about $175. But this is my life. I'm a retired teacher, and this is how my husband and I spend our time. I travel four months out of the year."

Lynn Pribus has more than one specialty. She writes in the areas of health, parenting, fitness, and travel. Why did she choose those areas to specialize in? "Well, I noticed an awful lot of articles on those topics, they seemed to be popular. And when I sent out queries on those topics, I got a lot of go-aheads."

Dead Lines

Writer Lynn Pribus shares her tips on the care and feeding of editors—ignore them at your peril: 1) submit on time, 2) hit your word counts, 3) use correct tenses, 4) check all numbers for accuracy, and 5) submit perfect copy.

Pribus has now worked with enough editors in those fields that sending out query letters is a rare occurrence; she now just picks up the phone and pitches a story straight to someone she knows. At this point in her career, she has made 750 free-lance sales—not 750 individual articles, mind you, but 750 sales. Some sales were for the same article sold over and over. "My most-printed article is a 700-word parenting piece I wrote in 1978 called 'The Love Bucket,'" she says. "I have sold it 30 different times."

Pribus's successful career poses an interesting question: Should you try to develop more than one specialty? Early in your career, stick to just one. But as your success grows and new niches occur to you, go ahead and investigate those, too.

The Straight Scoop

As you'll learn, developing yourself as an expert in a particular topic could well lead you to writing your own books on the subject. It might also lead you to writing books for other people, too. Huh? Ever heard of ghostwriting? As your profile as an expert free-lancer increases, it could lead to calls about "ghosting" books. That is when high-profile folks get book deals and then ask other people to actually write the book for them. As an established personal finance writer, co-author Jennifer has been approached to secretly write books for high-profile money folks. That could easily happen to you, too.

Books 'R Us

Where else can building a writing specialty take you? Quite far, actually—perhaps as far as a book contract! In the next chapter, we'll talk more about how to decide whether a particular article can be spun into a book, but for now let's just look to see what kind of writers get book contracts these days.

Publishers are always on the lookout for experts in their field. Although the most common image of a book editor is someone who sits in a New York office surrounded by stacks of manuscripts submitted by hopeful agents, a little-known pastime of many a book editor is flipping through magazines and other publications. Why? They are on the lookout for writers who have a good writing style, a command of their topic, and an interesting take on things. Of course, they're also looking for writers who are writing about a topic with a potentially large book-buying audience. Sometimes, out of the blue, an editor will pick up the phone and track down a writer to begin discussing the possibility of a book contract.

"I worked as an acquisitions editor for years," says Jennifer, "and I got several of my best writers by finding them in magazines."

Richard Poe wrote an article for *Success* magazine in the mid-1980s on what was considered a taboo topic—multilevel marketing, such as selling Amway products. "It turned out to be their single best-selling issue ever," Poe recalled with pride. With his article and that amazing fact—that this topic obviously appealed to large numbers of readers—he ended up with a contract for a book called *Wave 3*. Who was the editor who signed him? Surprise, surprise, it was co-author Jennifer. And how did his book do? Was the fact that so many people bought copies of that issue of *Success* a good indicator? You betcha. *Wave 3*, and the several sequels and updated editions that Poe has published since, have all been best-sellers.

And it all started with just one article he wrote for a business magazine. You just never know where your writing will take you!

Well, as we've pointed out, you too could write a book. Read on to learn from one of the best literary agents in the business—co-author Sheree—when to pitch your article as a book.

The Least You Need to Know

➤ Specializing in one particular market is a very smart and potentially profitable way to approach your writing career.

➤ Specializing in one topic can help you establish yourself very quickly, much faster than if you were pitching all types of articles to all types of publications.

➤ Building a reputation in one area of expertise can lead to book contracts, speaking engagements, and other opportunities.

➤ Follow writing etiquette to the letter. If you are specializing, you have only a limited pool from which to draw; if you make a bad impression on one editor, the pool becomes much smaller.

➤ You might have to develop a specialty in an area that you don't exactly love but that you recognize to be a steady market.

Chapter 22

Hey, Is This a Book?

In This Chapter

➤ So, you want to write a book

➤ Is it a good idea?

➤ Searching for ideas

➤ It's no secret: you'll need an agent

➤ How three writers did it

Every freelancer has a dream—the dream of someday seeing his or her name on the spine of a book. Well, hopefully it won't be one of those books that are collections of reject letters. In this chapter, we'll give you the inside scoop, straight from the New York publishing world, on how to turn your articles into books.

Sheree and Jennifer know whereof they speak (and now that Lynne has written her first book—this one—she's pretty knowledgeable, too). Sheree has written more than a dozen books and also is a literary agent who has worked as a packager developing book ideas. Jennifer is the successful packager of several best-sellers, a former acquisitions editor, and the author or co-author of more than 20 books. Oh yes, and Sheree and Jennifer also write one of the best-selling books in the entire *Complete Idiot's Guide* series—*The Complete Idiot's Guide to Getting Published*. So go pour yourself a cup of good coffee and settle in for our lecture.

The Lure of the Book

You're probably feeling pretty good by now. You've stuck with it and have placed one or more articles. Perhaps you even have an editor or two who court you regularly for magazine pieces. Or, you might even have established a column for yourself. Perhaps there is a subject about which you've become especially knowledgeable. You have a right to be proud. You're a writer—even if it's not what you do full-time ... yet.

Still, there's something nagging at you. You keep hearing it, in your head and from other people: "When are you going to write that book?" The idea begins to seduce you.

By now you might have noticed that making a living just writing articles is a difficult thing to do. You endlessly generate ideas, pitch them, and wait excessive lengths of time for replies. And when you get right down to it, a dollar a word just isn't going that far these days.

You start thinking about writing a book—which in itself is a good idea. And many book ideas are generated by people who sit down and tell themselves that they want to write a book. Still, the best book ideas seem to come from the need for a book rather than the need to write a book. And, ultimately, that's what you'll be up against when you do finally come up with an idea that at first blush seems to have merit.

The first and best question to ask yourself when you come up with a book idea is, "Will people need this book?" The following is a sort of litmus test of other questions to help you determine whether you should write that book.

A Litmus Test for Book Ideas:
Twelve Questions to Ask Yourself

1. Is there a need for this book?

2. Who will need this book?

3. Could I say everything I need to say in an article instead?

4. On what shelf in the bookstore will I find my book?

5. What are the other books on that shelf?

6. How will my book be different from and better than the other books on the shelf?

7. Do I have the right "expert" credentials to write this book?

8. Do I have the right "writing" credentials to write this book?

9. Can I reasonably expect people to walk into a bookstore and ask for my book?

10. How big is the audience for this book? Is it a potential best-seller?

11. Would I read this book if someone else wrote it and not me?

12. Will it cost more in terms of time and expense to write this book than I could expect to earn from it?

In General, Generalize

When it comes to writing a book, the more you can generalize your expertise, the better off you'll be. For example, if you've written an award-winning article about growing a particularly large and healthy form of radish in your garden, that's not likely to become a big, best-selling book idea on its own. However, you are now established as a gardening writer. There are millions and millions of gardeners, and not just in the United States.

Let's say you've written lots of articles about different types of vegetables, and in your research you've found that more people are interested not just in gardening but in organic gardening. You go to the bookstore and try to find a book about growing large, healthy vegetables without pesticides, and you just can't find a book that pleases you. Voilà! A book idea.

Of course, your book not only will include information about growing that perfect radish, but it also will include information about growing large and healthy forms of every kind of vegetable that people might want to grow organically.

The Straight Scoop

Jennifer runs a book packaging business, Big City Books. She comes up with an idea for a book that will sell, sells the proposal to a publisher, and then hires a writer. How does she get her ideas? She always keeps her eyes open to ideas for what kinds of books the world needs. When she spots a hole in the marketplace, she works to fill it. Here is an example of how a packager thinks: Quote books sell well. Women's quote books have been steady sellers for years. Women are making big strides in the corporate boardroom, with more high-profile women CEOs than ever. But there is no quote book that gathers together women's business wisdom. Surprise—there is now! *The Quotable Businesswoman*, packaged by Big City Books, will be published by Andrews McMeel in the fall of 2001.

Make Friends with an Expert

Let's say that you have that idea but you really don't know enough about gardening to write such a book. Or, you know a lot, but you're not confident that others will trust your credentials. Don't give up. Try to find an expert to team up with.

Establish a rapport with an expert—for example, the owner of the organic farm down the road—and write the book as a team. Most experts relish the idea of becoming a published author—especially if they don't have to write anything! All they have to do is talk about their expertise, and you'll do the rest.

A writing team like this will share the credit for the book and arrange an equitable distribution of earnings. And you'll both promote the book and perhaps even sell individual copies for a profit. Win. Win. Win.

The Magazine Writer's Guide to Writing Books

On the one hand, as an established magazine writer, you're in a great position to become a book author. Magazine editors have already deemed you to be publishable. They've paid money for the sentences you have crafted. They've found an audience for what you've had to say. That's a huge plus for you.

When you begin the process of trying to get your book published, you'll find that it's a big plus to send some magazine clips or at least to say that you're a published writer. You're a pro.

On the other hand, as a magazine writer, you've learned to be concise, to take huge ideas and boil them down to their essence. Your forte is bare-bones, no-frills—yet interesting, needed, and cleverly written information. The better the magazine writer you are, the better you do this. You're used to writing an article in a week. You've never had a topic before that took you six months to a year to research and write. You've never stuck with any one topic that long. And you're not used to thinking in terms of chapters. What do you mean 12 chapters? What do you mean 80,000 words? Yikes! What are you getting yourself into?

Furthermore, you're used to thinking in terms of subjects that would make for good magazine articles. Boiling the perfect three-minute egg might make for a great article in a cooking magazine, but it's not likely to make its way into a bookstore, except as a sidebar, a chapter in a cookbook, or a book about homemaking tips.

With that bit of advice, it's time to start thinking of book ideas. You're going to have to use a different area of your brain for this one, magazine writer. And the best place to start doing it is the bookstore.

Dead Lines

Take a close look at the kinds of books piled on the bargain table. These are books that are no longer selling well, so don't waste your time thinking about writing a book on a similar topic. Finding a similar book on the remainder table is a good indication that the topic is dead or that the market is too crowded for a book on that topic.

Finding Ideas in Your Friendly Neighborhood Bookstore

When you started thinking about writing for magazines, you began to read every magazine you could get your hands on. Now you need to immerse yourself in the world of full-length books. Spend time with your neighborhood bookseller. Check out the best-seller shelf. Compare the books you find there with *remaindered books* on the bargain table. Do the topics on the remainder shelf seem dated? What kinds of topics seem to come up repeatedly on the best-seller shelf?

Check out the people, too. What are they reading? You might even want to talk to some people about their selections.

Then walk on over to the magazine section and pick up a copy of *Publisher's Weekly*, the weekly trade magazine of the book-publishing industry.

Study the best-seller list. Do the same with *The New York Times* and *Los Angeles Times* best-seller lists. If you're thinking about a business book, look at *The Wall Street Journal* best-seller list. Are you starting to see a pattern? Can you picture your name on one of those lists?

The Write Words

Remaindered books are books that have been sold by the publisher to a discounter for a fraction of their worth. These books end up on the bargain tables at a bookstore.

The Straight Scoop

What if none of your articles or ideas seem like potential books? Can you use someone else's magazine article as the basis for a book? Yep—and you better do it fast before they do! You shouldn't, of course, claim credit for another person's work or plagiarize the article, but you certainly can use it as inspiration. You might even want to clip it and use it in your book proposal as proof that people are interested in this topic.

Virtual Thinking

Don't limit your research to physical bookstores. The world of virtual books is but a keystroke away. Amazon.com and barnesandnoble.com have proven to be a great boon to writers.

Not only do they provide ever-changing (by the hour!) best-seller lists of all the books in English available throughout the world, but they also maintain best-seller lists arranged by category. You can research what books are available in different subjects, find out how well they're doing, and see how people like them. Online bookstores welcome readers' comments about books.

When you're ready to sell your book idea to an agent or publisher, you'll definitely want to pick up some information online for your book proposal.

As a matter of fact, you needn't limit your brainstorming at all. If you send your antennae up looking for book ideas, you just might find yourself with 3, 4, or 12 good ideas. The combination of reading as much as you can, listening to what people are talking about, and paying attention to what books are working will ultimately pay off for you.

The Straight Scoop

Online bookstores can give you a wealth of information about book sales. Amazon.com gives the sales rank on all titles. If a book on a topic you're interested in pursuing has a sales rank number that is less than 50,000, it might not be a bad idea. If books on your topic have sales rank numbers that are higher than 50,000—say, 750,000—forget it. This is a topic that is not moving. And Barnesandnoble.com will give you another valuable piece of information: In the Search field, type in the category of book you're interested in—personal finance, for instance—to get a listing of the top 25 best-selling books in this category. That's very solid information for book proposals.

Eureka!

You're finally ready. You have a brilliant book idea. You even spent some time coming up with a tremendous title. And, yes, you're the perfect person to write this book. It hasn't been done quite this way, yet all the books on the shelf prove that there's a huge audience for this subject. Now what?

Now you're going to have to learn a little about the business of book publishing—at least enough to become an expert book proposal writer (which is yet another challenge to your writing talents). And you're going to have to learn a little about finding and working with agents.

A full-blown discussion of how to pitch a book idea and generate a book proposal is a little beyond the scope of this book. We recommend that you read the best-selling *The Complete Idiot's Guide to Getting Published.* We're not saying this because two of us wrote it, either. In fact, we don't care if you read a different book on the subject (yeah, right!). But we do advocate that the more you know in advance of getting published, the more likely you'll be successful.

Our *Complete Idiot's Guide to Getting Published* contains an entire chapter on writing book proposals. For more in-depth instruction, check out *How to Write a Book Proposal,* by Michael Larsen, or *Write the Perfect Book Proposal,* by Jeff Herman and Deborah Adams.

Book Proposals

Most nonfiction books are sold on the basis of a *book proposal,* a short document of approximately 10 to 40 pages that fully explores the range, scope, content, need, and everything else about your book idea. When one finishes reading a great book proposal, one feels completely knowledgeable about the book while still craving more. And here's where your skill at being concise will serve you well. It will be your job to compellingly condense your entire book idea into the size and framework of a standard book proposal.

Basically, a book proposal consists of a three- to five-page "pitch," describing different aspects of your book:

➤ The idea

➤ The market

➤ The competition

➤ The publicity and promotion potential

➤ The author

Dead Lines

Books that are connected to dramatic events—such as the death of JFK Jr. or the U.S. Women's soccer team winning the World Cup—need to be on the bookstore shelves just a few days or short weeks after the event. These are called "instant books," and are difficult for solo writers. Stick to topics with a longer life span.

The Write Words

A **book proposal** is a packet of information about the writer's book idea. A proposal typically contains a description of the book's content, the potential market for the book, competition, author's credentials, and marketing ideas. It also contains a table of contents, an extensive book outline, and at least one sample chapter.

The pitch then is followed by a complete and detailed table of contents. After that comes some sample material from your book, usually a representative chapter or two (emphasis on "representative"). And, if you have them, include a few sample writing clips or promotional videos, photos, or tapes—ideally on the subject of the proposal—to help round out your presentation. Put it all nicely in a pocketed folder, double-spaced and unstapled and, ta da, you have one book proposal.

The Write Words

An **agent** is a well-connected professional who tries to interest publishers in your book in exchange for a percentage of your earnings from the sale of that book.

Dead Lines

Thinking about trying to sell the book to a publisher without an agent? And then if that approach fails, getting an agent? Think again. If your project gets turned down by all the major publishers, why would an agent want to represent you? Try first to get an agent. Then if you absolutely can't get an agent, go ahead and try selling it yourself.

Okay, Now What?

Now you're in the market for an *agent.* While most magazine articles are placed by authors, most books are placed by agents. As you learn when you read *The Complete Idiot's Guide to Getting Published* (another shameless plug for our book!), you need an agent for four reasons: 1) contacts; 2) contracts; 3) money; and 4) guidance.

Agents have the contacts (contacts with editors and publishers), know contracts (publishing contracts are peculiar documents), can get you more money than you could on your own (a bigger advance), and can guide you through not just your first book, but your entire publishing career.

Getting an Agent

So how are you going to get an agent? Start by getting a list of members from the Association of Authors' Representatives (AAR). Send a SASE and $6 to the AAR at P.O. Box 237201, Ansonia Station, New York, New York, 10023. Because member agents must abide by a canon of ethics to remain members, those who represent the kind of book you're writing are your best bet.

Another good resource for finding an agent is Jeff Herman's most current edition of *The Writer's Guide to Book Publishers, Editors, and Literary Agents,* from Prima Publishing. This excellent book lists agents and describes agencies in detail.

Another good source is from Writer's Digest Books, its *Guide to Literary Agents.* Again, use the most current edition. It's important that you have the most up-to-date addresses and information.

Approaching an Agent

When you know which agents you would like to represent you, you'll have to woo them. Although it's acceptable to query several agents at one time, unless there's a good reason to hurry, we recommend that you approach them individually the standard way—namely, with a carefully constructed one-page query letter and self-addressed, stamped envelope (typically referred to as a SASE). Here again, your powers of compelling and flawless conciseness should put you in the best light.

Wait a week or two to hear from each agent. If you don't hear anything or aren't satisfied with the response, move on to your next prospect.

Agents and Articles

Will your new agent now represent you to magazine editors? Probably not. Most agents cultivate relationships with book editors primarily and can't afford to spend their time pitching ideas to magazine editors; the commission is usually not lucrative enough to warrant it. But there is a big exception to this rule of thumb—namely, first serial rights.

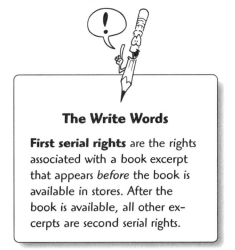

Agents sometimes hold on to *first serial rights* for their clients and pitch them to magazine publishers. More typically, however, publishers with vast subrights departments, not agents, pitch the serial rights to magazines and take a commission.

When serial rights are placed for a book, everyone wins. The author and agent (and sometimes the publisher) get some money, and the book gets some extra publicity. In the end, the best thing that can happen is that your magazine articles will help get you book deals, and your book deal will help get you article assignments.

The Write Words

First serial rights are the rights associated with a book excerpt that appears *before* the book is available in stores. After the book is available, all other excerpts are second serial rights.

Success Stories

Here are a few examples of authors who parlayed their article ideas into successful published books—to get your mind racing with possibilities!

Sally Richards

"I'd been writing short historical pieces for the local newspaper the *San Mateo Times*, about the history and the characters who were in this part of California long ago," Sally Richards says. "It was fun, a welcome change from my regular writing about the Silicon Valley high-tech world. I loved spending time digging through the archives at the library. And then the phone rang. It was a publisher who wanted me to tie together the two kinds of writing I'd been doing, to write a book about the Silicon Valley that stretched back to before the 1800s, up to where we are today, and then forecasting 100 years into the future!" Richards's book, *Sand Dreams & Silicon Orchards,* was published in April 2000.

Richard Poe

Richard Poe's example is great: He wrote an article for *Success* magazine on the topic of multilevel marketing. The issue in which Richard's article appeared was the best-selling issue in the history of *Success* magazine, and the requests to reprint his article poured in from multilevel marketing companies around the country. Hmmm ... perhaps this should be a book? The resulting book, *Wave 3,* was a *Business Week* best-seller and led to several more successful business books for Richard.

Heidi Evans

Heidi Evans wrote an amusing piece for the *Wall Street Journal* on married women who hide money from their husbands. The piece got so many letters and such a reaction that she thought, "Oh, is there a book here?" The result? *How to Hide Money From Your Husband and Other Time-Honored Ways to Build a Nest Egg,* published in hardcover by Simon & Schuster.

So get out your pad and paper (or fire up your laptop) and start brainstorming. Publishing books can be a powerful career move. And imagine the day when you can stroll into a bookstore and see your very own name on the spine of a book. Get to work today!

The Least You Need to Know

➤ Research book ideas in bookstores, on best-seller lists, and online.

➤ Magazine writers are in a good position to become book authors.

➤ Make sure that your book idea can't be fully explored in an article.

➤ The best route to getting a book published is through an agent.

➤ Agents usually don't represent articles, except as first serial deals.

Chapter 23

Setting Up Your Business

In This Chapter

➤ The frugal freelancer

➤ Equipping yourself electronically

➤ Gadgets you may or may not need

➤ Organizing your time

➤ When they won't pay you

In chapter after chapter, we've given you an inside look at the business of writing. We've talked about how to come up with ideas, how to pitch those ideas, and how to write the article once you get the assignment. But prospective freelance writers often have even more basic questions, such as "What kind of computer do I need?" or "How am I going to find the time to write?"

So let's take a closer look at the world of freelance writing, turning a practical eye toward answering practical questions. We'll see how freelance writers organize their time, their offices, and their finances. We'll also talk about hard drives, software, extra tools, and what to do when the check "is in the mail."

The Basics of Freelancing

What is it that you really need to begin life as a freelance writer? Not much. Here's a list of basics that every writer should have:

➤ A telephone

➤ A computer with word-processing capability

➤ Access to a fax machine

➤ Online access and an email account

And that's pretty much it. A phone and a computer would be enough to get you started. Access to a fax machine is something that you don't really need to have in-house in the beginning. Online access is something you'll want to have as soon as you can manage it. Meanwhile, if your neighborhood has an office supply store or other kind of business that rents computer time and lets you send and receive faxes, you probably can get by for now.

Booting Up

The choices available for word-processing programs are myriad. As a writer, you must decide which one is the best for you. One thing to keep in mind is that the type of software and word-processing program you use is not going to dramatically affect your writing ability. Some wannabe writers believe that if they could just find the right program, their careers would take off. That ain't gonna happen. Success is not a magic software program; it is a combination of persistence, hard work, and creativity.

Still, you want to have the best setup you can, one that frees you up to concentrate more on writing than on the hardware and software themselves.

Hardware

Just what kind of computer should you have? Co-author Jennifer is a firm believer in any PC. She has had trouble in the past with co-writers who use Apples. "It seems like the files just never correspond," she says. "Someone always ends up doing more work, and it is usually me. So, I make it a point only to work with other writers who are PC-based."

For another viewpoint, though, we checked with longtime freelancer Sally Richards. She writes primarily about the high-tech world of the Silicon Valley and has a much more sophisticated attitude toward equipment. "If you are going to write on an Apple computer, you will need to learn how to make your files readable to PC people," Richards says. "It is not really that big of a deal. It is a big deal, however, if you don't know how to work with what you've got. If you write a story and send it in to your editor and she can't read it, that is a problem."

You can't go wrong choosing a computer with a Pentium chip, tons of memory, and a 56K modem. Shop around—you should be able to find one for less than $2,000.

Software

Microsoft does rule, at least until the U.S. Justice Department tells us otherwise. And in word-processing programs, Microsoft rules all the more. Does your word-processing program make a difference in your ability to write well? No. But your software program can make a difference in your ability to communicate well with others.

250

The Straight Scoop

Consider a laptop as your primary computer. They're fast enough and screens are big enough now that you really won't be missing that much. Hard drives are smaller, but if you're only using it for word processing and e-mail, you'll be fine. You'll be portable, which is a big asset for a freelancer. Only drawback—they are more expensive than a desktop system.

We recommend using Microsoft Word. Everyone in the publications world, both online and off, can read files written in Microsoft Word. So just give Bill Gates your money and get it over with.

If you'd like to get a few more opinions on the matter, ask around among the other freelance writers you know. Find out what works best for them. It could be the perfect excuse for you to get to know them better and ultimately could lead to you learning more from the pros.

Cool Tools

Wonder up and down the aisles at Office Depot, and your head will be turned by some extremely cool stuff that looks like it would be fun to own—like one of those silver metal wireless phones, the ones that make you look like a Hollywood agent.

The more your career develops as a freelancer, the more you might need to acquire some extra things. Don't make the mistake of spending tons of money on fancy and expensive equipment right off the bat, though; buy them as the need arises. Otherwise, you may end up selling it all on eBay.

Here are a few extras you may find that you need as your career evolves:

➤ **Mini tape recorder.** These are great when conducting lengthy interviews. Make sure that you have a fresh tape and fresh batteries before starting an important interview, though.

➤ **Camera.** "I suggest that writers buy a basic 35-millimeter camera and take shots to accompany their stories," says Sally Richards. "Editors are relieved that they don't have to go to the trouble of sending a photographer, and you can make extra money too!" A word of warning: Learn the basics of photography so that you can take decent pictures. Editors won't buy crummy photos.

➤ **Color printer.** When writing for the Web, printing color copies of your writing in all its Web-based glory looks much cooler in color.

➤ **Second phone line.** A dedicated line for business purposes and interviews is handy, particularly if you are going to spend much of your time online, tying up your phone line.

➤ **Laptop computer.** Some writers swear by their laptops. "I live in California, where there could be a fire or an earthquake at any time," Richards says. "So I like the idea that in an emergency all I have to grab is one small laptop, and my life will go on as before." Less dramatic reasons to have a laptop include the ability to write on the go and the freedom to move from room to room in your house, or even outside your house, as you search for the perfect spot to write.

➤ **Account with a package delivery service.** Yes, they will be delivering things (checks, you hope), but they also will be picking things up. You want an account with one of the major delivery services so that you don't have to rush out at the end of the day to drop stuff off. They come to you.

➤ **Accountant.** What's this, an accountant on a list of cool things to have? Sure. The more involved you become with writing, generating income from writing, and taking deductions for business expenses associated with writing, the more complicated your life will become. An accountant can help sort it all out. We'll delve more deeply into this subject in Chapter 24, "Taxes and the Writer."

➤ **Business cards.** Nothing fancy, just black and white with your name, phone/fax, address, e-mail, and Web site if you have one. It may seem stupid, but you'll really be glad you have them. *Always* carry them in your pocket to pass out. Freelancers never know when they'll make contacts! You can get them cheap at Kinko's or at iprint.com.

The Straight Scoop

Although some professional writers swear by their scheduled pickups from FedEx and UPS, Jennifer likes to go out and drop hers into the box herself. Why? Because it gets her the heck out of the house. The life of a writer is a solitary one. It also gives you more time to finish your work if you know the location of the box with the latest scheduled pickup time.

From the Crazy Mixed-Up Files of ...

Be prepared to disappear, slowly but surely, under a stack of files—files of ideas for new articles, files of contact information for new magazines and other publications to approach, and files with research on each and every article you have written. (Weren't we supposed to be living in a paperless society just about now?)

How Long Do I Keep It?

How long do you have to hang on to all this stuff? Here's what you should hang on to until your house collapses around you:

➤ Copies of everything you've ever written for anyone. No matter how old or obscure, you just never know when a clip will come in handy.

➤ Copies of every contract that you've signed. Almost every contract is different in terms of the type of rights that you have sold.

➤ Copies of any tax information, business expense receipts, and so on (sure, you're "supposed" to hold on to that stuff for three years, but better safe than sorry).

The Straight Scoop

Jennifer's method for keeping copies of clips of magazine articles neat, tidy, and easy to retrieve is this: She has a shelf full of what the office supply store calls "24-sleeve presentation books." It's like a photo album with clear plastic sleeves inside. When she receives a copy of a publication in which she has a story (or prints a color copy off the Web site of the online publication she has written for), she carefully pulls out those pages and slips them inside the plastic sleeve. When copies are needed to send to an editor, she takes the whole book with her to Kinko's and pulls out the page when she gets there, rather than risk getting it all crumpled and torn on the way down.

Here's what you can keep for just a few months and then pitch:

➤ The research for a particular article. Save the phone numbers and e-mail addresses of the contacts, but go ahead and pitch the pages of notes and miscellaneous information.

Yes, there is a chance that you might one day need this information again, but when will "one day" finally arrive? As long as you remember *where the information came from,* you can get it again if you someday need it. Otherwise, you run the risk of turning your house into a serious firetrap.

Secret Files

"I keep files on *people,*" one professional writer maintains. "Not on *topics,* but on the people themselves who are involved in a particular topic. You just never know whether it might turn into a book. But the company information I can find on the Web. The Internet makes it possible to not have file after file of info on hand. Just go look it up on the Web when you need it."

Time Management

One of the biggest challenges of freelance writing—as with any profession, especially work-from-home professions—is managing your time wisely. Some of these challenges you may not even have thought of.

As a writer, time and talent are all you have to sell. Use it wisely, and prosper. Squander it, and your career will go nowhere. Meeting deadlines is the supreme mark of a professional, and effective time management can determine whether you will meet that mark again and again.

"As Long as You're at Home All Day ..."

Once you announce to the world that you intend to become a freelance writer, the world just might ask you to run a few errands for them.

"Make sure that your neighbors know you *work* from home," Sally Richards advises, "with an emphasis on the word *work.* Otherwise, your life will fill up with too many requests for help. Let them know you are working! Otherwise, if they see your car in the driveway all day, they will assume that you are there to help them—help feed the dog while they are out of town, bring their paper in, meet the dishwasher repair guy ...."

Self (Yawn) Starting

If you are working from home full-time as a freelancer, you need to understand that there will be days when it is pretty hard to get your "get up and go" going. Another long day of sitting in front of a computer keyboard is not an exciting prospect— nowhere near as glamorous as you thought it was gonna be when you started.

The life of a writer, as we've stressed elsewhere, is a quiet one, most days. Get up, turn on the computer, make a few phone calls, write, write, and write again. It's all too easy to buy into the idea that your life as a writer will be filled with really cool experiences (remember some of the examples we gave back in Chapter 1, "So, You Want to Be a Freelance Writer?") and forget that most of it is sitting on your behind trying to make something sound good on the page.

There will be days when, for a change of scenery, you might take your behind to a different chair. If your walls are closing in on you, take a pad and paper (or a laptop, of course) and sit in a café, the library, a placid park, or any place that you can keep on writing. Just remember to do exactly that—keep on writing so that the work gets done.

Time management tips? There really aren't any, other than to sit down, do the work, and turn it in on time. No editor is interested in hearing your excuses about why a piece won't come in on time. Regardless of the reason, the editor is still screwed because there's a hole in the publication that now needs plugging fast.

Dead Lines

Many a stay-at-home mom dreams of a spare-time career as a writer. But be warned: Writing and caring for children do not mix. The concentration required to write is impossible to achieve while the children are awake. What to do? Wait until they fall asleep, or hire a baby sitter.

The Straight Scoop

How do we manage our time as writers? In different ways. Co-author Lynne has four small children and a day job as a high school teacher. She writes in the early morning or late into the evening after the kids are in bed. Jennifer works full-time as a writer from home, but she lacks what you could call a real routine. Some days she starts out with phone calls and filing; other days she sits right down to start typing. It's all determined by the deadlines she faces that day.

But how much of the writing life is really just writing? Don't writers also have to find the time to do research, clip interesting articles, surf the Web, and deal with correspondence? Yep. So, in addition to having the discipline to write and meet deadlines, you must commit to keeping up with the busy work required.

It all sounds so confusing—sit down and write, or pick up the phone and call a fresh source? Deadlines will determine your priorities. And as you write more and more, you will develop your own routines. Some writers use the morning hours for research

and basic office work, and the afternoons for writing. Some business writers do their work in the daytime but save their late-night hours for work on the Great American novel!

Learning to Deal with Sporadic Income

Before you take the plunge as a freelance writer—especially if you have a family to support—please give it some serious thought. A writer's life is really a constant struggle for money.

Well, that's an uplifting thought, isn't it? We drag you along through 20-plus chapters of how cool it is to be a writer, and then we tell you that—surprise!—you could starve to death waiting for success. Even success brings a never-ending watch out the window for the postman and his bag of mail.

Dead Lines

Got a great excuse about why your magazine piece won't be turned in on time? Who cares? Not your editor. Regardless of why the work isn't done, the publication needs to go out on time and have all the spaces filled. This is a very time-sensitive business. Meet your deadlines, or risk never working as a freelance writer again.

The Straight Scoop

"How do you find the time to write?" This question is raised time and time again, generally by writer wannabes who dream of writing someday but never actually sit down to do it. At a publishing seminar in San Francisco, Jennifer choked on the cup of weak hotel coffee she was drinking as an agent on the panel fielded that very question from a member of the audience. "Sit your ass in the chair," the agent replied. "If you want to be a writer, sit down and write."

The ideal way to start your life as a freelance writer is to have enough money in the bank to tide yourself over when checks are slim. That isn't possible for most of us. How do freelancers do it?

Answer: Most of them work other jobs. The world of magazine writing is filled with folks who work day jobs as doctors, travel agents, financial consultants, multilevel marketers, photographers—you name it, someone does it and writes at night.

Of the three of us working to write this worthy tome together, Lynne is a high school teacher by day and a magazine writer by night; Sheree is a literary agent by day and a writer by night; and Jennifer is a book packager by day and a writer by night.

Are any of us full-time writers? Yes, we all three consider ourselves full-time writers! But we're full-time writers who have grown accustomed to the wait between checks and have made sure that other monies were coming in from other work.

"My income as an agent is just as sporadic as my writing income," Sheree offers. "I am continually looking for new opportunities. As a writer, you can't ever relax and think that the next check is taken care of. Fun and exciting as this lifestyle may be, when it comes down to security, you have to understand that there just isn't any. You have to keep working; you can't coast."

Is the Check *Really* in the Mail?

The wait for a check from a publication can seem endless, particularly if you're being "paid upon publication." You hate to seem like a nag, but it's hard to resist calling the editor to ask, "Is the check on its way to me yet?"

And sometimes, a piece that you worked long and hard on just seems to drop off the face of the earth. A 2,000-word article that Jennifer wrote for a national magazine in early fall 1999 was scheduled to appear in a December issue (thereby triggering a $2,000 check). And then it was scheduled for January. And then February. Still nothing, and in the meantime the editors have changed jobs. So it is entirely possible that she will never be paid for a large piece for which she invested a daylong trip (on her own dime) to Southern California. Live and learn.

Many writers have developed extremely thick skins when it comes to asking for money. "Don't be shy," one full-time magazine writer advised. "This is your livelihood. Get used to the idea that you will sometimes have to pester people in order to be paid." Is it worth the legal hassle to sue if you are never paid? We've never had to do it, but others have. By joining an association such as the American Society of Journalists and Authors, you will have access to their legal advice staff.

On the other hand, you could be paid for something that never gets published. It happened to Sheree: "The first article I ever sold was called 'Wheel of Torture,'" she explains. "It was a first-person account of my appearance on the *Wheel of Fortune* television game show. The first line read, 'I won $34,000 on *Wheel of Fortune* and had the worst time of my life.' I pitched the article idea to *Woman* magazine, got the go-ahead, wrote it, and turned it in. They paid me a dollar a word not long after I turned the story in, $1,500. The issue was typeset and ready to go to press, and then the magazine folded. I thought about re-selling it elsewhere, but by then it was too dated. In addition to the $1,500 I was paid for an article that never saw print, I have recycled that material endlessly in speeches and in books. So it was far from a total disappointment."

Sally Richards is quite skilled when it comes to collecting the money she is owed. Her advice? Don't be shy about negotiating your terms.

The Write Words

A **boilerplate contract** is a standard contract, the same contract that a company uses over and over again. Boilerplates tend to favor the company that paid to draw them up, not the person being asked to sign them.

The contract that you will be sent will be a "boilerplate," the same contract that the publication sends to everyone. Needless to say, a *boilerplate contract* is drawn up to favor the publication's company, not necessarily the writer.

"You need to work your own stuff in there," Richards says. "I am most particular about when I get paid. I add something to the contract that stipulates when the magazine will run the piece. Magazines can hold a piece for many, many months, so I always try to get them to agree to pay me within two weeks of submitting the manuscript. Sometimes it works, sometimes it doesn't." (We'll talk more about contracts in the very last chapter.)

What Else Is in the Mail?

What else will you have to keep track of as a writer? Not just who owes you what, but when. You'll also have to know whom you have queries out to and who has rejected your work.

As your success as a writer grows, you will also be receiving 1099 forms from the publications for whom you've done the most work. We'll go over this is the next chapter, the one about taxes. Guess we aren't saving the best for last ....

The Least You Need to Know

➤ All the fancy equipment in the world won't help if you aren't determined to succeed as a writer. Sell a few pieces before investing in anything expensive.

➤ All you really need to get started is a computer (or access to one) and a phone. However, you'll need to move online if you're going to compete with other writers, so you'll eventually want to consider getting a modem and an extra phone line.

➤ Most editors are PC-based and use Microsoft Word. However, it's possible to save files in a PC- and Word-compatible format if you have a different setup. Be sure that you're up to speed on how to do this.

➤ Guard your worktime. Don't let neighbors and others get you to help them because you're at home all day. Let people know that you *work* from home.

➤ Learn to deal with sporadic income. Budget wisely and write incessantly.

Chapter 24

Taxes and the Writer

We've thrown an awful lot of material at you in this book. Some of it was meant to inspire you, some of it was meant to warn you, and some of it was meant to make you laugh. In this chapter, it's meant to make you pay attention. Now we're talking about taxes.

Entire books are devoted to taxes and writers, and we can't cover everything in one chapter. But we will give you a solid overview of just how your life as a freelance writer breaks down on a properly filled-out tax form.

Did we mention that we aren't tax professionals? We aren't, so do not consider this legal advice. We are simply explaining the rules as we understand them as working writers. So, before you take deductions of any kind, check with a tax professional. End of disclaimer.

Setting Up Your System

We began this book with a lecture about adopting a businesslike attitude toward becoming a freelance writer. We told you that the people who succeed in this quirky business, the people who sell the most stuff and command the highest prices, are the ones who *treat it like a real business*.

And we return to that stern lecture now in the context of taxes and the writer. This is not a game for you to play with the IRS: "Gee, let's see how much I can write off before they catch me ...."

The first step in setting up any business is to set up a system for keeping track of the money—the money in, the money out. We talked to writer and organizing expert Terry Prince about putting together a solid record-keeping system any writer can understand. Here is what she advises.

Folders Galore

Run down to the office supply store and buy a packet of ordinary file folders. Save the receipt—this is a business expense, after all.

Mark two of your folders "expenses." Within one of those add two subfolders marked "Expenses—Charge, Current Year," and "Expenses—Cash, Current Year." It's always a good idea to keep track of cash and credit purchases separately—it just makes it easier on yourself.

Put receipts in the appropriate cash or credit file until you process them. *Process* sounds like a scary word, but we just mean until you sort them out by type and write down the expense on your master expense list. You also could use a software system such as QuickBooks; many writers find that makes dealing with taxes so much easier.

Once processed into a system like Intuit's QuickBooks, move them into the second folder.

Dead Lines

Don't toss it all in a shoebox. Spend time each week filing your receipts and entering your data. "The better your records, the easier it will be to file your taxes—and smoothly undergo an audit," says organizing expert Terry Prince. "Just a few minutes a week will save you hours and hours at tax time."

➤ Set up a folder for the current-year bank statements for your business accounts. Mark this one "Bank Statements, Current Year."

➤ Set up a file marked "Taxes—Current Year." Include letters that acknowledge donations.

➤ Set up a file for "Business Bills to Be Paid." This is where you'll stick the office phone bill when it comes in, or the printing bill for your business cards.

➤ Set up a file for "Accounts Receivable." All invoices and correspondence related to it go in this folder. This is where you keep track of the people who owe you money!

➤ Set up "Payments Received." Once those people you sent invoices to have paid up, move the paperwork (check stubs and invoices marked "paid") into this file.

➤ Set up a "Quarterlies" file to keep the forms and records of what (if anything) you have contributed to charity so far. This way when you sit down to try to figure your quarterly tax payments, you'll have it all there.

➤ Set up a *Schedule C* historical file to keep copies of all your yearly Schedule Cs (more on the Schedule C follows). This will help you keep an eye on how well you're doing from year to year.

The Write Words

Schedule C is the tax form that you need to file to declare your freelance writing income.

Once you have this kind of a filing system set up, dealing with your taxes will be a snap. The paperwork is where you need it to be, your receipts are all neatly filed, and you won't lose track of who owes you what.

The Straight Scoop

"You should definitely have a business checking account," says Terry Prince, author of *Surviving and Thriving in the Home Office*. "At least have a separate account. That makes it so much easier for bookkeeping purposes, and you won't have to continually reimburse yourself from your home account. Trying to run a business from your family checkbook is a big hassle." You can get a copy of Prince's book by sending a $25 check (from your business account) to: Terry Prince, P.O. Box 2607, Elk Grove, CA 95759.

Records, Records, Records

The first rule of record keeping for the freelance writer is this: If you want to write it off, you have to write it down.

Jennifer carries a daytimer everywhere and writes down all appointments, short trips to the post office, and major expenses. She also writes down the amount of checks she receives and when she receives them.

Dead Lines

You can't just declare yourself a writer and start writing off everything you do in your life. It doesn't work that way. Acquaint yourself with the tax laws that apply to writers and their incomes. The January edition of *Writer's Digest* magazine always has a good feature on writers and their taxes.

If you want the IRS to believe that you are a business—as a freelance writer, that's what you are, a business—you must behave that way. And that means a professional level of record keeping.

Writing It Off

What can you write off? The most common items are these:

➤ Research materials such as magazine subscriptions, books, and newspapers

➤ Business-related travel expenses

➤ Almost anything having to do with your computer and your Internet connection

➤ Phones, faxes, and other office equipment

➤ Postage and shipping costs

Writing It Off: An Example

Not long ago, Jennifer traveled from Granite Bay, California, down to Redwood City, California, to cover a large women's venture capital conference late in January 2000. Although she originally planned to attend the event to write it up in her USAToday.com column, she also pitched a story to the Fortune.com Small Business site and got the go-ahead from them. She printed out the e-mail and filed it away.

Dead Lines

Always check the current income tax regulations regarding mileage. It used to be 32¢ per mile, then for a time it was 31.5¢, and currently it's 31¢. A cent or two may seem petty, but it adds up. Take steps to get it right.

Driving down the night before, she spent the night on the couch at the home of a friend who was covering the same event for *Newsweek*. So far her expenses were just mileage and bridge tolls.

The event began at 7 A.M. with a breakfast, and there was complementary valet parking. Still a pretty cheap trip. Lunch was provided (a really cheap trip!). She tipped the valet a few dollars.

Here are the expenses she logged from that trip:

➤ Two bridge tolls

➤ Round-trip mileage of 250 miles at 31¢ a mile

➤ Fresh batteries for her mini-tape recorder

➤ A new set of blank mini-tapes

➤ A bottle of wine and dessert for her host

What? A bottle of wine and dessert? That last item might well be subject to debate, but Jennifer plans to write it off anyway—as a business gift. It saved her a night in an expensive Silicon Valley hotel, and this woman is a valuable colleague with whom Jennifer shares many contacts and advice. She is by no means alone in that practice.

Jennifer writes off thank-you cards and all kinds of small business gifts as well. "This is a business where the nicer you are to people, the further it gets you," she explains. "So why not give business gifts?"

Another writer agrees: "It's not like we give away Tiffany paperweights."

The limit is $25 per client or customer per year, according to the most recent tax books, but most writers get nowhere near it.

No Hobby Here

Professional-level record keeping benefits the freelance writer in another way: It helps document your strenuous attempts to produce an income—a *profitable* income.

Ever heard of a "hobby business"? That is what the glinty eye of the IRS might reveal your writing pursuit to be if you don't work hard enough to make a profit. And while income from a hobby is taxable, the expenses from a hobby business are allowable only up to the extent that you have generated revenues from it. So if you have no income, you can't deduct anything.

If your freelance writing has produced a profit in three out of the past five years, the IRS says you are indeed in business. But if year after year after year you make only a few hundred dollars selling articles, and you try to write off thousands of dollars of expenses against that ... well, it just ain't gonna cut it with the IRS.

Mysteriously, if you were engaged in horse breeding instead of writing, the rules are somewhat different. When breeding, training, racing, or showing horses, you have to show a profit in only two of seven consecutive years. Guess the IRS gives horses a few years to grow up and bear a saddle, but you as a writer have to be out of the starting gate from the get-go! So put that bit in your mouth—and produce!

Scheduling Your C

A Schedule C is the tax form that you need to file to declare your freelance writing income. It's not just for writers, but for anyone who is self-employed.

"If you have never before filed a Schedule C form, get yourself a copy as soon as possible," Lynn Pribus, author of more than one hundred published articles, suggests. "Take a look at the categories of expenses that are there on the form. And then set up your expenses file with categories to correspond to them." That way you won't spend all night on April 14th trying to decide which of your expenses are "Legal and Professional Services," "Depletion," "Office Expense," or any of the other 27 categories on the form.

The Schedule C form can be intimidating at first glance (what part of a tax form isn't?), so getting used to the way it is organized is great advice. Thankfully, as writers, we really don't have to fuss with that whole "Cost of Goods Sold" section on the back!

This form can seem like a bit of a struggle, but take heart. Unlike the guy who owns a bagel shop, you just have to worry about two things—income and expenses. Everyone else in the business world needs to fuss with inventory, payroll, depreciation of assets, and all manner of other tangles.

So fill it out and file it.

Do It Four Times a Year

How often do writers pay taxes? The ones who make money do it very often, four times a year. Self-employed folks need to pay as they go, lest they end up with a big tax bill at the end of the year that they can't afford to pay. And you don't want to fall behind in your taxes, no siree. As your income from freelance writing grows, send off to the IRS for the forms you'll need to file every January 15, April 15, July 15, and October 15. Think of it as a badge of honor, a symbol of your success as a freelance writer! Think of it as more than that, actually, because the IRS could ding you for not paying your taxes quarterly if they think you make enough. Check this out with your accountant.

As your freelance income grows, you also will need to check into the self-employment tax. This is necessary for full-time writers, those whose income is 100 percent derived from their own efforts. And it might also be necessary for your part-time writing income, as well. The IRS publication #533 can help you decide whether you qualify for this cumbersome task.

But as with filing your Schedule C or paying quarterly taxes, when it comes to the self-employment tax, just pay it and move on. Don't tangle with the IRS. The life of a writer is hard enough without fighting the government at the same time.

Home Office Deduction?

More than one waggish writer has suggested that you turn the largest room in your house into your office to take the biggest deduction possible, particularly if you live alone.

If you are pursuing this career with a serious bent, you should check out the home office deduction. Long believed to be a red flag for an audit, more Americans are qualifying for a legitimate home office deduction.

According to the IRS, if you use a room in your house for "exclusive and regular" business use in the pursuit of an income, then you may take the home office deduction. You may deduct the percentage that the office makes up of the entire square footage of your home. Math wasn't your strong point, that's why you became a writer, huh? Well, if you live in a 2,500-square-foot house and your office is a room that is 500 square feet, you may take a 20 percent deduction. And that means that 20 percent of most of the costs attached to your house—your mortgage, utilities, property taxes, insurance, and so forth—is also deductible.

So, Is This Vacation a Business Expense?

Well, is it? So many of us dream of how swanky our writing lives will be, with the endless pursuit of tantalizing topics in equally tantalizing locations. And, of course we'll be able to write it all off, right? Maybe.

Most professional writers handle the question of writing off trip expenses this way: They send off query letters to editors pitching story ideas related to the trip they are going to take a few months *before they go*. This way, even if they don't successfully market any stories from this trip, there is a paper trail for the IRS that documents their intentions of trying to sell material related to it.

> **Dead Lines**
>
> If you have declared one room of your house to be a home office, you must use it like an office—only an office. Not a place where the kids can come and play video games in the afternoon, and not a place where you store your winter wardrobe. Just an office.

> **The Straight Scoop**
>
> As the author of several books, Jennifer likes to contact a Borders or Barnes & Noble near her destination when planning a family vacation. Book a talk, and write off at least a small portion of your trip. When traveling to Hawaii with her husband and children, she gives talks at area bookstores and writes off the rental car expenses for the day of her talk, and one night of the hotel for each talk. She does not, however, try to write off part of the plane ticket. Why be greedy?

Writers take trips all the time in pursuit of a story, to do research on a story, or to attend an event that they are covering. Expenses incurred on these kinds of trips are usually legitimate business deductions. But you must be honest in your assessment of just what portion of your trip was devoted to the business side. This is the only portion of your trip that you can legitimately write off.

265

Tracking Your Money Before the Tax Man Does

After working on her own as a full-time writer and book packager, Jennifer thought she was doing pretty well—especially considering that most writers average somewhere around $15,000 a year and she was way ahead of that. Or so she thought.

While writing her weekly column for USAToday.com about being self-employed (talk about a fishbowl life!), Jennifer began to sort through her quarterly expenses in anticipation of paying her quarterly taxes. And suddenly realized that she was looking at a loss. She had spent more money in the last few months than she had made. Oh. Whoops.

So she picked up the phone and called Ellen Rohr, the author of *Where Did the Money Go?* to learn a better way of keeping track of her financial life. "Financial statements are just like scorecards," Rohr advises. "Your financial statements reflect your company's performance—for better or worse." But—here is the great thing—just by paying closer attention to what you have written down, you will actually improve!

"Ever hear of the Hawthorne Effect?" Rohr asks. "It is an old productivity study in a light bulb factory that showed that productivity goes up just by virtue of the fact that it is being studied. As long as the workers—or, in this case, you—know that someone is paying closer attention to what they are doing, they really do make more of an effort."

So Jennifer changed her system. She started paying closer attention not only to her expenses, but to where her income was coming from, who owed her money, and who paid best and fastest. She learned that when she ran the numbers more often, she did two things:

➤ Stopped spending money immediately—no more lunches out, no more books, no business trips until more money came in!

➤ Picked up the phone to hustle up more work.

So pay attention to your money. Writers are frequently described as scatterbrained, too creative to really pay attention to the money side of things. Remember that this is a business, and treat it that way. The IRS will, too.

Writers Talk Taxes

Judy Fertig Panneton starts off every January 1st with a blank book for mileage and high hopes. "But within a month or two I've lost the book entirely," she admits. If she is handed a printed receipt—for a book, a lunch, or office supplies—she files it.

"But the stuff that I have to remember and keep track of … it's hard enough keeping track of manuscripts, let alone money. What's going out and what's coming back. Manuscripts versus checks. I just need to remember that it really is not that hard, and that like the ad says, just do it!"

Panneton, a freelance writer and television reporter, wisely skips the home office deduction because the room is not dedicated to "exclusive and regular" use for business purposes. "I keep my entire wardrobe in the closet in my office," she confesses, which is not at all what the IRS has in mind for a home office.

The Straight Scoop

On the subject of taxes, one freelance writer we spoke with had these words of advice: *"Get an accountant. It's worth every penny."*

Don Dachner sat down across from an IRS auditor years ago who took one look at his occupation—travel writer—and snorted in derision. "Oh yeah," the auditor said, "A travel writer. I took a course myself on how to become a travel writer. I know you only do it for fun!"

But as Dachner tells it, he hired a tax attorney and fought to be allowed to deduct his writing-related travel expenses. "And not only did I win, but I got enough back from the IRS to pay my attorney and make an extra $1,800 that I got from mistakes I'd made in past returns!" Dachner also got a letter from the IRS stating that he was indeed a for-profit writer. He won his case because he keeps pristine records. He *is* a professional writer.

And you owe it to yourself to treat freelance writing as a profession. If your goal in reading this book has been to learn how to succeed in this business, then treat it like a business. The business will treat you like a professional in turn.

The Least You Need to Know

➤ A businesslike attitude toward record keeping, together with a thorough filing system, are central to a successful freelance writing business.

➤ As a freelance writer, you can deduct expenses for newspapers, magazines, and books you use in your research.

➤ Most professional writers pay their taxes on a quarterly basis rather than save up for one annual tax bill. File a Schedule C with your tax return to declare your writing income and expenses.

➤ If your writing pursuits have produced a profit in three of the past five years, the IRS considers you a business. If you claim loss after loss for years, however, the IRS might decide that writing is just a hobby for you.

➤ It's a good idea to query editors with story ideas several weeks or months before you leave on your trip. This way you have proof that you tried to market your travel stories.

➤ You may write off travel-related expenses only to the extent that your trip was devoted to business. When mixing business and pleasure, you cannot deduct 100 percent of the trip.

Chapter 25

Contracts and What They Really Mean

You've learned how to keep the IRS happy and know the basics of how to set up your business. Now we take care of the final business aspect of freelancing—the contract. In this chapter, you learn about your rights as a contracted writer. You'll get the ammunition with which you can arm yourself, retain some rights, and earn more income per article.

Beggars *Can* Be Choosers

You've managed to get your foot in the door with a publication, and you don't want to blow the deal by being "difficult" when it comes to the contract. We understand the dilemma. On one hand, you want the assignment—bad! On the other hand, you don't want the publisher to get the best of the deal and make extra money for work you did. What do you do?

Well, first, understand that your power as a writer increases with your reputation. In the beginning, you may have to accept a few ho-hum contracts to build your reputation. It isn't necessarily a bad thing to bite the bullet a few times early in your career.

That said, keep in mind that editors expect a little negotiation for certain items within a contract. You won't be out of line by asking for a few alterations to a proffered contract.

Thus, if you do give away some rights in your first few assignments, don't let your generosity persist. Take a stand and start negotiating. You may walk away from an assignment because a contract is bad—and that's okay. You're your own business. Do what's best for the business. With that all said, let's take a closer look at contracts and the rights that are up for grabs.

The Straight Scoop

When your gut says, "I'm unhappy with this contract. It bites!" don't sign the contract. But don't beat yourself up afterward either for losing an assignment. You will need to make some tough decisions regarding the value of the goods you sell—your writing—by choosing this career. Everything you write comes from you. Don't sell yourself short, and furthermore, trust that you as executive director of your own freelance business know what's best for the business, even if that means nixing the deal in the end due to a lousy contract.

Rights: A Primer

First, what do we mean when we talk about rights? Well, rights give both you and the publisher protection—peace of mind, per se. Just as you would sign a contract with a guy who builds a pool in your backyard before he begins digging dirt, you sign a contract before beginning to write an assignment or giving the publisher the right to print an unsolicited manuscript. In the pool-building contract, both your obligations as the person asking for the watery hole (the cost, payment, and timeline for completion) and the contractor's obligations (the size, cost, and timeline for completion) are listed.

When you and the pool company agree on all the components of the deal, you both sign on the dotted line, thereby giving both of you certain rights. For instance, you maintain the right to a functioning pool after paying for the work. The pool guy maintains the right to payment after digging a hole, putting in the plumbing, and laying the cement.

When we talk about magazine rights, we mean, specifically, your rights to whatever you write and the rights of the magazine or newspaper to whatever you write and they pay for. Just because your article appears in one publication doesn't mean that it can't appear in another—or even within another medium, such as the Web or television. Rights give you or the publisher the chance to cash in on those other worlds of wealth. You want to make sure that the one cashing in on your hard work is you, not the publisher.

Let's say that you sell a story to *Shoe Digest* on Victorian shoes. *Victorian Shoes* prints it in the next issue. Now *Women's Shoe Daily* wants to reprint the story, and the Society of Antique Shoe Lovers wants to include the article in a press kit. Here are two more opportunities for someone to make money off your article for *Shoe Digest*. Do you think that *Shoe Digest* should have the right to sell the piece to the Society of Antique Shoe Lovers and also sell it to *Women's Shoe Daily?* And keep the cash? Or, do you think the author—you—should have the say over what happens to the article and should keep that cash? We thought so.

Here a Right, There a Right, Everywhere a Right, Right

Generally, there are six rights with which freelance *serial* writers should be familiar:

➤ First serial rights

➤ One-time rights

➤ Second serial rights

➤ All rights

➤ Electronic rights

➤ Dramatic, television, and motion picture rights

Let's take a closer look at each.

> **The Write Words**
>
> When you hear the word **serial,** don't think killer. Instead, think publication. A serial describes anything published periodically, at regular intervals. Newspapers and magazines are both serials, and if you write for them, you're a serial writer.

First Serial Rights

First serial rights grants the publisher of a periodical the right to print your article before anyone else, and that publication can print it only one time. You retain all other rights.

Sometimes the geographic area is specified with this right, as in first *North American* serial rights. This means that you grant the publisher the right to print your piece first—and only in North America. The writer has the option to publish it simultaneously on another continent.

The Write Words

No need to spell out **first North American serial rights,** or even say it aloud in its entirety. Savvy writers say **FNASR** and use the acronym when they write it, too.

One-Time Rights

One-time rights means that you give the magazine the right to publish your article once, yet you also retain the right to sell it simultaneously to another publication. You don't give the magazine the exclusivity of publishing the piece first. All a publisher receives is your article and the opportunity to print it—once.

Second Serial Rights

Remember gym class? Everyone wanted to be picked first. Second was, well, not as good. But second proves great for writers if it means retaining second serial rights.

Second serial rights are also called reprint rights, and they earn the publisher big bucks. Reprint rights mean that the periodical has the right to sell your article to another publication after it has already appeared in the publication. The time frame specifies when the publisher must stop reprinting for "free." If the publisher, for instance, wants to reprint an article you wrote for the publication after, say, 90 days (the time the contract specifies), then the publisher cannot sell the piece. The publisher must send the prospective buyer back to the writer to negotiate a price. If the publisher has reprint rights with no timeline, the writer is out of luck. That publisher can sell it again and again. Sometimes the author is granted a percentage of that sale. But what's better—a percentage of the sale, or the whole enchilada? If you retain second serial rights, you can sell the article somewhere else, and the money is all yours, honey.

All Rights

All rights are all wrong for the freelancer when a publisher receives them. If you sign a contract granting all rights to the magazine or newspaper, then that publication owns the article lock, stock, and barrel. The publication makes all the money off the sale of the piece to other media. If an association wants to reprint the article in a brochure, for example, that "cha-ching" you hear means money in the magazine's pocket—not yours. If a Web site runs the article, surfing for dollars becomes the sport of the publisher—not you. Avoid signing away all your rights.

Electronic Rights

E-gad! By far the trickiest right around is electronic rights. In fact, we'll look into electronic rights more closely later. For now, just know that electronic rights is a blanket right that includes the right to reprint in all forms of electronic media. Web sites, online magazines, CD-ROM anthologies, interactive programs, databases—all these and any emerging media fall under the term electronic rights.

We hate to say it, but the electronic boom brought about some tricky play by publishers. Suddenly, there was this whole world of rights without bounds. The Web and the way content is delivered is currently undergoing round after round to determine who owns what right in our courts. Writers suddenly gain thousands upon thousands of potential online magazines to which they may resell articles. Publishers, however, want the exclusive right to post the article on their Web sites or sell the information (and make big bucks) in CD-ROM anthologies. Here's another problem: With technology continually developing, no one is sure where we'll all be in two weeks, two months, or two years. It's in the publisher's best interest to try to cover every possibility with work-for-hire contracts that specify all rights.

But what about the writer? It's in our best interest to retain as many rights as possible, because who knows what medium or number of venues we may be able to find to resell an article. It's actually pretty screwy. Both parties—publishers and writers—are currently trying to protect their interests and rights in what may come.

That said, when you retain your electronic rights, you open yourself to the possibility of a world of extra income.

The Straight Scoop

Before you sign any publisher's contract, navigate to the Contracts Watch section of the American Society of Journalists and Authors (ASJA) at www.asja.org. A search engine within the Web site leads writers to either the publishing group (such as Condé Nast) or the individual magazine. If the magazine's contractual reputation stinks—if they have an all rights contract they shove down freelancers' throats, for example—the ASJA will alert you.

Dramatic, Television, and Motion Picture Rights

As a nonfiction writer you generally don't need to concern yourself with the intricacies of dramatic, television, and motion picture rights. Fiction writers try to keep these rights so that they can sell their novels to a film company for big bucks. But suppose that you write an article about an intriguing, true-life tale, and a studio wants to buy the rights to your story and spin a screenplay from it? Voilà! If you retained and specified dramatic, television, and motion picture rights in your contract, you may have won the writer's lottery.

The Straight Scoop

On September 24, 1999, the landmark copyright case *Tasini et. al* v. *The New York Times et al.* gave freelancers a first rights victory. Here's what the U.S. court asserted that helps the freelance writer: First, online and database uses of articles that originally appeared in print may not be considered part of the *first rights* sold. Instead, these uses are additional and should be negotiated and paid as such. Second, additional uses of an article are not permitted without a contract signed by both parties that specifically grants the additional usages. In other words, first rights means that no one can use your article online or in a database without express consent by you, the writer.

Showdown on the Electronic Frontier—Writers and Their Rights

With the technological boom, a need has come about for electronic rights. Not since the 1978 Copyright Law has so much hullabaloo over rights come down in the magazine arena.

There was a time when FNASR was the standard. When a writer's article hit the newsstand, the life of the article in that publication ended with that issue. When the next issue appeared, the article began a new life—that is, it could be sold to another publication or elsewhere as a reprint.

With electronic rights, however, an article's shelf life can be extended significantly. Why? Because of the Internet. An article can change hands indefinitely online, through CD-ROM anthologies of articles, through other online magazines, and in so many ways that, in short, we can't list them. This means that an article can enjoy several reprints and uses in electronic form alone.

If you give the publisher electronic rights to a piece, you've not only given away any rights to ever sell the piece electronically, but you've also given up multiple income opportunities. Keep in mind that the term "electronic rights" doesn't just mean the magazine's online equivalent. It means the possibility of a number of different online incarnations for your article.

Think about it this way. Actors receive payment every time a television show appears in rerun. You, the writer, should retain your online rerun rights in whatever form your article is rerun.

The Straight Scoop

Lynn Pribus, a freelance writer, offers this tidbit regarding rights: "I like to type my own name into search engines like mamma.com, dogpile, or egosurf, to see what comes up. I have found articles that I've written for newspapers included in their sites. Articles for which I only sold one-time rights! So I remind the papers of that fact. 'I didn't sell you the story, I only rented it to you. If you rent a car from Hertz you don't get to park it in your driveway forever.'" Right on, Lynn! And the rental car analogy is an apt comparison. Rental cars get driven over and over by different parties.

Unfortunately, publishers often see only the bottom line when it comes to the World Wide Web phenomena and the technological boom. Many top publishing groups—Condé Nast, for one—insist on retaining electronic rights. Sometimes editors will offer you more money for these rights. Many writers, however, are telling the magazines and papers where to shove the contract and are moving on to more lucrative writing gigs.

The one thing you, the neophyte freelancer, can do is this: Include the word *print* in front of *serial* in your contract. Make the contract read "first print serial rights." By adding that one word, you protect yourself from any ambiguity. *Print* means any printed form, and that includes electronic print.

The Write Words

A **contract** is an agreement between two or more parties. It is enforceable by law and may contain specific terms within the document.

What if they won't go for adding the word *print* to the contract? An optimum solution may be dividing the income from electronic rights. In this case, the *contract* specifies what percentage or dollar figure you'll receive if the magazine sells your piece for reprint. This way everybody wins.

The Straight Scoop

Co-author Jennifer holds perhaps the best online rights deal you can get. For her *USAToday* Online column, Jennifer did indeed sell away electronic rights. The online publication has sole and exclusive rights ... for the first 24 hours. After the sun rises and sets once, Jennifer is free to turn around and sell the column to other people. Try cutting a deal like Jennifer's.

Dead Lines

Never sign a contract giving the publisher all rights if you can help it. You could potentially sign away thousands of dollars in reprint income. A freelancer for *The New York Observer* refused to sign an all rights contract, citing the fact that he earned about $66,000 off reprint rights one year. All rights gives the publisher everything and you nothing.

Remember that the electronic beast is continually evolving. We offer this advice for the future:

➤ Be wary of signing away your electronic rights.

➤ Keep abreast of current rights law by frequently perusing the American Society of Journalists and Authors Web site for updates at www.asja.org.

A Paragraph-by-Paragraph Explanation

No two contracts are completely alike. Some may specify the number of sources you must use in an article, while others won't. One contract may stipulate a deadline, while another makes no mention of it. Certain ideas are common to all freelance agreements, however. Let's go paragraph by paragraph and try to explain what you'll most likely come across in a contract.

The writer's agreement begins by defining the two parties engaging in the contract:

> *Marvelous Magazine* Corporation ("Publisher") is engaged in the business of publishing. The person whose name is written above ("Author") has written a work which he/she has submitted for publication in a forthcoming edition of *Marvelous Magazine*. Publisher and Author agree as follows:

> 1. Author transfers and grants the Publisher the right to print, publish, sell, lease, and license the Work in the United States and throughout the world, including the right to publish the Work electronically in the form of a computer database.

Sounds like all rights, doesn't it? It is. But read on—there's more.

2. The transfer and grant described in paragraph 1 is an exclusive transfer and grant until 90 days after the first publication of the Work by *Marvelous Magazine*. Author agrees to authorize or permit publication of the Work by any other persona until 90 days after the first publication by *Marvelous Magazine*.

Okay. So it's all rights, but only for 90 days. After 90 days, the rights revert to the writer. That's not a great arrangement for the writer, but it's not a terrible one either.

3. Author may authorize and permit others to publish the Work on a nonexclusive basis beginning 90 days after Publisher has first published the Work.

Pretty clear, huh? After 90 days, you can sell the piece again. You should be sure, however, that the other buyer knows the piece was published exclusively prior to its new home.

4. In full consideration for the transfer and grant of rights under this agreement, Publisher shall pay Author the sum of $_____ upon execution by both parties for this agreement and within four weeks of publication of the Work. For the right to reprint the Work or a portion of the Work, the publisher agrees to pay the Author the sum of $_____ within four weeks of publication of the reprint.

Paragraph 4 tells you how much pay you will receive for the article. Moreover, this publisher is giving you a piece of the pie if he sells a reprint of your article during those first 90 days. Typically, the reprint fee is a percentage of the original payment.

5. Publisher shall have the right to edit the Work and make changes and revisions to it as Publisher deems appropriate. Publisher reserves the right to not publish the Work at any time.

You're authorizing the editor to work her magic in this paragraph. A relatively harmless decree, typically. According to the ASJA, writers should be wary of the word *augment* when it appears in this type of paragraph, warning, "You don't want to be responsible for what someone else writes." Typically, any edits or changes an editor makes will pass through you for approval. In fact, an editor probably will ask you to correct something or add something. The intent in this paragraph is good.

The Write Words

Your **copyright** is the exclusive right to the publication, production, or sale of the rights to your article granted by law. Once you conjure an idea and write it, copyright protection automatically kicks in—whether or not you've filed for a copyright with the government.

6. Author warrants that he/she is the sole author of the Work, that Author is the sole owner of all the rights granted herein, and that Author has full power to enter into this agreement; that the Work is original and is not in the public domain; that Author has not previously assigned the Work or published it in any form; and that the Work does not violate the rights of privacy of any person, is not libelous or obscene, and does not infringe on the *copyrights* of anyone.

Here you are asserting that you wrote it and no one else. Moreover, the publisher worked in a mention of libel. What if the work does violate privacy? Shouldn't the publisher take some responsibility? A better wording to negotiate might be that the Author "believes to the best of her knowledge" that the Work "does not violate the rights of privacy of any person ...." Yes, you should warrant that you wrote it; but you can't foresee the future. What if someone falsely claims that the piece is libelous? The publisher needs to back you up. Don't release the publisher of all liability.

7. Author agrees to indemnify, defend and hold Publisher harmless against any claim, demand, suit, or proceeding that may be brought against Publisher by reason of any of the following matters regarding Author's Work: (1) any violation or infringement of any proprietary right or copyright; (2) any libelous or unlawful matter contained in the work; (3) any invasion of the rights of privacy or other personal rights possessed by any person or entity; (4) Author's breach of any term, covenant, representation, or warranty of this agreement; or (5) anything whatsoever that might prejudice the securing to Publisher or his assigns of the full benefit of rights herein granted. Publisher agrees to use reasonable efforts to notify Author of any claim, demand, suit or proceeding regarding Author's Work, and Author agrees to fully cooperate with Publisher in the defense thereof by counsel selected by Publisher.

Whew! What a mouthful. And basically, it's telling you you're on your own in the event that anything you write results in a lawsuit. Pretty yucky, considering that you don't have a crystal ball. As a journalist, you may follow ethics and do the best you can with the information presented, without any malice, and someone still might sue over something you wrote. Chances are pretty good that if you're writing an article with potential legal ramifications—like Jeffrey Toobin's coverage of the O.J. Simpson trial for *The New Yorker*—the magazine's legal department will be scrutinizing every detail to ensure that the I's are dotted and the T's are crossed. Still, another "to the best of the Author's knowledge" phrase might help here, as it would in paragraph 6.

8. If any action is filed in relation to this agreement, the prevailing party shall recover its costs of suit, plus reasonable attorneys' fees. In addition, the parties agree that, in the event any suit or action is instituted to enforce or interpret any of the terms of this agreement, the suit or action shall be prosecuted in the court of competent jurisdiction located in *Marvelous Magazine* Town.

This paragraph is straightforward. If you, the writer, sue the Publisher over the breach of this contract, or vice versa, whoever loses pays the court costs. Let's say that *Marvelous Magazine* never paid you for the article. You secure an attorney and win a judgment for payment. Moreover, let's say that it cost you $250 to take *Marvelous Magazine* to court. You'll also receive $250, in addition to the fee payment. If the mag sues you and you lose, you pay the publication's court costs.

9. The parties acknowledge that this is the entire agreement; it supersedes all prior agreements and understandings, whether oral or written; and cannot be modified except by a written instrument signed by each party.

This is pretty clear. Paragraph 9 acknowledges that the contract is binding. If you want to make changes—such as request more money or different rights—you need to write another contract, and both parties must sign it.

These nine paragraphs offer a glimpse into the world of magazine and newspaper contracts. But contracts vary. The most important thing to remember is to keep your eyes wide open. Read the contract carefully. Ask questions. Negotiate any details that don't sit right with you. If you don't, you could end up losing a lot of money.

Dead Lines

Although a presumption exists that any unspecified rights remain the writer's rights, don't rely on ambiguity in your contract. Specifying your rights could make you a whole lot richer.

Dead Lines

Think about this: When you don't look closely at a contract and give away your rights—especially the continually morphing electronic rights—to a magazine, you contribute to and help establish a standard against the freelancer. Fight for your monetary rights and the rights of other freelance writers by demanding fair contracts.

The Straight Scoop

On January 1, 1978, The Copyright Law went into effect. The Copyright Law basically stated that, unless the freelancer stipulates otherwise, a magazine gets only first serial rights (one-time rights) with the purchase of an article. Any further rights had to be spelled out in a contract. Thus came the advent of contract negotiations for the freelance writer.

Some Final Words

We've said it before, and we'll say it again: Editors expect some negotiation concerning rights and the contract. The dilemma for the writer remains understanding how much you can comfortably sign away without walking away.

Some rights are unalienable when selling an article—first North American serial rights, for example. Don't try to negotiate one-time or nonexclusive rights. Keep in mind that two popular options are adding *print* in front of *serial* (to keep your electronic rights) and offering to divide income from reprints. Finally, remember that these are turbulent times for writer's rights. Keep abreast of developments.

The Least You Need to Know

➤ Retaining ownership of your work remains one of the most important aspects of the freelancing business.

➤ The contract is the vehicle by which the writer and the publisher designate rights.

➤ The most common rights are first serial rights, one-time rights, second serial (reprint) rights, all rights, electronic rights, and dramatic, television, and motion picture rights.

➤ Read your contract thoroughly, and don't be afraid to negotiate the best deal for yourself.

Glossary

advertorial   A combination of the words "advertising" and "editorial," usually identified at the top of the page with the words "special advertising section." An advertorial looks and sounds like the rest of the magazine, and is frequently written by the magazine's staff.

agent   Well-connected professional who tries to interest publishers in your work in return for a percentage of the book's earnings. Most agents do not sell magazine pieces.

alliteration   The repetition of consonant sounds for effect.

artist   A person who does anything well with a feeling for form and effect.

boilerplate contract   The standard contract a publication uses, before you have requested any changes.

book   Slang within the magazine industry for a magazine. An editor may refer to an issue as the book.

book proposal   A packet of information outlining a book idea.

byline   The author's name as listed at the end of the article.

captions   Explanatory copy that may identify the Who, What, Where, When, Why, or How of a picture, but may also tell something extra to amplify a message or illuminate a point.

clips   Samples of your published work included in a pitch for an editor to peruse.

content   Written material found in a magazine or on a Web site. Content is always distinguished from advertising.

content provider   Someone who provides content—in other words, a writer. Also called a content developer.

contract   An agreement between two or more parties. It is enforceable by law and may contain specific terms within the document.

contributor's copies   Copies of the magazine sent to the writer in which his work appears. Typically, a magazine will send you at least one copy of the issue containing your article.

copyright   Your exclusive right to the publication, production, or sale of the rights to your article granted by law. Once you conjure an idea and write it, copyright protection automatically kicks in whether or not you've filed for a copyright with the government.

coverlines   Pithy, suggestive, and teasing lines of copy on the cover of a magazine.

deadline   The final day a writer has to turn in an assignment.

decked heads   The brief opening or short introduction, giving the reader an idea of what the feature will cover; the decked head is usually one to two sentences.

departments   Sections in a magazine devoted each issue to one area. For instance, if a magazine covers health, beauty, and finance in every issue, each topic is termed a department (i.e., Beauty Department, Health Department, Finance Department).

domain name   The name of a Web site, the words that follow the www. designation.

dominant photo   The primary visual element of a magazine article spread.

downstyle   Describes the grammatical device employed when the first word and only the proper nouns are capitalized in a headline. All major words in an upstyle headline, however, are capitalized.

editorialized   Subjective response in a piece.

editor-in-chief   Supervises the editorial staff and oversees every story, department, and column, shaping the content, tone, and personality of the magazine. Depending upon the size of the publication, the editor-in-chief may wear many hats.

element   Anything put into a layout within the pages of a magazine. The text, the artwork, the headline are all examples of elements.

embossing   A special process that creates a raised image on the page of either an article or an advertisement in a magazine. Embossing is another design element that adds to the glitz of a glossy.

essay   Composition articles infused with editorial; one's opinion piece.

first serial rights   The rights associated with a book excerpt that appears (or is serialized) prior to the book's publication. After a book is published, all other rights are second serial.

five Ws and H   Who, What, When, Where, Why, and How.

FNASR   Acronym for First North American Serial Rights.

folio   The page number, usually positioned in the bottom corner of the page.

foreshadowing   A device by which the writer creates suspense and also hints at what may come later in the story.

freelance writer   One who writes for a publication or Web site without being employed by them.

front of the book   The first section of a magazine, before the major features begin.

glossies   Shiny photographic prints for sharp reproduction; magazines using glossy paper.

headline   The title of the story.

honorarium   Payment in copies of the periodical or a token monetary amount.

HTML   Hypertext Markup Language, the computer coding by which text appears on a Web page.

hyperbole   An exaggeration of the truth for a humorous effect or greater emphasis.

imagery   The literary device of using descriptive words to recreate sensory experience for the reader. Imagery is an important device for writers to master, because it is through this device that you bring visual images to paper and put pictures in the reader's mind.

kill fee   The amount paid a writer if the story proves unacceptable or unsatisfactory for print.

lead   The introduction of your article, several sentences of stylistic device, to "lead" the reader into the body of your article. A lead can also possess a hook—an idea that catches the attention of the reader.

lead-in   The first words of a story, drawing the attention to the copy and often set apart typographically for emphasis and style.

link   A way of connecting one Web site with another via a highlighted icon that the Web visitor can click.

masthead   A list of all the editors, artists, designers, editorial staffers, and sometimes advertising executives for a publication, typically found within the first few pages of the publication.

media kit   The publicity and marketing material that a magazine sends out to a potential advertiser.

metaphor   Metaphors compare two things more directly. Example: Time is money.

newspaper   A publication issued daily, weekly, or at frequent intervals, containing news and advertising.

"on assignment"   What a writer is when an editor asks him or her to produce a specific article for a fee.

op-ed   The opinions and editorial pages, or the opinions and editorials that appear on those pages.

paraphrasing   Rewording the thought or meaning of something that has been said or written before.

pay in copies   Some smaller publications don't pay money, but rather send free copies of the magazine in which your piece appeared.

pay on pub   Payment for a piece that is not sent out until the article has appeared, been published.

penny press   Inexpensive printing of all kinds.

piece   The work that a writer produces; the piece of writing.

plagiarism   Copying another writer's work and claiming it as your own.

platform   An author's proven ability to sell their books through a Web site, public speaking, radio show, or newspaper columns.

pseudonym   A fictitious name used in place of your own for an article's byline.

pulled quotes   Words pulled from the text of an article and displayed boldly in quotes as a visual.

query   A letter to an editor "pitching" a story idea of yours and offering to write it.

SASE   Self-addressed, stamped envelope.

Schedule C   The tax form used to declare freelance writing income.

screen   A page of Web content.

serial   Describes anything published periodically, at regular intervals. Newspapers and magazines are both serials.

shelter magazines   Home design magazines.

simile   A figure of speech that makes a comparison between two things using the words *like* or *as.*

slant   A device used in articles to appeal to the readership. For instance, one magazine may insist on inspirational endings, while another magazine may begin all articles in first person.

sound bite   The term reporters, producers, and editors use to denote a quote pulled from the tape and used in the story.

spec   Short for "on speculation" and means writing a piece on the chance that the publication may purchase the rights for it.

strippable   Denotes magazines whose covers can be stripped off and returned to the publisher for credit if the magazine doesn't sell.

symbol   A person, place, activity, or object that stands for something beyond itself. For example, a heart symbolizes love.

target audience   The group of people who will be interested in reading your article.

tear sheet   The actual page, torn from a magazine or a newspaper, with your article.

tools   On a Web page, tools are interactive functions such as calculators or spreadsheets that help the viewer accomplish a task.

transcribing   The act of transferring the interview from the taped recording to a written document.

unsolicited manuscript   When you send an editor your entire article without her asking for it.

Zapf dingbats   Decorative fonts used by magazine designers to start captions or copy, as an endmark, or to break unindented copy into paragraphs. Each magazine's style dictates the Zapf dingbats used.

'zines   Originally an inexpensive homemade publication for fans of particular celebrities, rock bands, or lifestyles. Now also means an online publication.

Recommended Books

Allen, Moira. *Writing.com.* New York: Allworth Press, 1999.

Blundell, William E. *The Art and Craft of Feature Writing.* New York: Plume, 1968.

Bly, Robert. *Write More, Sell More.* Cincinnati: Writer's Digest Books, 1998.

Bykofsky, Sheree, and Jennifer Basye Sander. *The Complete Idiot's Guide to Getting Published.* Revised second edition. New York: Alpha Books, 2000.

Callahan, Christopher. *A Journalist's Guide to the Net: The Net as a Reporting Tool.* Needham Heights, MA: Allyn & Bacon, 1999.

Holm, Kirsten C., ed. *Writer's Market.* Cincinnati: Writer's Digest Books, updated annually.

O'Neil, Peat. *Travel Writing: A Guide to Research, Writing, and Selling.* Cincinnati: Writer's Digest Books, 1996.

Schumacher, Michael. *The Writer's Complete Guide to Conducting Interviews.* Cincinnati: Writer's Digest Books, 1993.

Stewart, James B. *Follow the Story: How to Find the Idea, Report the Facts, and Write Successful Non-fiction Narrative.* New York: Scribner's, 1998.

Yudkin, Marcia. *Writing Articles About the World Around You.* Cincinnati: Writer's Digest Books, 1998.

Sample Contracts

Example #1: Sample Online Content Contract, Exclusive Content Contribution Agreement

This is an "Agreement" between "You," having name, address, and age provided at the end of this Agreement, and PUBLISHER.com, Inc.

1. Content Submissions. The purpose of this Agreement is to create an understanding about the "Content" that you are submitting, what PUBLISHER rights are to this Content, and how you will be compensated by PUBLISHER. You and PUBLISHER agree that this Agreement is about the following Content.

Please check the following Content categories that apply.

Cartoons and/or Other Drawings

Articles and/or Other Writings

Graphic Designs and/or Other Artwork

2. Compensation. For each item (a cartoon, article, etc.) of Accepted Content, PUBLISHER agrees to compensate you according to PUBLISHER'S standard compensation terms as of the date of PUBLISHER'S acceptance, as described in the attachment. PUBLISHER'S rates and compensation terms may be changed from time to time. Please contact PUBLISHER to confirm current rates and terms.

You agree that no compensation will be provided for items, materials, writings, and other content that is not submitted by You, even if it is similar to Content that You submit.

3. Rights Granted to PUBLISHER. You agree that, for any and all Content that you provide to PUBLISHER, without any particular time limit, PUBLISHER may (but is not obligated to) reproduce, display and publish such Content anywhere in any form and medium and may create new works of authorship based on and including the Content. You agree that, after you have received the compensation that is described above, no more compensation will be required for these rights and that these rights cannot be revoked. You agree not to take any action that would diminish or deprive PUBLISHER of these rights.

PUBLISHER and You agree that the rights granted to PUBLISHER in this paragraph are exclusive to PUBLISHER (also excluding You) for all media and forms.

4. Legal Stuff.

Content Rules. With the exception described below, You agree not to submit any Content that You did not create by yourself, (a) that contains images, designs or writings of others, (b) that makes real people falsely appear to be immoral, incompetent, or undesirable, (c) that contains images of people who are not public figures who want to remain private, or (d) that contains the commercially valuable names or images of others. The exception to these content rules is that you may include the commercial images of others if your Content is primarily educational in nature or is a satire making fun.

Liability. You and PUBLISHER agree that neither will be liable to the other for any consequential, incidental, special or indirect damages of any kind or nature, under any theory of law or equity, related to or in connection with this Agreement, whether or not advised of the possibility of such damages.

Your Information. You promise to PUBLISHER that the information you have inserted in this Agreement below is completely true.

Other Stuff. This Agreement cannot be changed or any of our rights waived unless both You and PUBLISHER agree in writing. This Agreement can be assigned by either You or PUBLISHER to another person only if there is reasonable notice to one another before the assignment, and only if the new person (the "Assignee") agrees in writing that this Agreement applies to the relationship. Any notices related to this Agreement need to be given in writing to one another at our addresses below, or any new address that is given in such a notice. The laws of the State of _____ apply to this Agreement. This Agreement is the entire understanding between You and PUBLISHER about the Content.

5. Effectiveness. This Agreement becomes effective on the date of PUBLISHER's acceptance of this Agreement, after receiving a copy signed by You. This Agreement is intended to continue in effect until and unless terminated as permitted by law, or until You and PUBLISHER agree to terminate this Agreement in writing. However, termination of this Agreement is not intended to terminate or otherwise affect the provisions of this Agreement that concern "Rights Granted to PUBLISHER" or "Legal Stuff."

Agreed by You: _____

Your name (please print clearly): _____

Your signature: _____

Your birth date: _____

Your Social Security number: _____

Your postal address: _____

Your e-mail address: _____

Agreed by PUBLISHER: _____

This Agreement becomes effective only after signature by PUBLISHER. PUBLISHER will return a copy of the Agreement to your address above after signature by PUBLISHER.

PUBLISHER'S signature: _____

Editor's name: _____

Editor's signature: _____

Company name: _____

Address: _____

E-mail address: _____

Example #2: Sample Print Contract, Agreement for Contributors

This is an agreement between _____ Magazine and "Writer," an independent free-lance contributor.

1. Writer will write an article on an agreed-upon subject for publication in _____ Magazine. Both a hard copy (double spaced) and a version on disk must be submitted (Labeled ASCII disc REQUIRED).

2. Upon receipt, review and acceptance of the manuscript, on agreed-upon subject, fee will be paid. The fee includes a maximum of one substantive rewrite, if necessary, and writer agrees to cooperate with _____ Magazine during the editing process. Final editorial authority to edit, abridge, or augment the article belongs exclusively to _____ Magazine.

3. The fee shall be paid within 60 days of acceptance of the article whether or not publication has occurred. If _____ Magazine deems the article unacceptable, it will pay a kill fee of 20 percent of the agreed-upon fee. Unless otherwise stated, writer's fee shall include all expenses incurred in preparation of the article.

291

4. If the writer fails to meet the scheduled deadline, _____ Magazine will have no obligation to accept the article and have no obligation for fees or expenses to the writer.

5. _____ Magazine shall receive all rights to the use of this article for a period of 60 days from the date of publication and writer agrees not to allow publication of any similar articles or any other articles using the same research or interviews within North America during this period. If another publication or syndicate requests permission from _____ Magazine to republish the article within 60 days of the date of publication, writer shall receive one-half of the fee received by _____ Magazine for this republication. After 60 days all rights to the article revert to the writer except that _____ Magazine retains the right to use the article, or elements thereof, for promotional, advertising, reprint, historical, or anthological purposes in print or electronic formats.

6. Writer agrees, at _____ Magazine's option, to allow the use of his/her name and/or photograph to promote the article.

7. Writer represents that the material submitted is original, has not been previously published and does not infringe on anyone else's copyright or any other rights.

8. Writer represents that he/she has used all reasonable care to ensure that all facts and statements in the work are true and accurate and that the article does not violate the privacy of anyone else, and does not misappropriate anyone's persona or likeness. Writer agrees to inform the editor in the event that the work is based, in whole or in part, on confidential sources, and to cooperate with the editor and the magazine's attorney upon request.

9. Writer agrees to keep and maintain all notes, tape recordings, and working papers used in connection with the work for a period of two years from the date of first publication of the article, and to produce all notes, tape recordings, and working papers to _____ Magazine on request.

10. _____ Magazine will provide liability coverage under its publishers' liability policy.

Sincerely,

_____

Editor's Name

_____

Title

AGREED

Please sign and return one copy of this letter, indicating your acceptance of this agreement with us for all future publication of material you submit. For our records, we request that you supply all information requested below.

Print name: _____

Sign name: _____

Date: _____

Social Security #: _____ Phone: _____

Address: _____

Article: _____ Fee: _____

Date Assigned: _____ Date Due: _____

Intended Issue of Publication: _____ Word Count: _____

Sample Writer's Guidelines

Sample #1: Women's Glossy

Editorial Guidelines for Writers' Submissions

SAMPLE MAGAZINE welcomes inquiries from previously published writers. Please send published writing samples to Editor, SAMPLE MAGAZINE, ADDRESS.

Generally, contributing writers work on assignment, and SAMPLE MAGAZINE does not publish unsolicited material. If the writing samples meet the standards of SAMPLE MAGAZINE, the editor will contact the writer and request that the writer submit story ideas for the magazine's departments or features, which include:

Topics that encourage readers to improve their emotional, spiritual, or physical well-being.

Topics that give readers tools to manage and enhance their careers.

Topics that encourage readers to increase their financial security.

The male perspective on relationships or issues affecting women.

Lightly humorous end page.

Travel article.

Topics relevant to entertaining.

Features: A variety of topics.

Story ideas should be two or three sentences summarizing the proposed topic and communicating how the piece will be written (interviews, sidebars, etc.).

SAMPLE MAGAZINE generally does not accept first-person narratives, poetry, or fiction.

Articles range from 800 to 2,500 words, depending on the department or feature. Topics need to be of interest to all women.

Sample #2: Parenting Glossy

Submission Guidelines for SAMPLE MAGAZINE

SAMPLE MAGAZINE is published 10 times a year, with combined issues in June/July and December/January.

SAMPLE MAGAZINE provides parents of children from birth to age 12 with the newest thinking, information, and advice they need to raise their families in a constantly changing, time-pressed world.

Freelance writers are invited to submit query letters only on the following topics:

Children's health

Parenting and marital relationship issues

Child behavior and development

Personal essays pertaining to family life

SAMPLE MAGAZINE purchases first-time rights for articles and pays upon acceptance. Fees vary depending on length and positioning of articles.

Writers must include clips of previously published work and a self-addressed, stamped envelope (SASE) with their queries.

Address all correspondence to:

Submissions
SAMPLE MAGAZINE
ADDRESS
ADDRESS

Please allow eight weeks for a reply.

Sample #3: Travel Magazine

Writers' Guidelines

Thank you for your interest in SAMPLE MAGAZINE. The most useful thing a prospective contributor can do is read the magazine, which is available on newsstands or in bookstores. If the magazine is not available locally, we'll mail you one for $6 ($11 for non-U.S.). Subscriptions cost $24 per year ($33 for non-U.S.).

SAMPLE MAGAZINE (eight times a year as of January 2000) is a travel magazine that focuses on islands around the world: urban, rural, tropical, or windswept, well-known or virtually undiscovered. We strive for geographical and topical diversity and encourage articles with a well-defined focus and point of view. Our purpose is, in effect, to take the reader to the island. To that end, we seek informative, insightful, personal pieces that reveal the essence of the place.

In every issue there are usually several feature articles, ranging from 2,500 to 4,000 words. There are also occasional shorter features of about 1,500 to 2,000 words.

Front-of-the-book sections include XXXXXX (columns on the arts), with brief book and record reviews (staff written), short profiles, and Q&As with artists and writers, as well as short pieces on museums, films, and other arts topics. XXXXXX includes regular columns by contributing editors on the Caribbean and Hawaii, as well as department-length pieces (750–1,500 words) on slices of island life. These can be essays or narrative experiences—profiles or topics that range from sports to nature to encounters with islanders.

For the opening XXXXXX section, see the separate guidelines.

XXXXXX is our back-of-the-book section of service information. Within XXXXXX, XXXXXX relates specifically to the features and is staff-written. XXXXXX (850 words) is a Top 10 list of not-to-be-missed things to do in on-the-beaten track island destinations. XXXXXX pieces (750–1,000 words) showcase a great place to stay, a great place to eat, or a special island experience. For a hotel or restaurant to be an appropriate subject, it must be more than something new or luxurious. There must be a good story behind it.

Prospective authors should submit material on speculation or send a detailed proposal of each article idea (no laundry lists, please), including an estimate of travel expenses (for features only), and samples of previously published work. Do not send query letters without samples of writing. In general, we look for accomplished feature writers with many assignments to their credit. Less-experienced writers may have better luck submitting articles on speculation or proposing shorter pieces.

Be sure to enclose a self-addressed envelope with adequate postage to ensure the return of your material. Allow at least two months for a response. We receive a large volume of inquiries and need time to consider each thoughtfully. You may also send queries or articles on speculation via e-mail to E-MAIL ADDRESS. (We may request writing samples via regular mail.)

SAMPLE MAGAZINE pays $.50 and up per word for articles. The fee is paid within 30 days of acceptance of the manuscript. If an assigned article is rejected, a kill fee of 25 percent is paid within 30 days of rejection.

Contributors receive three complimentary copies of the magazine in which their article appears.

We hope you continue to enjoy the magazine.

Great Web Sites for Writers

www.asja.org

The American Society of Journalists and Authors is a membership organization, but even nonmembers will find good information here on contracts and conferences.

www.brillscontent.com

Read back issues or the current issue of *Brill's Content* magazine, a good source for what is going on in the media industry.

www.craigslist.org

You'll find an ever-changing list of job opportunities for writers in the Writing and Editing Jobs section of this site. Many are freelance.

www.inkspot.com

Billed as "The Writing Resource, Writers' Community," this site has been named the best Web site for writers. It's filled with all manner of useful information and links.

www.mediaweek.com

This site includes breaking news and gossip about all aspects of the media world, from newspapers and magazines to movie companies.

www.powerfulmedia.com

From the folks who started *Brill's Content* magazine, this site promises to be just as media-gossip-filled.

www.thewell.com

The Well requires a monthly subscription fee, but it has a very active ongoing conference/chat room for freelance writers called Byline.

www.verio.com

Here's where you can register your own URL or Web address to promote your books or writings. Also try www.register.com.

www.writersdigest.com

Run by the folks who publish books and magazines about getting published, this site has a wealth of information for freelancers, including access to writers' guidelines from major markets, information on writers' conferences, and even a featured Market of the Day.

www.writersmarkets.com

Sign up for a free subscription to this site's email newsletter, with information on freelance markets and opportunities. You can also download the free e-book *How to Be a Freelance Writer.*

www.writersonlineworkshops.com

This online educational forum run by the Writer's Digest folks offers online classes on how to polish and improve your writing skills.

Index

phone books, 104
reports, 103
studies, 103
specialized writings, 229.
See also niches
book contracts, 236-237
building a reputation, 233
market research, 229-231
competition, 231
editors, 231
selecting topics, 232-233
writers' stories, 234-235
staccato leads, 211
staff reporters, 128
statistics, magazine article ideas, 80
studies (research source), 103
style of Web writing, 174
attitude, 176
informative, 175
samples, 175
short, 175
versus printed articles, 176
submission guidelines, 295-297
success stories
freelance writers
Beckerman, Ilene, 33-35
Clark, Brooks, 30-33
Thornton, Jim, 36-37
Wiley, Kim Wright, 28-30
published books, 247
Evans, Heidi, 248
Poe, Richard, 248
Richards, Sally, 247

summary leads, 209
supply and demand (newspapers), 125
synergies, 70
system (record-keeping), 259
file folders, 260-261
write-offs, 261-263

T

tape recorders, 112
Tapper, Joan (editor), advice for freelancers, 43-44
target audiences, 79
magazine article ideas, 84-85
taxes
accountants, 252
home office deductions, 264
payment schedules, 264
profitable income, 263
record-keeping system, 259-261
Schedule C, 263
tracking money, 266
write-offs, 261-262
samples, 262-263
travel expenses, 265
team of writers, 241
television rights, 273
The Well Web site, 299
Thornton, Jim (freelance writer), 36-37
time management, 254-256

time frames, saving files, 253-254
Times of My Life: And My Life with the Times, 66
titles, 197, 204-205
tones (query letters), 92
tools
freelance writers, 251
interviews, 111
e-mail, 113-114
notebooks, 112
pens, 112
tape recorders, 112
trade magazines
Amy Hamaker's interview, 149-151
editor expectations, 145-146
income, 148
networking, 147-148
pitching ideas, 148
research versus experience, 144
versus glossies, 144
Transitionsabroad Web site, 170
travel writing, 7-8
advice from Joan Trapper, 44
tax write-offs, 265
Web magazines, 169-170
Travel Writing: A Guide to Research, Writing, and Selling, 287
trends
magazines, 137-138
newspapers, 128
Tripsmag Web site, 170
turn-around time, 140